# 微观西安

（汉英版）

屈胜文 主编

SINCE 1897
商務印書館
The Commercial Press
2014年·北京

摄影：贾庆华

策　　划　聂晓阳　周洪波
主　　编　屈胜文
编　　写　陈　静　陈　颖　高　雅　闫　斌　王晓英
　　　　　刘　瑾　常宇江　孙　欢　翟小雪　贾庆华
　　　　　李平选　屈胜文
审　　订　聂晓阳　王广新

英文翻译　祝伟婧
英文审订　魏令查　陈德彰
英文编辑　李昆之　刘　珏

责任编辑　储丹丹
装帧设计　东方美迪
项目统筹　《汉语世界》杂志社

Producer　Nie Xiaoyang　Zhou Hongbo
Chief Compiler　Qu Shengwen
Compilers　Chen Jing　Chen Ying　Gao Ya　Yan Bin
Wang Xiaoying　Liu Jin　Chang Yujiang　Sun Huan
Zhai Xiaoxue　Jia Qinghua　Li Pingxuan　Qu Shengwen
Reviewers　Nie Xiaoyang　Wang Guangxin

English Translator　Zhu Weijing
English Reviewers　Wei Lingcha　Chen Dezhang
English Editors　Li Kunzhi　Liu Jue

Executive Editor　Chu Dandan
Art Design　EmDesign
Project Coordinator　THE WORLD OF CHINESE

序

# 让珍贵的文明资源活起来

魏民洲

西安是中华文明的根。几千年来，在这片山水环绕、川塬相接的土地上，先辈们用勤劳和智慧创造了历史上最早的“天府之国”，成就了周秦汉唐的辉煌文明，留下了无数的古迹遗址、史书典籍、掌故传说。礼乐儒理的秩序思想深深融入民族血脉，汉赋唐诗的浩瀚美丽至今滋养国人精神。作为中国文明的荣耀之地，西安在传统文化的推陈出新、继承弘扬上有义不容辞的责任。

西安还是中华文明发展的缩影。著名城市学家刘易斯·芒福德说，贮存文化、流传文化和改造文化，是城市的三个基本使命。千百年来，西安这座城市的文明精神不仅永恒地矗立于遗址文物，更鲜活地存在于市井里巷，生动地演绎于市民生活。西安的一切都有中华文明的深深印记，秦岭巍峨俊秀、水清木华，秦腔激越酣烈、沉郁苍凉，秦人忠勇担当、直率坦荡，甚至舌尖上的西安味道都勾连着几百年几千年的皇宫故事。

作为一个生于斯、长于斯的西安人，我对这方水土、这城百姓充满了依恋、热爱和敬仰。这里的一山一水、一砖一瓦、城墙街巷、方言俚语……构筑起最美丽的乡愁。在西安生活多年，我越来越深切地感受到，包含着先哲们无穷智慧的优秀传统文化，和人民群众的日常生活密不可分。深厚的文明积淀不但是西安人精神的底色、心灵的纽带、信心的源泉，也是生存的背景、生活的元素、生命的因子。西安人深深浸透在悠久灿烂的文明中，举手投足都展示着对文化的关注和渴慕。我们启动汉长安城遗址区保护建设、城墙南门区域综合提升改造，就是希望护住古都文明根脉，满足群众文化情结，让西安大地上的文明遗产真正融入群众生活，真正深入人心、造福黎民。

习近平总书记指出，“要系统梳理传统文化资源，让收藏在禁宫里的文物、陈列在广阔大地上的遗产、书写在古籍里的文字都活起来”。众心同欲者胜，民心相齐者强。让西安丰富广袤的文明资源都“活”起来，需要全社会的关注、参与和支持。守护民族珍贵的历史记忆和精神价值，需要每个人都积极响应、担当作为。不管是严谨精深的研究、深入细致的挖掘、持久用心的保护，还是生动活泼的普及、热情真诚的宣传、创新方式的运用，都有助于把富有永恒魅力、具有当代价值的优秀传统文化从禁宫、大地和古籍中唤醒，成为城市发展重要的生产力和软实力，成为人民生活不可分离的精神光芒和灵魂力量。

《微观西安》用微博的形式，通过一个个词条对西安文明进行了回溯和展示。这本书深入到城市肌体的各个脉络，从一个地名、一段故事展开，从一道菜、一个话题道来，深入浅出、图文并茂，把西安悠久的、丰富的、多元的、时尚的文明资源全方位展现在读者面前，是一部在微时代整合和传播西安文明、让普通百姓和社会精英都深刻感受到文化“活”起来的诚意之作。

细微处常见精神，希望关心西安、锐志于文明传承的朋友们都读一读这本书，从微观角度感受文明的博大丰富和绵亘深沉。愿我们共同努力，让“活”的文化在和社会主义核心价值观，和现代城市生活的密切交融中更生动精彩、充满魅力，构筑群众的精神故乡和心灵家园。

（作序者为中共陕西省委常委、西安市委书记）

Preface

# Enliven Precious Cultural Heritage

Xi'an holds the roots of Chinese civilization. For thousands of years, our forefathers, diligent and intelligent, have changed the land of plateaus, basins, rivers and mountains into one of the earliest "Land of Abundance" in the world. They created brilliant civilizations in the Zhou, Qin, Han and Tang dynasties, leaving behind numerous historic sites, records and legends. Confucian philosophy and rites have sunk deep into the veins of our nation; the marvelous Han and Tang poetry has nourished Chinese souls until the present day. A glorious land in Chinese civilization, Xi'an is obliged to inherit, renovate, and promote traditional Chinese culture.

Xi'an is also the epitome of the evolution of Chinese civilization. Well-known American urbanologist Lewis Mumford pointed out that preserving, passing on, and remodeling culture are a city's three fundamental missions. For centuries, the spirit of Xi'an not only rests permanently in its historic relics, but finds its vivid expression in its neighborhoods and daily life. Everything about Xi'an bears the imprint of Chinese civilization. From the imposing and gorgeous Qinling Mountains with its flourishing trees and winding rivers, to the passionate and melancholy Qinqiang opera, from the brave and candid people to the superb cuisine, all can be traced back to imperial tales from hundreds and thousands of years ago.

Born and bred in Xi'an, I have deep attachment, affection and respect for this land and its people. Every hill and every drop of water, every brick and every roof tile, city wall and street, even the dialect and slang, all evoke a wave of nostalgia within me. My years in Xi'an have made me realize the interrelationship between traditional and modern culture. The city's profound cultural tradition, which encompasses endless ancestral wisdom, serves as its spiritual essence, the common soul and the source of confidence of the Xi'anese; it is also their common background and an indispensable element of daily life. Deeply entrenched in the long standing and glorious civilization, the Xi'anese have developed and nurtured a thirst for this culture.

The recently launched preservation projects, such as the Chang'an relic of the Han Dynasty and the renovation of the south gate area show our determination to guard the cultural roots of this ancient capital, realize people's long-cherished cultural dreams, and let the cultural heritage of Xi'an merge into everyday life and benefit the populace.

President Xi Jinping has called for "systematic sorting out of traditional cultural heritage, so as to enliven all artifacts kept in forbidden palaces and scattered over the vast land, to make alive the texts residing in ancient classics." Unity of the will and mind ensures success. For the affluent cultural resources of Xi'an to "come alive", it will require the awareness, participation, and support of society as a whole. The preservation of our nation's historic memories and spiritual values entails everyone's active response and action. Rigorous research and scrupulous exploitation, sustained protection and lively popularization, zealous publicity and creative application are all conducive

to waking up our permanently fascinating traditional culture, which, albeit dormant in forbidden palaces, our vast land and ancient texts, still has value at present. Cultural heritage is expected to become an important driving force and soft power for the city's development and an inalienable spiritual support and strength for the people.

In the form of microblogging, the book *Xi'an: Back to the Future* traces back and demonstrates different aspects of Xi'an's culture in hundreds of entries. It taps into the life-blood of the city via the name of a place, a story, a dish, or a topic. Nicely illustrated and elegantly narrated, the book is an earnest effort to showcase and disseminate the civilization of Xi'an in an era of the internet. Meanwhile, it presents to the reader a panorama of the rich, diverse, and long standing culture of Xi'an. Above all, it is a sincere book for both the elite and the masses to experience a real and living culture.

Sincerity manifests itself in every tiny detail. If you are interested in Xi'an and determined to carry its splendid culture forward, it is advisable for you to read the book for a personal feel of the extensive and profound civilization from a micro perspective. I'm confident that our joint efforts will make the resurrected ancient culture more vivid, glamorous and splendid if we mingle it with socialist core values and modern urban life. After all, culture is the home of the soul.

*Wei Minzhou*

August, 2014

1960年代 钟楼

# 目 录 | Contents



2013年 钟楼

摄影：翟小雪

# 地理·印记

Geography and Landmarks

**天府之国**
**The Land of Abundance**

关于西安一直有种误解，以为西安地处黄土高原，条件较差，作家朱鸿释疑说："实际上西安在关中平原，属九州膏腴之地。"关于西安的资质，思想家荀子说："山林川谷美，天才之利多。"战略家张良说："金城千里，天府之国也。"文学家韩愈说："天街小雨润如酥，草色遥看近却无。最是一年春好处，绝色烟柳满皇都。"

There is a misconception that Xi'an is disadvantaged because it is located on the Loess Plateau. Zhu Hong, a famous writer, explains that "in fact, Xi'an is on the Guanzhong Plain, one of the richest lands in ancient China." Xunzi, a great thinker (c.312 - 230 B.C.), remarked on Xi'an: "The mountains, forests, rivers and valleys are marvelous, as are the talents." Strategist Zhang Liang (262 - 189 B.C.) said: "The state's forts hold strong, such is the Land of Abundance." Litterateur Han Yu (768 - 824) elaborated in a poem: "The royal streets are moistened by a creamlike rain. / Green grass can be perceived afar but not near-by. / It's the best time of a year late spring tries in vain. / With its capital veiled in willows to outvie."

**中为贵**
**The Middle Is the Superior**

身处自古富庶繁华地的关中，西安人有强烈的"中为贵"意识，喜欢把别处以东南西北命名，自己天然地立足于坐标系正中。比如，他们把大荔、韩城一带统称"东府"，把凤翔、扶风、眉县一带称"西府"。在介绍省内其他地市时，不用行政区划的地名，而是概括为"陕南""陕北""渭南""渭北"……

Living in Guanzhong, a land of prosperity, the Xi'anese contend that "the middle is the superior". They tend to name other places after north, east, south, or west, which puts Xi'an at the center of the world. For example, they call the area of Dali and Hancheng the "East Prefecture", and the area of Fengxiang, Fufeng, and Mei County the "West Prefecture". When introducing other places in the province, they prefer "West Shaanxi", "North Shaanxi", "South of the Wei River", and "North of the Wei River" to the correct administrative term.

**最古老的留学生社区**
**The Foreign Students Community**

盛唐时期，长安城的人口超过百万，是人类历史上第一个人口过百万的城市。这其中，仅留学生就达十万人。在西安的大小"学习巷"，盛唐时期曾居住着数万名外国人，大家都在那里学习汉语，因此得名。若昔日有"长安话四六级考试"，不知道会难倒多少外国友人。

During the heyday of the Tang Dynasty, the population of Chang'an exceeded one million, making it the first city with a million people in history. Among the residents, 100,000 were foreign students. In the "Study Alleys" resided tens of thousands of foreigners studying Chinese. If there had been a "Test on the Chang'an Dialect", how many foreigners would have failed?

**庵与寺**
**The Convent and Monastery**

西安东门外的八仙庵，名为庵，实则是西安市最大的道教观院。八国联军入侵北京后，慈禧和光绪来西安避难时曾住在这里。距它不远处的罔极寺，虽叫寺，却是庵堂。这座太平公主为纪念武则天而修建的寺院曾发生许多重大历史事件，如今仍有十几个尼姑在此修行。

Although its Chinese name indicates it is a convent, the Temple of the Eight Immortals outside the East Gate is actually the largest Taoist monastary in Xi'an. Empress Dowager Cixi (1835 - 1908) and Guangxu Emperor (reign 1875 - 1908) took refuge here when Peking was seized by the Eight-Nation Alliance. Not far from here situates the Wangji Temple, a convent in fact. Built by Princess Taiping in honor of Empress Wu Zetian (reign 690 - 705), this temple witnessed many significant historic events. Nowadays, a dozen or so nuns are still practicing Taoism here.

**最早的"百家讲坛"**
**The Earliest "Lecture Room"**

央视"百家讲坛"名噪一时。但鲜为人知的是，早在汉代，老祖宗们就已经开设了传播各种学术的"百家讲坛"，天禄阁就是汉代学者经常"开坛"的场所之一。今天的汉城遗址上，曾经的未央宫、石渠阁、建章宫等皇家宫阙都已化作阡陌田野上的一个个孤零零的大土包，唯有天禄阁伴着一间小祠庙留存至今。

While the CCTV program "Lecture Room" enjoys popularity at present, few people know that our ancestors had already established various academic "lecture rooms" in as early as the Han Dynasty (206 B.C. - 220 A.D.), including Tianluge, where Han scholars often convened for lectures. On the ancient site of Hancheng, imperial palaces like the Weiyang Palace, Shiquge and the Jianzhang Palace have all ended up mere mounts on the vast plain. Only Tianluge survived by a small ancestral hall.

**瘦身的朱雀大道**
**The Avenue Slimming Down**

阿根廷布宜诺斯艾利斯的七月九日大街被认为是当今世界上最宽的马路，足有 140 米宽。但相比于唐朝西安的朱雀大街，它还是要逊色一点。当年的朱雀大街叫天街，是唐朝皇帝城南祭天走的街道，是西安城的主干道。不过一千多年来，朱雀大街"瘦身"很快，只剩下 30 多米宽，总长度也不及原来的三分之一了。

The world's widest avenue, 9 de Julio Avenue in Buenos Aires, Argentina, is 140 meters wide. It is, however, eclipsed by Xi'an's Zhuque Avenue in the Tang Dynasty. A main road in ancient Xi'an, it was called the Heaven Avenue because the Tang emperors walked along it to the south of the city to make sacrifices to heaven. Over the last dozen centuries, however, Zhuque Avenue has "slimmed down" fast to only 30 meters in width, and less than a third of its original length.

**书院门**
The Academy Gate

从南门进城，向前几十米右拐便是书院门古文化街。街口牌楼上书有“碑林藏国宝，书院育人杰”的对联，隐含着这街上的两个重要地标——碑林博物馆和关中书院。街道两旁是清一色的仿古建筑，关中书院便“隐身”其中。如果不是伫立在街边的一尊礼学大师冯从吾塑像，路过者也许会错过“他”身后的书院。

Enter the city via the South Gate, turn right after dozens of meters, and you'll hit the Ancient Culture Street by the Academy Gate. On the archway at the intersection writes the couplet: “The Beilin hides the national treasure. The ancient academy produces the best scholars”, alluding to the two significant landmarks on this street: the Beilin Museum, and the Guangzhong Academy. Among the ancient structures that line up the street “hides” the Guangzhong Academy. If it weren't for the statue of great master Feng Congwu (1556 - 1627) by the street, passersby could easily miss the academy behind.

**关中书院**
The Guanzhong Academy

今天的西安，高校众多，其中知名度和影响力较大的有西安交通大学、西北工业大学和西北大学等。而在一百多年前，西安最著名的“高校”是关中书院。400年来，关中书院始终作为传道、授业、解惑的场所传承至今，目前仍是西安师范学院校址，是一座国内少见的“活的书院”。

Xi'an is home to many universities, the best known and most influential of which include Xi'an Jiaotong University, Northwestern Polytechnical University and Northwest University. More than a century ago, however, the best known “university” was the Guanzhong Academy. Throughout 400 years, the Guanzhong Academy has remained an institute for teaching ancient wisdom and answering questions. One of the few surviving academies of its type in China, the site still houses Xi'an Normal University.

**艺术感十足的霍去病墓**
The Mausoleum of Huo Qubing

西安周边的陵墓非常多，贾平凹向外地的朋友介绍：“你如果是政治家，请去参观秦兵马俑以张扬你的气势；你如果是艺术家，请去参观霍去病墓以寻找浑然整体的感觉。”霍去病墓最具特色的是它的石刻，这里的石刻都依石拟形，是中国目前发现的年代最早、保存最完整的一批大型石雕艺术珍品。

Since Xi'an is surrounded by mausoleums, writer Jia Pingwa told his nonlocal friends: “If you are a statesman, visit the terracotta warriors and parade your power; if you are an artist, visit the Mausoleum of Huo Qubing(140 - 117 B.C.) for its wholesome feel.” Most distinctive about Huo's mausoleum is the stone carvings, with each shaped very naturally. They are the best-preserved and most ancient stone treasures in China.

摄影：尚洪涛

## 闯关中
Migrating to Guanzhong

一百多年前，一些山东人离开老家，驾着马车，推着独轮车，挑着担子，携老扶幼，风餐露宿，跋涉上千公里，来到陕西，在渭河北岸的黄土地上建起新家园。与同时期移民东北的山东人“闯关东”相呼应，谱写了一部“闯关中”的传奇。阎良区的谭家村，就是这样一个由山东人建起来的移民村。

Over a century ago, some people in Shandong left their home, rode on carriages, pushed carts, carried shoulder-poles, and brought their entire families along on their journey. They slept and ate in the wild, trudged over a thousand kilometers, arrived in Shaanxi, and built their new homes on the yellow earth north of the Wei River. Similar to those who migrated northwest, the people to Shaanxi passed into a legend of “migrating to Guanzhong”. For instance, Tanjia Village in Yanliang District is an immigrant village built by Shandong people.

**地名值得玩味**
**Fascinating Names**

西安的地名值得再三咀嚼。冰窖巷是因为明代秦藩王宫和清代满族官僚夏季藏冰于此而得名；五味什字则得名于中药的甘、辛、酸、苦、咸五味，明清两代直至民国初年，这里药业汇集。还有许多诸如粉巷、书院门、大差市等古代沿袭下来的名称，读来就能感受到盛唐时期的繁华热闹。

The street names in Xi'an are pregnant with culture. Bingjiao (literally, "ice vault") Lane received its name for functioning as an ice store in summer for the aristocrats during the Ming(1368 - 1644) and Qing(1616 - 1911) dynasties. Wuwei Shizi (literally, "five-flavor crossroads") got its name for being the center of traditional Chinese pharmaceuticals from the Ming and Qing dynasties to the early Republic of China years. The "five flavors" are sweet, spicy, sour, bitter and salty in traditional Chinese medicine. Other names like Fen Xiang (Powder Alley), Academy's Gate, and Dachaishi (Important Matter's Market) all offer a glimpse into the prosperity of the Tang Dynasty(618 - 907) in its heyday.

**道北今昔**
**North of the Railway**

冯小刚的影片《一九四二》中，对大量河南灾民逃往西安之事有不少表现。西安北门外的铁路沿线以北，就是当年河南灾民聚居区，简称“道北”。道北曾是“赤贫、落后”的代名词；而如今，这里高楼林立，且伴有大明宫遗址保护区，昔日的旧模样一去不复返。

*Back to 1942*, a film by Feng Xiaogang, portrayed large groups of Henan refugees fleeing to Xi'an, who gathered and settled along the railway outside the north gate of the city. Their residential district was called Daobei, literally, "North of the Railway". It used to be a synonym for poverty and backwardness. With tall buildings and the Daming Palace National Heritage Park, this area has taken on a new look now.

**古市与今市**
**Ancient and Modern Markets**

现在西安叫“市”和与“市”相关的街道依旧比比皆是。竹笆市，唐代尚书省对着的一条街道，明代因竹木家具集中在此地而得名，如今此街作用依旧。骡马市，自古就是繁华街市，明清时成为骡马市场，如今是大型商业步行街。炭市街，过去卖的是煤炭，而非白居易《卖炭翁》中的木炭，近现代以卖海产品为主。

Xi'an has evovled from a town of many markets, so a number of street names here are related to certain markets. Zhubashi (literally, "bamboo fence market"), for instance, a street opposite to the Tang Dynasty's Department of State Affairs, received its name for being the center of bamboo and wooden furniture in the Ming Dynasty, a function still served today. Luomashi (literally, "the mule and horse market"), a hustling street since ancient times, evolved into a livestock market in the Ming and Qing dynasties, and is now a major shopping street. Tanshijie (literally, "coal market street"), a street that used to sell coal (not charcoal), mainly vends marine products nowadays.

## 玄奘长眠之地
## The Resting Place of Xuanzang

提到唐僧，很多人会想到西安以及西安的大雁塔，而很少有人会注意到大唐护国兴教寺。这座坐落于西安城南少陵原的寺院正是玄奘法师长眠之地，为唐代樊川八大寺院之首。从公元 669 年建成至今，寺院几度兴衰，但玄奘和两位弟子的舍利塔却一直得以保存。

The mere mention of Buddhist monk Xuanzang (602 - 664) reminds many of Xi'an and the Giant Wild Goose Pagoda, yet few would think of the Xingjiao Temple in Shaoling Plateau in southern Xi'an, which ranked first among the top eight famed temples in Fanchuan in the Tang Dynasty partially because it was the palace where Xuanzang rests in peace. Since its establishment in 669, the temple has gone through multiple ups and downs, but the dagobas for Xuanzang and his two disciples have been preserved.

摄影：尚洪涛、刘潇

**有历史的丰镐路**
Fenghao Road

丰镐路是西安城西的一条东西向主干道，许多外地人初来都会念错这个路名，把镐（hào）念成了 gǎo。可别小瞧这个路名，十三朝古都西安第一次成为全国性都城就是这西周的丰镐，丰镐是西周文王所建丰京和武王所建镐京的合称，丰在沣河西，镐在沣河东。丰镐遗址在如今西安西南方的户县。

Fenghao Road is a major road that runs east and west in west Xi'an. Many freshly-arrived nonlocals get the name wrong, pronouncing it "gao" instead of "hao". This name, however, is not to be underestimated. Xi'an began its history as the capital of 13 dynasties in Fenghao when the Western Zhou Dynasty (1046 - 771 B.C.) established its capital here. Located in Huxian, a county southwest of contemporary Xi'an, Fenghao was the twin settlements of Fengjing on the west bank of the Fenghe River and Haojing on the east bank, with the former established by King Wen (reign c.1099 - 1061 B.C.) and the latter by King Wu (reign c.1046 - 1042 B.C.). The actual Fenghao site is located southwest of Xi'an in Huxian.

**坊**
Wards

唐长安城的坊就是居民区，纵横交错的道路将盛唐的长安城分作 110 坊，也成就了中国历史上城市布局史无前例的广阔与独特。长乐坊、安仁坊、回坊……一些坊的地名西安沿用至今，走进这些里坊，依然可追寻昔日门庭若市的兴旺景象。

In the Tang capital Chang'an, the residential ward was called "Fang". Intersecting roads divided the city into 110 wards, which marked unprecedented scale and distinctness for Chinese urban planning. Such names of wards as Changlefang, Anrenfang, Huifang are still in use today. Walking in these wards, one can still retrace the once bustling and prosperous scenes.

摄影：翟小雪

**墓区公园**
Cemetery Park

陈忠实的小说《白鹿原》里，白灵提到过一个万人坑。历史上，北洋军阀刘镇华曾率十万人围困西安。至解围时，包括阵亡将士在内，西安城内有五万多人死亡。后来，在于右任的主持下，修建公墓和纪念馆，并以公墓为基础建设革命公园。如今，公园已成为守城之战的记忆。

In Chen Zhongshi's novel *White Deer Plain*, Bai Ling speaks of a Revolution Park where tens of thousands of bodies were buried in a pit. In 1926, Xi'an was besieged by ten thousands of soldiers led by warlord Liu Zhenhua. The warfare left over 50,000 dead. Later, Yu Youren (1879 - 1964), a famous scholar, advocated the construction of a public cemetery and a memorial museum. The Revolution Park was based on the cemetery in honor of the courageous defense.

**乐游原**
Leyou Plateau

在大雁塔的东北方，有一块高出平地数十米的黄土台塬，名叫乐游原，这里曾经是唐朝长安城的最高点，文人墨客登高远眺时，往往才思泉涌，留下许多脍炙人口的诗句。李商隐登临乐游原后，留下了“夕阳无限好，只是近黄昏”这一佳句。

To the northeast of the Giant Wild Goose Pagoda lies a highland called Leyou Yuan, once the highest point in Chang'an during the Tang Dynasty, which commanded a panaromic view. Standing here and looking afar, literati often felt inspired and produced household poems. In the wake of his trip here, Li Shangyin (813 - 858), a Tang poet, left the world the famous stanza "To see the sun, for all his glory, buried by the coming night".

**西风残照，汉家陵阙**
The Cold Wind Blows, the Sun Sets, over the Mausoleum of the Han

“西风残照，汉家陵阙。”唐代诗人眼中的景象，在今天的关中平原仍能感知。汉阳陵外藏坑遗址保护展示厅的入口处，有一幅巨大的照片：夕阳正落于南阙门和阳陵封土之间，染红天边的云霞。今天看到的人，仍不免如诗人般发出故国兴亡之感叹：“青山依旧在，几度夕阳红……古今多少事，都付笑谈中。”

"The cold wind blows, the sun sets, over the mausoleum of the Han." This scenery that the Tang poet once marveled at can still be seen on the Guanzhong plains today. At the entrance to the Outside Pits Exhibition Hall of the Yangling Mausoleum of the Han Dynasty, there is a gigantic photo: the setting sun is lodged between the South Gate Tower and the grave mound, dying the clouds red on the horizon. People, witnessing this scene today, cannot help but recite the lines about the fall of one's country, just like another poet did, "Yet stand of old the hillocks green / How many sunsets red went by and / days of present or past, more or less / O throw to gossip and jest".

摄影：尚洪涛

## 鸠摩罗什与草堂寺
## Kumārajīva and the Straw Hut Temple

人人都知《金刚经》，却少有人知道《金刚经》译者鸠摩罗什的舍利就安放在西安市户县草堂寺。公元 401 年，龟兹高僧鸠摩罗什受后秦国王姚兴邀请东入长安，在此苫草建堂译经，草堂寺因此得名。今日草堂寺，远眺有秦岭，近看有莲花，气度庄严不差千年之前。

Many know the *Diamond Sutra*, but few know that the stupa of Kumārajīva (the translator) stands at the Straw Hut Temple in Xi'an's southern suburbs. In 401, Buddhist master Kumārajīva traveled east to Chang'an from Kucha at the invititaion of the Later Qin King Yao Xing (reign 394 - 416). A thatch-roofed house was built for him to translate Buddhist scriptures, hence the name Straw Hut Temple. At the temple today, the Qinling Mountains hover on the horizon, and lotus flowers blossom close at hand. Its grandeur and solemnnity remain the same as it was thousands of years ago.

## 西安也产大米
## Rice and Xi'an

在以面食为主的关中，大米多来自外地。很多人都不知道，其实西安也产大米，南郊的长安区就有 400 多亩的水稻种植基地。这里种植水稻的历史可以追溯到三千多年前的西周。《诗经·小雅·白华》里有这样的话：“滮池北流，浸彼稻田”。滮池在今西安西南的长安区灵沼，可见当时这里就已经种植水稻了。

In Guanzhong where the staple diet is wheat flour, rice mostly come from other provinces. Few know that Xi'an produces rice as well. In the southern suburbs, there is a rice plantation base as large as 400 *mu* (266,700 square meters) in the Chang'an District. The history of rice cropping here goes back more than 3,000 years to the Western Zhou Dynasty. It is recorded in "Xiao Ya" (Minor Court Hymns) in the *Book of Odes* that "the Biao Pool flowed north, watering the rice fields". The Biao Pool is located in the Chang'an District, giving evidence of early rice plantation here.

## 香米园
## Fragrant Rice Garden

香米园，一个好听的名字，那里有多条小巷，交织成片。也因为这个名字，总让人觉得那里曾经应该是稻田葱绿。而事实上，香米园的命名与米无关。它的真正来源是：北宋时期宰相寇准在陕为官时，给位于此处的自家花园题名“香墨园”。久而久之，“香墨园”就演变成了谐音“香米园”。

With a beautiful name, Xiangmiyuan (literally, "fragrant rice garden") is an intersection of several alleys. This name seems to be a reminder of a green rice field. Yet its origin had nothing to do with rice. When Kou Zhun (961 - 1023), a chancellor in the Northern Song Dynasty (960 - 1127), was appointed as an official here, he named his garden "Xiangmoyuan" (fragrant ink garden). Over time, Xiangmoyuan evolved into Xiangmiyuan.

**钟楼的搬迁**
**The Relocation of the Bell Tower**

钟楼位于西安市中心。很多人不知道，钟楼最早并不在现在的地方。据《钟楼碑》记载，明洪武十七年（1384年），钟楼始建，选址在今日的西大街与广济街口。两百年后的明万历年间，随着城市中心东移，城门改建，钟楼显得日益偏离城市中心，于是向东进行了整体搬迁，移至现址。

The Bell Tower is located in downtown Xi'an, yet its original site remains obscure to many. According to the inscriptions on the Bell Tower Stele, the tower was built in the 17th year of Emperor Hongwu's reign (1384) at the crossing of West Street and Guangji Street. Two hundred years later, during the Wanli period (1573-1620) of the Ming Dynasty, with the city center shifted east and some city gates refurbished, the Bell Tower seemed to be gradually off-centered; therefore, it was moved east to its current location.

**姑娘村**
**The Girls' Village**

西八里有个姑娘村，在20世纪90年代叫作姑娘楼。由于当时村子富裕，专门为姑娘们建了一座楼，如果姑娘不外嫁，女婿上门，两人就可住进姑娘楼内，享受村子里的优厚待遇。这样的村子在西安原有很多，现随着观念的改变和城中村的拆除，姑娘村已经慢慢淡出人们的视线。

There was a Girls' Village in Xibali. In the 1990s, Xibali was rich and local girls were reluctant to marry out, so a "Girls' Mansion" was built to house couples if the wife was a villager and the husband chose to marry into the village. How great a favor it was! There used to be many such villages in Xi'an, but as social views changed and "villages in the city" got demolished, girls' villages have gradually faded out.

**骡马市**
**The Mule and Horse Market**

骡马市位于钟楼东边，明清时期因交易骡马而得名。20世纪80年代初，当西北的百姓还穿着中山装时，就有人尝试从南方购进时髦服装在此摆摊。这条南北长365米的街上，有着近千家个体经营户，每天客流量达40万人次，时尚风暴席卷整个西北。经过改造升级，老街面容一新，如今仍保持着时尚风向标的地位。

The Mule and Horse Market (Luomashi) located to the east of the Bell Tower attained its name for its livestock trade during the Ming and Qing dynasties. In the early 1980s when ordinary people in northwest China still wore the Mao suits, pioneers stocked fashionable clothes from the south and set up stalls in the Mule and Horse Market. The 365-meter street stretching from north to south held nearly a thousand private businesses and received about 400 thousand customers each day, sparking a fashion storm that swept through the entire northwest region. With renovation and upgradation, this ancient street puts on a brand new look and remains the trendsetter.

摄影：贾庆华、翟小雪

## 韩湘子与湘子庙街
## Han Xiangzi and Xiangzi Temple Street

韩湘子，传说中的道教八仙之一，据说是文学家韩愈的侄孙，从小放荡不羁，常饮酒醉卧，偏偏练就神仙之道。韩湘子在洒金桥碰见铁拐李和吕洞宾，受到点化，修炼多年后得道。于是，后人在韩湘子修行的这条街上，盖了一座庙，叫湘子庙。这条街，就叫湘子庙街，现位于西安南门里西侧。

Han Xiangzi, one of the Eight Immortals of Taoism, is said to be the grandnephew of essayist Han Yu. He led a wild life in his youth and often lay drunk and idle. Yet he mastered the way of becoming an immortal. Legend has it that Han Xiangzi encountered Iron-Crutch Li and Lu Dongbin on the Sajin Bridge. Enlightened by their wisdom, he attained immortality after many years of practice. On the street where he practiced Taoism, a temple was later built in his honor, hence the name Xiangzi Temple Street. Today the street is located in the west side of Nanmenli, stretching westward.

摄影：贾庆华

### 诗人最爱渼陂湖
### The Poets' Favorite Lake

渼陂湖位于西安西南，渼水发源于终南山谷，流经于此蓄积成湖。唐代地理专著《十道四番志》中记："地有五味陂，产鱼甚美，因名之。"杜甫、韦应物、苏轼等都为渼陂留下不少美词好句。这里至今还有宋时为纪念杜甫而修建的空翠堂，还有秦始皇母亲住过的行宫遗址和周文王父亲的墓冢。

In the southwest of Xi'an, Meibei Lake is fed by the Mei River originating in the Zhongnan Mountains and trickling down to form the lake. According to *Chronicles of Ten Prefectures and Four Dependent States*, a Tang Dynasty geography book: "There's a pond called 'Flavorful Lake' (the original name for Meibei Lake), which produces delicious fish; it was named consequently." Famous poets Du Fu (712 - 770), Wei Yingwu (737 - 792) and Su Shi (1037 - 1101) were all inspired to write beautiful poems about the lake. Today, Kongcui Hall, built in memory of Du Fu during the Song Dynasty (960 - 1279), still stands by the lake, along with the temporary abode of Emperor Qinshihuang's (259 - 210 B.C.) mother, and the tomb of King Wen of Zhou's father.

### 崔护和樊川
### Poet Cui Hu and the Fanchuan Plain

"去年今日此门中，人面桃花相映红。人面不知何处去，桃花依旧笑春风。"这首诗是唐代诗人崔护在落第后重游樊川时所作。樊川是西安城南少陵原与神禾原之间的一片平川，诗中的农家已无处可寻，樊川这个名字却因为崔护和这首诗而代代相传。

"This day last year at this doorway, a maiden face and peach blossoms were shining bright and gay. She is here no more; while the peach blossoms in the spring breeze are smiling as before." This poem was written by Tang poet Cui Hu during his trip to Fanchuan after he failed the imperial examination. Fanchuan is a plain in the south of Xi'an that spreads between Shaoling Plateau and Shenhe Plateau. Although the farmhouse mentioned in the poem is nowhere to be found, the term "Fanchuan" has become a household name thanks to Cui's poem.

### 报话大楼是"劳模"
### The Model Worker of Xi'an

在现代化建筑林立的今天，西安人对西华门的报话大楼仍有着特殊的情感。它于 1963 年竣工并投入使用，作为西安市的标志性建筑之一，几十年来一直是西安人心中的"北京时间"。时钟每小时报时一次，钟声洪亮，响彻市中心，如今已经整点报时 50 多年了。网友 @寻找老西安 感叹："这才是西安真正的劳模啊！"

Among the forest of modern buildings stands an iconic structure, the Baohua Tower. It came into use in 1965 and has endeared itself to the locals as an announcer of Beijing Time. The big clocks on its top strike every hour and the sounds resonate through downtown. It has been loyally fulfilling its duty for more than 50 years. Netizen @寻找老西安 (In Search of Old Xi'an) praised: "It is the true model worker of Xi'an."

摄影：贾庆华

## 史上最著名澡堂子

### The Most Famous Bathhouse in History

临潼华清池，千年之前就是皇家温泉离宫。现今景区内还保留着唐玄宗御用的莲花汤、杨贵妃沐浴的海棠汤遗址，瞬间穿越至白居易《长恨歌》中的“春寒赐浴华清池，温泉水滑洗凝脂”。这座史上最著名的澡堂子，如今周边遍布着各式疗养院、星级温泉酒店，皇家享受不再神秘。

Famous for its hot springs, Huaqing Pool in Lintong became an imperial resort a thousand years ago. The relics of the Lotus Pool used by Emperor Xuanzong (reign 712 - 756) of the Tang Dynasty and the Crabapple Pool by Yang Guifei (719 - 756), the emperor's consort, will bring alive the scene depicted by poet Bai Juyi (772 - 846) in “The Song of Everlasting Regret”: “On a cold spring day, he bestowed upon her the honor of bathing with him at the Huaqing pool; The water of the hot spring was smooth, and washed over her creamy skin.” The most famous “bathhouse” in history is now surrounded by various sanatoriums and star-rated hotels. The royal treatment is no longer mysterious to the common people.

**兴庆宫公园**
Xingqing Palace Park

兴庆宫在唐朝曾是唐玄宗与杨贵妃居住的地方。李白的名句“云想衣裳花想容，春风拂槛露华浓”即写于此。今日的兴庆宫公园是 1958 年为配合西安交通大学整体搬迁而修建的，是我国第一个在文物遗址原址上扩建的文化公园，其设计沿用了当年兴庆宫的格局，是市民休闲娱乐的好场所。

The Xingqing Palace Park is the first cultural park built around a historical relic in China. The Xingqing Place was the imperial residence for Emperor Xuanzong and his concubine Yang Guifei. Poet Li Bai's (701 - 762) famous stanza of Yang, "Her robe is a cloud, her face a flower; her balcony, glimmering with the bright spring dew", was written here. The Xingqing Palace Park was built in 1958 to accommodate the relocation of Xi'an Jiaotong University. The design followed the layout of the original Xingqing Palace, but the park itself has become a great place for local residents to hang out.

**离西藏最近的地方**
The Place Closest to Tibet

广仁寺又名喇嘛寺，位于西安古城墙内西北角，是全国重点寺院，也是陕西省唯一的藏传佛教寺院。它 1703 年由清圣祖康熙帝敕建，寓意“广布仁慈”，历史上起着凝聚西北边陲多民族、促进团结的作用。这里也被誉为陕西“离西藏最近的地方”。

The Guangren Temple, also called the Lama Temple, is situated in the northwest corner inside the city wall. One of the key temples in China, it is the only Tibetan Buddhist monastery in Shaanxi Province. By order of Kangxi Emperor (reign 1661 - 1722) in 1703, the temple was built "to widely spread benevolence". Since then it has played an important role in increasing social cohesion and ethnic unity in the northwest. Today, it is hailed as the place closest to Tibet in Shaanxi.

摄影：王幼健

**端履门**
Duanlümen

西安的一些地名，往往会误导外地游客。例如东大街附近的端履门，这个地方的来历与鞋子无关，且现在也没有城门。端履门这个地名，从明代西安秦王府城的“端礼门”一脉相承而来。“礼”和“履”读音相近，后来成了端履门或许只是一种误读。

Some of the place names in Xi'an could mislead tourists. For instance, the origin of the place "Duanlümen" (literally, "Decorous Shoe Gate") near the East Street has nothing to do with shoes or a gate. It was derived from "Duanlimen" ("Decorous Propriety Gate") of the Prince Qin's Mansion in the Ming Dynasty. The pronunciations *li* and *lü* closely resemble each other; therefore, the name Duanlümen could just be a misinformation.

**辋川**
Wangchuan

诗人王维曾在蓝田辋川隐居 20 余年，他最好的诗句都写于这里。位于终南山下的辋川因此成为历代文人的“朝圣之地”。今日辋川，不仅有王维故居、宋之问别墅旧址，还有刘邦与秦军最后决战的峣关、蒉山古战场。在辋川，佐史佐实，也许更能体会王维笔下“行到水穷处，坐看云起时”的意境。

For over 20 years, poet Wang Wei (701 - 761) lived a hermit life in Wangchuan Town, Lantian County, where he wrote his best poems. As a result, Wangchuan, situated at the foot of the Zhongnan Mountains, became a holy place for the literati. In today's Wangchuan, there's not only the old residence of Wang Wei, but also the villa of Song Zhiwen (656 - 712), a Tang Dynasty chancellor, let alone the ancient battlefields in Yaoguan Pass and Kuishan Mountain, where Liu Bang (reign 202 - 195 B.C.), the founder of the Han Dynasty, defeated the Qin army. In Wangchuan, with history and relics, you may have a better understanding of Wang Wei's poetic lines: "Walk leisurely to where the stream end, sit and watch the clouds rise."

**四个“二府庄”**
Four "Erfu Zhuang"

西安有四个“二府庄”。雁塔区有两个，莲湖区有一个，未央区有一个。一城之内有四个地方使用同一地名的确少见，这主要是历史传承原因所致：或为官员住地，或为皇亲庄园，或为官府田庄，个个得名都很有来头。因此，如果您来西安打车去二府庄，一定要向司机说清楚是哪个街办辖区的二府庄，以免南辕北辙。

In Xi'an, there are four places named "Erfu Zhuang": two in Yanta District, one in Lianhu District, and one in Weiyang District. It is indeed rare for a city to have four places under the same name, but it is due to historical evolution. Each one of these places used to be the residence of an official, the mansion of a royal, or the land of the magistrate. Each was named with significance. If you take a taxi to Erfu Zhuang in Xi'an, remember to clarify its district and street, or you may end up at the other side of town.

摄影：尚洪涛

**骊山**
**Mt. Li**

骊山其实很小，以其色如苍黛、形如骏马得名。山虽小，故事却很多。周幽王为讨爱妃褒姒一笑，烽火戏诸侯发生在这里；项羽没能杀掉刘邦的鸿门宴也在这里；李隆基与杨贵妃演绎的绝世爱恋在这里；改变中国现代史的“西安事变”也是在这里。

Mt. Li, literally, “Black Steed Mount”, is in fact quite small. The mount resembles a black horse. Tiny as it is, it’s full of history. This is where King You of Zhou (reign 782 - 771 B.C.) faked warning beacons and fooled his nobles in order to amuse his favorite concubine Baosi. This was also the venue for the Feast at Hong Gate (206 B.C.), when Xiang Yu (232 - 202 B.C.) spared the life of Liu Bang only to be defeated by Liu later on. This is also where Li Longji, Emperor Xuanzong of Tang, and Yang Guifei had their romance. Moreover, it is the site of Xi’an Incident (1936) that changed the course of modern Chinese history.

**西安北郊**
**The North Suburbs of Xi’an**

以前，西安人把铁道以北称为北郊。这里曾是唐朝皇帝办公的地方，后来却成了西安落后的一角，直到上世纪30年代陇海铁路向西延伸，才有所好转。如今，随着行政中心北迁以及大明宫遗址公园等西安新名片的建成，西安北郊已成为城市新核心。2000年以前一到晚上就漆黑一片，现在却变成了不夜城。

In the old days, the Xi’anese called the area north of the railway “northern suburbs”. Although Tang Dynasty emperors tended state affairs here, it became an under-developed corner of the city. The situation didn’t improve until the 1930s when the Longhai Railway extended westward. Now, with the relocation of the municipal government to the north and the establishment of new landmarks like the Daming Palace National Heritage Park, the northern suburbs has become a new center of the city. At night this area was completely dark before 2000 but brightly lit at present.

**开通巷**
**Kaitong Alley**

要在名胜古迹之外寻觅一道西安的怀旧风景，开通巷是不错的选择。这条从明清时代延续下来的老街道，过去鲜有商铺、单位，是比较纯粹的居住区，如今沿街尽是店铺。巷内有百年老树，路边不时可见磨光了的石礅，许多居民家还在沿用老式的砖木门头，还有几户值得探访的百年老屋。

If you are seeking a nostalgic trip aside from well-known historic attractions, Kaitong Alley is a good choice. This street dates back to the Ming and Qing eras and used to be a pure residential area with few shops or institutes. Nowadays, it is lined up with stores, but you can still find hundred-year-old trees and worn stone stools along the alley. Many residences kept their old-fashioned brick wooden transoms; a few century-old houses are also worth visiting.

**西安有个杏花村**
**The Apricot Blossom Village**

杜牧诗中“牧童遥指杏花村”中的杏花村到底在哪儿，已很难说清楚。但西安有个村子却是名副其实的“杏花村”。蓝田县华胥镇阿氏村，原名娲氏村，据说女娲曾在此居住，以出产娲氏大杏闻名。村中种植的杏树，有的已逾百年。每年三月，漫山遍野的杏花开放，整个村庄浸在花海之中，如诗如画。

The actual Apricot Blossom Village in Du Mu's (803 - 852) famous verse "a cowherd boy points, far away, to the Apricot Blossom Village" is difficult to locate now, but there is one in Xi'an. The Ashi Village in Huaxu Town of Lantian County is famous for its large Washi apricots. Originally named Washi Village, it is said to be Godness Nüwa's residence. Some of the village's apricot trees are over a hundred years old. Every March, apricots blossom all over the fields and hills, drowning the whole village in a dreamy floral sea.

**香积寺的日与夜**
**The Life at the Temple of Heaped Fragrance**

“不知香积寺，数里入云峰。古木无人径，深山何处钟。”唐代诗人王维笔下静谧闲淡的古刹意境，今天在香积寺仍可感知。这个位于子午大道边的千年寺院幽而不僻，静而不寂。寺中 30 多位僧人至今延续暮鼓晨钟、早课晚课的传统生活。世界变幻，但古朴苍凉的寺院永恒。

"Not knowing the way to the Temple of Heaped Fragrance, under miles of mountain-cloud I have wandered; through ancient woods without a human track, but now on the height I hear a bell." What the Tang poet Wang Wei had depicted can still be felt today. Located by Ziwu Boulevard, the thousand-year-old temple is covert yet not secluded, quiet yet not lonely. Over 30 monks here have kept the traditional Buddhist lifestyle: chanting sultra in the morning and evening, ringing the bell at dawn and striking the drum at dusk. The world changes every day, but the ancient temple remains simple.

### 宅门深处有人家
### Families Deep in the Courtyards

新中国成立前，西安城中曾流传"高家的墙，马家的房，米家的金子拿斗量"，说的是北院门的三大富户。但今人更感兴趣的不是他们曾经的富有，而是他们留下的已有三四百年历史的极具关中特色的老宅。现今北院门144号就是当年高家宅院之一；马家老宅在北院门路西中段；米家的房产在北院门路西的南段。

Before 1949, it was well-known in Xi'an that "tall are the walls of the Gao family, grand are the houses of the Ma family, and bright is the gold of the Mi family." These lines were about the wealth of the three families in Beiyuanmen. What interests us today is not their past wealth, but their Guanzhong-style residences that are three to four hundred years old. No. 114 of Beiyuanmen Road is one of the Gao family's old residences; the Ma family had their old house located at the mid-section of Beiyuanmen Road, while the Mi family had property on the west side at the south section of the road.

### 楼观变迁
### The Changing Views on Louguan Peak

"关中河山百二，以终南为最胜；终南千峰耸翠，以楼观为最名。"这个曾以老子著《道德经》闻名的圣地，如今被冠以"财神庙"标签着力宣传。从"无为而治"的恬淡寡欲，到祈求财富的世俗功利，世风人心的变化也尽在其中了。

"Among the 120 mountains and rivers in Guanzhong, the Zhongnan Mountains is the most beautiful; and among the thousands of towering green peaks of the Zhongnan Mountians, Louguan Peak is the most famed." The sacred place where Laozi (c.571 - 471 B.C.) wrote *Tao Te Ching* is now heavily promoted under the label of "Temple of the God of Wealth", bearing witness to the shift of moral values from indifference to fame and gain in Laozi's doctrine of "action without action" to the sheer secular pursuit of fortune.

摄影：王旭东

## 张学良公馆

The Former Residence of General Zhang Xueliang

建国路 69 号，三幢三层砖木结构西式小楼里，家具陈设依然保留着上世纪 30 年代模样，主人的公文包、笔筒、戎装、皮靴一样不少，就连美国通用公司当时生产的“别克世纪 210C”黑色轿车都仿佛刚刚入库。1936 年 12 月 12 日，就是这处小院酝酿出震惊世界的西安事变，它的名字叫作张学良公馆。

At 69 Jianguo Road, in three little Western-style buildings, the furniture arrangement still stands like that in the 1930s, with the briefcase, pen container, military uniform and leather boots remaining in place. Even the black Buick Lesabre 210C by General Motors looks like a new arrival in the garage. On December 12, 1936, the plan for the world-shaking Xi'an Incident was born in this courtyard, the Former Residence of General Zhang Xueliang (1901 - 2001).

摄影：王旭东

**书市**
The Book Market

西安城的东六路是书市，全长不足 800 米的街面上，集中着大大小小百余家书店，门面散乱错落，看起来不打眼，各种门类的最新版书却是一应俱全。《美文》杂志的常务副主编穆涛爱书，他说：“每个周末都要去东六路转一圈，一是搜买新书，二是呼吸那里乱乎乎却亲切的空气。”

Less than 800 meters long, the 6th East Road of Xi'an is a hub of over one hundred bookstores in varying sizes. Seemingly messy and unimpressive, the stores offer the latest editions of all kinds of books. Mu Tao, deputy editor-in-chief of the magazine *Mei Wen* (*Beautiful Prose*), is a book lover. He said, “Every weekend, I go to the 6th East Road to look for new books and enjoy the bustling yet friendly atmosphere.”

**低调的董仲舒墓**
The Low-key Tomb of Dong Zhongshu

陕西的黄土埋着数不尽的王孙显赫，这其中最“低调”的当属坐落在和平门内的董仲舒墓——下马陵，相传汉武帝路过董仲舒的墓也要下马步行。虽然陵墓就在西安城墙内，而且是陕西省首批重点保护文物，但很多当地人也不了解，它至今还藏在路边的一所院内，很少被外界关注。

The yellow earth of Shaanxi is the final resting place of countless royals and aristocrats. The tomb with the lowest profile is that of a Chinese philosopher, Dong Zhongshu (179 - 104 B.C.), located in Xiamaling (literally, “get off the horse”) inside Heping Gate. It is said that Emperor Wu of Han (reign 141 - 87 B.C.) would get off his horse and walk to pay his respect to Dong when passing by the tomb, hence the name. Although the tomb is located inside the city wall, and is one of the first important heritage sites under provincial protection, it is unknown to many locals. It is hidden away in a courtyard by the street, receiving little attention.

**名叫“浮沱”的村庄**
The Villages Named “Hutuo”

西安有不少称“浮沱”的村庄，比如南郊的金浮沱和沙浮沱，北郊的马浮沱和浮沱寨，这个“浮沱”是啥意思？有一种说法是凡是叫“浮沱”的地方都曾住过蒙古贵族，“浮沱”其实是蒙古语，意思是“水边的村镇”。据考证，这些称“浮沱”的村庄很多都出现在元代。

There are multiple villages called “Hutuo” in Xi'an, such as Jin Hutuo and Sha Hutuo in the southern suburbs and Ma Hutuo and Hutuo Zhai in the northern suburbs. Then what does “Hutuo” mean? One theory suggests that in all the places called Hutuo there once lived Mongolian royals, and “Hutuo” actually means “a waterside village” in the Mongolian language. According to research, most of these villages came into being during the Yuan Dynasty (1206 - 1368).

## 西安第一低调古庙
## An Ancient Temple with the Lowest Profile

东门里的东岳庙是西安为数不多的几处古代木构建筑，东岳庙里的壁画面积是陕西最大的，绘制水平也是全国所有东岳庙里最高的，至今栩栩如生。这里曾做过军营，也办过学校，但一直没有对外开放，因此被网友们称为“西安第一低调古庙”。按照规划，这里即将建成一座展示西安市井文化的民俗博物馆。

The Dongyue Taoist Temple inside the East Gate is one of the few ancient wooden structures that have survived in Xi'an. The area of the murals here is the largest in Shaanxi, and the drawing skill is the highest among the Dongyue Taoist temples in China. The murals are still vivid today. This temple was used as a military camp, then a school, but it has never been open to the public. Thus it is called "Xi'an's No.1 low-key ancient temple" by netizens. As has been planned, this temple will turn into a folk museum, exhibiting the lifestyle of the local people.

## 曲江初碧草初青
## Qujiang Lake in Early Spring

从皇家极地到大众乐土，曲江历经千年，盛衰几度。它在隋被圈为皇家禁苑，唐时成为平民最爱的公共园林，文人墨客常倾城而至，歌咏这里的迤逦幽远。2003 年“曲江新区”成立，大唐芙蓉园、大唐不夜城、曲江池相继开放，让这里再展“曲江初碧草初青，万毂千蹄匝岸行”的风貌。

From an imperial park to a public wonderland, Qujiang has gone through vicissitudes over the last millennium. It was designated as an imperial park exclusive to the royals in the Sui Dynasty (581 - 618), and in Tang it became a public wonderland. Men of letters often flocked here, praising its charm and tranquility. In 2003, Qujiang New District was established. With the Tang Paradise of Lotus, the Great Tang Ever-bright City, and Qujiang Lake open in succession, a poetic scene comes back: "When Qujiang just turned blue and the grass just green, millions of wheels and thousands of hooves pass by on the bank."

摄影：张宇明

**化觉巷安家老宅**
The An Family Mansion in Huajue Alley

化觉巷安家老宅是座青砖木门的小四合院，主人安守信是地道的坊上人。当整条街的人家都在推倒老屋建新房时，安守信对儿子说："我上午死了，你们下午再拆。" 1999 年，老宅入选中国和挪威联合实施的民居保护项目，经过两年修复原貌，经历了 200 年风雨的老宅荣获联合国科教文组织亚太地区文化保护遗产奖。

The mansion of the An Family in Huajue Alley is a little quadrangle with brick walls and a wooden gate. The owner An Shouxin is a typical resident of the Muslim Street. When other residents here demolished old houses and built new ones, An told his son, "I'll have to die in the morning for you to demolish our house in the afternoon." In 1999, the old mansion was designated as a historic residence under joint protection by China and Norway. After two years of restoration, this 200-year-old house won the UNESCO Asia-Pacific Award for Cultural Heritage Conservation.

**藻露堂和五味什字**
Zaolutang and the Five-flavor Crossing

藻露堂是西安老字号的中药店，比北京的同仁堂早了半个世纪。电视剧《大宅门》剧中有一个细节，说白家少爷避难投靠了长安城的沈家，沈家的原型即是藻露堂。今天的藻露堂仍在五味什字巷内，其实，五味什字的巷名也是由藻露堂而来，甘、酸、苦、辛、咸五味包容着，也散发着中药的药理。

Zaolutang, a time-honored Traditional Chinese Medicine pharmacy in Xi'an, is 50 years older than Beijing's Tongrentang, the most famous pharmaceutical company in China. In the TV drama *Grant Mansion Gate*, based on Tongrentang, there is one detail that the young master of the Bai family sought shelter from the Shen family in Chang'an, and this Shen family is based on Zaolutang. Today, Zaolutang is still located at Wuwei Shizi (literally, "five-flavor crossroads") Alley. In fact, the name of the alley has something to do with Zaolutang because Traditional Chinese Medicine's pharmacology features five flavors: sweet, sour, bitter, spicy and salty.

**很文艺的文艺路**
The Culture and Arts Road

文艺路，南起南二环，北至环城南路。从文昌门出来，目光所及是成立于 1957 年的西安市群众艺术馆，再往南走，省京剧团、省歌舞剧院、省戏曲研究院等文化演艺单位在路东顺次排列，文艺路由此得名。

Wenyi Road runs from the South Second Ring to Huancheng South Road. Out of the Wenchang Gate, the eastside of the road is lined from north to south by many art and entertainment institutes: Xi'an People's Art Troupe founded in 1957, Shaanxi Peking Opera Troupe, Singing and Dancing Institute, and Opera Research Institute, hence the name Culture and Arts Road.

## 大唐西市

## The Tang Dynasty West Market

大唐西市是丝绸之路的起点，也是唐时世界上最大的商贸中心。“五陵年少金市东，银鞍白马度春风。落花踏尽游何处，笑入胡姬酒肆中。”今日再读李白《少年行》，当年繁华仿若昨天。如今的大唐西市，是我国唯一在古遗址上恢复重建的大型商贸旅游区。如果您想感受市井文化，来大唐西市是一个不错的选择。

The Tang Dynasty West Market in Chang'an was where the Silk Road began, and also the largest commercial center in the world during the Tang Dynasty. “Into eastern downtown Chang'an comes a fine youth, blaz'ng like spring breeze, white horse with silver saddle, too. many fall'n flowers I've trodden; now where should I go? Laugh'ng, he enters Persian wine-house.” Reading this poem, “Youthful Adventures” by Li Bai, you may find that the prosperous scene feels like yesterday. Nowadays, the Tang Dynasty West Market is the only large commercial tourist zone restored on its original site in China. If you wish to get a feel of the quotidian urban life, a visit to the Tang market is a good choice.

摄影：刘珂、尚洪涛

**孝义王顺山**
Mt. Wangshun, a Symbol of Filial Piety

蓝田王顺山，古称玉山，有陕西“小黄山”之美誉，因中国古代二十四孝之一——王顺担土葬母于此而得名，距西安仅 55 公里，兼有华山之险、黄山之秀的特点，奇峰耸立，沟谷幽深。每年 4 月下旬至 5 月上旬，王顺山国家森林公园的千年杜鹃花海又是一景，给这座以“孝”闻名的王顺山披上绚丽色彩。

Mt. Wangshun in Lantian County, once called Jade Mountain, is acclaimed as Shaanxi's "Little Mt. Huang". It got its name because Wang Shun, one of the 24 Filial Exemplars in ancient China, buried his mother here. Only 55 km away from Xi'an, Mt. Wangshun is as precipitous as Mt. Hua (in Shaanxi Province) and as beautiful as Mt. Huang (in Anhui Province), with towering peaks and steep valleys. From April 20 to May 10 every year when Mt. Wangshun National Forest Park is a sea of azaleas, the symbol of filial piety appear all the more gorgeous.

**何家村唐代窖藏**
The Tang Dynasty Relics in Hejia Village

西安南郊的何家村，1970 年 10 月 5 日发生了一件大事，即后来被称为“何家村唐代窖藏”的文物出土。当时共出土文物一千多件，有些金银器皿连专家都叫不出名字，其中三件被定为中国国宝级文物，还有数十件国家一级文物。现在的何家村人已经住进了高楼大厦，文物都陈列在各大博物馆。

On October 5, 1970, a significant event took place in Hejia Village in the southern suburbs of Xi'an: the excavation of what later was named "the Relics of the Tang Dynasty". At that time, over 1,000 artifacts were unearthed, among which were gold and silver vessels that even experts could not identify. Three were designated as national historic treasures, and over 10 as first-class artifacts. Now, the villagers have moved into high-rise residential buildings, and the relics are on display at different major museums.

**颜真卿墓**
The Tomb of Yan Zhenqing

书法爱好者到西安，西安碑林是最重要的朝拜地。更资深的书法家，在集齐了太子太师颜真卿的《多宝塔感应碑》《麻姑山仙坛记》和其后期佳作《颜勤礼碑》后，会去位于蓝田的颜真卿墓凭吊一番。安史之乱时，颜氏与兄起兵抵抗，却在此地被奸臣所害。据说，以此墓土入墨，可得清正刚和气韵。

The Xi'an Beilin Museum is the most significant shrine for calligraphy lovers. Having collected Yan Zhenqing's (709 - 785) *Duobao Pagoda Stele, Magu Shan Xiantan Ji*, and his Magnum Opus *Yan Qingli Stele*, senior calligraphers would make a pilgrimage to Yan's tomb in Lantian County. During the An-Shi Rebellion (755 - 763), Yan and his elder brother put up a resistance, yet he died here in Lantian County because of a traitor. It is said that if the earth from the tomb is used in ink, then the writing will attain a bold and ethereal aura.

**咸阳古渡**

**The Ancient Ferry of Xianyang**

西安的东西两侧各有一座著名的桥，城东的是灞桥，城西的为咸阳桥。这两座桥都因离别而闻名，也各自延伸出“关中八景”中的一景，城东的是“灞柳风雪”，城西的则是“咸阳古渡”。“劝君更进一杯酒，西出阳关无故人。”唐代诗人王维的《送元二使安西》一诗，正是在咸阳渡口为朋友饯行时所作。

There are two famous bridges in Xi'an. Both of them are famous for being the place for departure, and both are among "Eight Scenic Spots in Guanzhong". One is "Snowy Willow Catkins of the Ba Bridge" on the east, and the other "Ancient Ferry of Xianyang" on the west. "Let's have another cup of wine, my dear sir; past the Yangguan out to the west, old friends there'll be none." The poem "Seeing Yuan Er off on a Mission to Anxi", by Wang Wei, was written when he bid goodbye to his friend at the Xianyang ferry.

**城墙肚子里的博物馆**

**The Museum Inside the City Wall**

西安城墙的城门，每一扇都有道不完的历史。含光门最独具一格，这里隐藏着一处完整的唐代皇城城门遗址。当年城墙倒塌，遗址露出真容，地上车辙清晰可见，使人怀想这里曾经车水马龙的繁华景象。修复后的遗址，外观以城砖包裹，与城墙一致，里面是框架结构的保护大厅，堪称藏在城墙肚子里的博物馆。

Every city gate of Xi'an has an endless story to tell. What distinguishes Hanguang Gate is that it hides a complete entrance to the Imperial City of the Tang Dynasty. It happened that when part of the city wall collapsed, the remains of the royal gate surfaced, and even the tracks of carriages were visible. It reminded people of how prosperous this place once was and how it was bustling with life. After the restoration, the relic site was covered with bricks on the outside, the same kind as the city wall, and inside is the exhibition hall built with reinforced concrete frame, forming a museum inside the city wall.

摄影：尚洪涛

**药王洞**
**The King of Medicine**

小北门里有条路叫药王洞，药王洞里曾经有个庙叫药王庙，顾名思义是为纪念药王孙思邈所建。从清代开始，每年农历二月初二，庙里都有隆重的庙会举行，人们祭奠药王、祈求健康。如今，庙宇虽早已拆除，但一年一度的庙会仍是街道里的一项盛事。

On Street Yaowangdong (the King of Medicine Cave) near the Xiaobeimenli once stood a temple called "the King of Medicine" in honor of Sun Simiao (581 - 682). Since the Qing Dynasty, people have been paying tribute to the King of Medicine and praying for good health at the temple fairs held annually on the second day of the second lunar month. Although the temple has been demolished, the annual fair remains a great festival in the vicinity.

**马清运与"玉山石柴"**
**Ma Qingyun and the "Jade Valley"**

诗人王维的画作《辋川图》是宋元明清历代画家的重要摹本，更是研究唐代建筑格局与风格变迁的重要依据。秉承此风，生于陕西蓝田、学贯中西的著名建筑师马清运，在辋川建造了现代建筑"玉山石柴"（柴 zhài，指栅栏、篱障）。由于马清运在国际建筑界的影响力，玉山石柴成为现代蓝田文化新的标签。

The painting "Wangchuan Villa" by Wang Wei, is an important work that painters from the Song to the Qing Dynasty often emulated. It also serves as a vital basis for studying the change in the architecture structure and style in the Tang Dynasty. Drawing on Wang Wei's legacy, Ma Qingyun, a Lantian-born famous architect well-versed in both the Western and Chinese traditions built the modern architecture "Father's House" in Wangchuan, which has become the new icon for the contemporary Lantian culture, thanks to his international fame in the world of architecture.

**湖北庄**
**Hubei Village**

西安北郊有个湖北庄，这里很多人都是湖北人的后代，也有一些商洛商南人的后裔。在清代甚至更早的时候，一些住在鄂西北、陕东南的人翻越秦岭，把家从秦岭南麓搬到了渭河南岸，他们白手起家，把荒草丛生的河滩地改造成了肥沃的耕地。时至今日，村里仍有部分家族保持着自己原籍的习俗和传统。

Most of the residents of Hubei Village in the northern suburbs of Xi'an are descendants of people from Hubei Province; some are descendants of people from Shangnan County, Shaanxi Province. During the Qing Dynasty, some of the families in northwest Hubei and southeast Shaanxi crossed the Qinling Mountains, and moved from the south ridge of the mountains to the south bank of the Wei River. Starting from scratch, they transformed the weed-savaged beachland into fertile soils. To this day, many families in the village still observe the customs and traditions of their native land.

**史上第一大人工湖**
**The Largest Artificial Lake in History**

在西安西南的斗门、细柳镇一带，曾有我国历史上第一大人工湖昆明池，其面积是西湖的四倍。相传是汉武帝为征讨南方的古昆明国而操演水兵所凿，北京颐和园内昆明湖的名字，也是乾隆联想到武帝的文治武功后仿照昆明池所起的。可惜，昆明池在唐末时已干涸，不过如今，西安正着手重现千年昆明池胜景。

There used to be an artificial lake called Kunming Lake around Doumen and Xiliu, two towns in southwestern Xi'an. The largest one of its kind, Kunming Lake was built for Emperor Wu of Han (reign 141 - 87 B.C.) to train his navy for military expeditions to southern states. Emperor Wu had learned that the extensive Dian Lake in the ancient Kingdom of Kunming was invincible, so a reservoir was constructed for navy training and it was named Kunming Lake. Unfortunately it dried up in late Tang Dynasty. Now, Xi'an is to restore the lake to its glory 1000 years ago.

**月登阁**
**The Moon Ascent Pavilion**

位于东郊的月登阁村，听名字就很浪漫。月登阁村的雏形可追溯至周朝，到了唐代，这里被称为月灯阁。相传，唐代新科进士及第后，除了在曲江池游赏宴饮、雁塔题名外，还会来此举办击球会，用马球比赛的方式庆祝及第。

The village of Yuedengge in the eastern suburbs has a romantic name that means "the moon ascends from the pavilion". Its history could be traced back to the Zhou Dynasty (1046 - 256 B.C.), yet the present came into use during the Tang Dynasty. It is said that the winners of imperial examinations would hold polo competitions in this village to celebrate, aside from "drinking on Qujiang Lake" and "having their names inscribed on the Giant Wild Goose Pagoda".

**杨虎城止园别墅**
**The Villa of General Yang Hucheng**

止园别墅位于西安市内青年路中段。为民国时期著名将领杨虎城将军主政陕西时所建别墅。名字取"止戈为武"之意，有"停止内战，联合御侮"的寓意。西安事变之后，杨虎城与周恩来曾在此商议救国大计。现在这座别墅已被辟为杨虎城将军纪念馆。睹物思人，令人对杨虎城将军的命运不胜唏嘘。

Located in the mid-section of Qingnian Road in Xi'an, Zhiyuan Villa is a residence built by Yang Hucheng (1983 - 1949), a famous general in the Republican period (1912 - 1949), during his governing of Shaanxi. Zhiyuan literally means "stop war" and, more specifically, "stop the civil war and unite against the foreign invasion". After the Xi'an Incident, Yang Hucheng and Zhou Enlai (1898 - 1976), the first Premier of the People's Republic of China, discussed the plan to save the nation in this villa, now called General Yang Hucheng Memorial Hall. Looking at his belongings, one can't help but sigh for his fate.

## 化觉巷清真寺

## The Great Mosque in Huajue Alley

西安市鼓楼西北化觉巷内的清真寺，始建于唐天宝元年（公元742年），与大学习巷内始建于唐中宗乙巳年（公元705年）的清真大寺，并称为西安最古老的两座清真大寺。化觉巷清真寺因在大学习巷以东，故又叫东大寺，是一座规模宏大的中国殿式古建筑群落。东大寺的米芾与董其昌手书碑刻是难得的书法真品。

The Great Mosque in Huajue Alley (built in 742) to the northwest of the Drum Tower, and the Grand Mosque in Daxuexi Alley (built in 705) are two oldest mosques in Xi'an. The Great Mosque, a typical Chinese complex of ancient halls, is also called "Eastern Great Mosque" for it's located in the east of Daxuexi Alley. Its stone steles with the hand-written scripts of Mi Fu (1051 - 1107) and Dong Qichang (1555 - 1636) are rare authentic calligraphic works.

摄影：翟小雪

摄影：翟小霄

**五星街天主教堂**

**The Cathedral on Wuxing Street**

位于西安市内五星街的天主教堂，始建于清康熙年间，曾是清代天主教陕西总堂。教堂的建筑为典型的古罗马风格与中国古建筑合璧遗存。历代均有扩建，最近的一次修缮在2004年。修缮一新后，常有游人来此观看，亦多有青年男女来此拍摄西式风格的婚纱照。现为陕西省教务委员会所在地。

St. Francis Cathedral on Wuxing Street was constructed during the reign of the Kangxi Emperor, and served as the Shaanxi Catholic headquarters during the Qing Dynasty. The cathedral combined ancient Romanesque and Chinese architectural styles. It has been expanded several times throughout history. And the latest renovation was carried out in 2004. Tourists have ever since frequented here. Many young couples also shoot Western-style wedding photos here. Now, the cathedral houses the Shaanxi Provincial Catholic Administrative Committee.

**汉未央宫遗址**

**The Weiyang Palace Relics**

未央宫始建于公元前200年，是皇帝处理国家事务的地方，因而成为汉长安城最重要的宫殿。西汉之后，又有七个朝代沿袭在此处理朝政，登基、寿诞、接受朝谒、发布诏书等重大活动均在这里举行。现在国内古玩界被奉为珍品的“长乐未央”瓦当，及其吉祥寓意的传说，均与此有关。

Built in 200 B.C., Weiyang Palace was the most important palace in Chang'an because emperors handled state affairs here. After the Western Han Dynasty(206 B.C. - 25A.D.), seven other dynasties continued to use the palace as the venue to handle state affairs and hold important events such as coronations, birthday celebrations, receptions, and edicts issuing. “Changle Weiyang” (literally, “endless happiness”) eaves tiles, deemed delicate treasures by the Chinese antique world, and relevant legends are all somewhat related to this palace.

**纺织公园**
The Textile Park

“东有纺织城，西有电工城”，这曾是昔日西安繁荣的标志。位于纺织城的纺织公园，尽管论规模、论特色，不及市内多所历史文化深厚的老公园，但伴随着纺织城崛起而问世的这座公园，铭刻着上世纪六七十年代纺织城繁荣鼎盛的印记，成为十几万纺织工人的后花园。如今，纺织城人依旧会在此娱乐休闲。

“The Textile City in the east and the Electric City in the west” was once the symbol of Xi’an’s prosperity. The Textile Park in the Textile City may not compare, in either size or charm, with other parks with long history and profound culture, but it was the backyard of tens of thousands of textile workers in the 1960s and 1970s, and bears the marks of the Textile City’s prosperity. Even now, residents nearby still come here to while away their leisure hours.

**汉长乐宫遗址**
The Changle Palace Relics

汉长乐宫规模宏大，大约占汉长安城的六分之一。长乐宫本是丞相萧何主持修建，供汉高祖刘邦处理政务的地方，后因专供皇后吕雉居住，遂得“东宫”之名。现存多处长乐宫遗址，已经只剩下一截截土峁。迷信的周边居民认为，未嫁的姑娘吃了用遗址的土壤种的菜，能嫁得好，降伏得了丈夫。

With a grand scale, Changle Palace covers an area one sixth of Chang’an City of the Western Han Dynasty. Built by Chancellor Xiao He (257 - 193 B.C.) during Liu Bang’s reign, the palace was where Liu Bang handled state affairs, and later served as the residence for Empress Lu Zhi under the name East Palace. Now, the multiple relic sites of the palace in Weiyang District have been dug into mounds by residents nearby. It is believed that after eating the vegetables grown in the soil from these sites a girl can marry well and tame her husband.

**《创业史》与柳青墓**
*History of an Undertaking* and the Tomb of Liu Qing

在作家路遥、陈忠实的记忆中，柳青的《创业史》是对他们影响最大的作品。路遥在回忆录中曾写到自己创作《平凡的世界》时，七次研读《创业史》。柳青（1916—1978）是陕西吴堡县人，新中国成立后曾任《中国青年报》副刊主编，为创作小说，1952 年落户长安县皇甫村。现该村保存有柳青墓及陵园。

Writer Lu Yao (1949 - 1992) and Chen Zhongshi (1942 - ) both regard Liu Qing’s (1916 - 1978) *History of an Undertaking* as the work that influenced them the most. Lu Yao recounted in his memoir that he read this novel seven times while writing *Ordinary World*. From Wubao County in Shaanxi, Liu Qing worked as editor-in-chief of *China Youth Daily Supplement* after 1949. To focus on writing fictions, he moved to Huangfu village in Chang’an County in 1952. Hence Liu’s tomb and memorial park are found here.

**国棉四厂职工楼**

**The Staff Quarter of the Fourth Cotton Factory**

位于西安东郊纺织城内的国棉四厂职工楼，因为王全安导演的电影《纺织姑娘》而闻名国内文艺界。还有国棉五厂、国棉六厂职工楼，均为20世纪苏联专家参与设计的苏式建筑。墙体为砖混水泥结构，屋面施红色机瓦。2009年《纺织姑娘》在蒙特利尔电影节获奖后，时有艺术爱好者来此流连。

Director Wang Quan'an's work *Weaving Girl* (2009) brought fame to the staff quarter of the Fourth Cotton Factory in the Textile City in the eastern suburbs of Xi'an. Along with those of the Fifth and Sixth Cotton Factories, the Russian-style quarters were designed by Soviet experts in the 1920s, with brick-concrete walls and red tiles. Since the *Weaving Girl* won an award at the Montreal World Film Festival, art lovers often linger around.

**韦曲杜曲出宰相**

**Weiqu and Duqu, Where Chancellors Came**

韦曲和杜曲是西安城南长安区的两个街道，汉唐时期这里就以人杰地灵著称。唐有韦曲镇，因诸韦聚居得名；以东五里即少陵原东南端，有杜曲，为诸杜世居之地，合称韦杜。这两个家族在历史上曾走出过30多位宰相，还有杜甫、韦应物等众多名人。不过唐亡后，韦杜家族开始衰落，今天这里已经难觅韦杜后人了。

Weiqu and Duqu are two streets in the Chang'an District in south Xi'an. During the Han and Tang dynasties, both were famous for talented scholars. Weiqu Town, established in the Tang Dynasty, was named after the Wei Family, who lived there for generations. A couple of kilometers to the east of Weiqu is Duqu Town in the southwest of Shaoing Plain, named after the Du Family. Together the two towns were called Weidu. The two families turned out over 30 chancellors as well as such celebrities as poet Du Fu (712 - 770), Wei Yingwu (737 - 792) and so on. Sadly, after the collapse of the Tang Dynasty, the two clans waned. And few of their descendents inhabit here at present.

**《胡笳十八拍》与蔡文姬墓**

**"Eighteen Songs of a Nomad Flute" and Cai Wenji**

“天无涯兮地无边，我心愁兮亦复然。人生倏忽兮如白驹之过隙，然不得欢乐兮当我之盛年。”《乐府诗集》中收录的感人肺腑的长篇骚体叙事诗《胡笳十八拍》，是中国历史上著名才女东汉蔡文姬的作品。该诗被郭沫若赞为“自《离骚》之后最值得欣赏的长诗”。蔡文姬墓位于现蓝田境内。

"Heaven has no limit, earth has no border; my heart's sadness is also like that. Human life is fleeting, like a passing white colt seen through a crack; but I have no chance to enjoy myself during my prime years." The touching narrative poem "Eighteen Songs of a Nomad Flute", from the *Collection of Yuefu Poems*, is the work of Cai Wenji (177 - 249), a talented female writer in Chinese history. Guo Moruo (1982 - 1978), a famous writer, deemed this poem "the best narrative epic poem since Qu Yuan's (340 - 278 B.C.) *Li Sao*". The Cai Wenji Tomb now lies in Lantian County.

### 梅兰芳与五四剧院
### May Lanfang and the Wusi Theatre

位于青年路曹家巷南侧的五四剧院，是建于 1954 年的苏式风格建筑。剧院外面悬挂的“五四剧院”四字为京剧大师梅兰芳所题，只可惜现在剧院外观经过了现代化维修，已经难见当年的建筑风韵。这座剧院，与北大街上同为苏式风格的和平电影院一起见证了西安人民半个多世纪以来的文化艺术生活。

Wusi (May Fourth) Theatre on the south side of Caojia Alley, Qingnian Road, is a Soviet-styled architecture built in 1954. The sign “Wusi Theatre” was inscribed by Mei Lanfang (1894 - 1961), a master of Peking opera. Unfortunately modern renovations have deprived the building of its exotic charm. With Heping Cinema on North Street, this theatre has witnessed Xi’an’s cultural life over half a century.

### 城墙厚度大过“身高”
### The Dimensions of the City Wall

登上城墙，青砖铺底，平整宽广，煞是壮观。明朝初年，明太祖朱元璋实行“高筑墙，广积粮，缓称王”，西安城墙就是根据此政策在唐皇城的基础上建成的。西安城墙完全围绕防御战略体系建成，厚度大于高度，稳固如山，过去城墙顶上可以跑车和操练，现在则可以举办国际马拉松赛事。

After ascending the city wall, you will find that the wall top tiled with grey bricks are smooth and wide. A gorgeous sight! The present city wall in Xi’an was built on the foundation of the Tang imperial city wall as an effort of Zhu Yuanzhang’s (reign 1368 - 1398) policy: “to built high walls, store abundant food and take time to be an emperor”. The city wall, durable and stable like a mountain, was constructed as a defensive system. Its thickness is greater than its height. In the past, on top of it, you might find carriages and military training on the top. Now, international marathon games take place there.

摄影：徐佳伟

# 历史·回望

## History and Nostalgia

**西安的由来**

**The Origin of Xi'an**

西安，号称十三朝古都，历史上曾称镐京、长安等，元朝时称奉元。1368年朱元璋建立明朝，第二年命大将徐达率部攻打奉元，元将弃城而逃，奉元光复后更名为西安，寓意“安定西北”。虽然西安早已经不是国家的首都，但是作为西北地区最大的城市，千百年来为西部的发展和稳定也做出了巨大的贡献。

Once called Haojing, Chang'an, etc, Xi'an served as the capital of 13 dynasties. During the Yuan Dynasty (1270 - 1368), the city was given the name Fengyuan. Zhu Yuanzhang established the Ming Dynasty in 1368. In the following year he ordered general Xu Da to attack Fengyuan. The Yuan army abandoned the city. When conquered, Fengyuan was changed into Xi'an, bearing the wish to bring peace to the Northwest. Although Xi'an is no longer the national capital, the largest city in the northwest has contributed significantly to the western region's development for centuries.

**古代文明活标本**

**The Living Specimen of Ancient Civilization**

“要了解中国的近代文明那就得去北京，要了解中国的现代文明得去上海，而要了解中国的古代文明却只有到西安了。”贾平凹说，西安至今仍全方位地保留着中国真正的传统文化，“具有了浑然的厚重的苍凉的独特风格，正是这样的灵魂支撑着它，氤氲笼绕着它，散发着魅力，强迫得天下人为之瞩目”。

“To know China's modern civilization, you have to visit Beijing; to know its contemporary one, you have to visit Shanghai; and to know its ancient one, you have to visit Xi'an,” said Jia Pingwa, who believes that traditional Chinese culture has remained intact in Xi'an, “thereby distinguishing the city with a forlorn profundity. It is the soul of the culture that underlies the city, reigns here, exudes glamour, and forces its way into the attention of the world.”

**忠良比国宝更珍贵**

**Honesty is More Precious than National Treasure**

“皇后之玺”是我国现存两汉时期唯一的帝后玉玺。今天我们在陕西历史博物馆能看到这件国宝，应该记住他——孔忠良。40多年前，13岁少年孔忠良在放学途中捡到一块白色石头，便与父亲将其上交到文物部门，当时就有专家认定这是吕后之印，价值连城，但他们还是毫不犹豫地无偿上交了。

“Seal of the Empress” is the only existing jade monarch seal of the Han Dynasty. When we admire this piece of national treasure in the Shaanxi History Museum, we should remember a man named Kong Zhongliang. One day 40 years ago, Kong Zhongliang, aged 13 then, happened to find a white rock on his way home from school. His father and he submitted it to a cultural heritage department when experts affirmed that it was the invaluable seal of Empress Lü (241 - 180 B.C.).

## 陕西的黄土埋皇上

Shaanxi, Known for Mausoleums

“南方才子北方将，陕西的黄土埋皇上。”中国目前已经探明的100多座帝王陵墓中有70多座都位于陕西。秦始皇陵、汉茂陵、阳陵、唐昭陵、乾陵等，这些举世闻名的帝王陵墓密集而宏大，以傲视古今的气势环绕着西安。

Traditionally it is believed that the South of China enjoys a reputation for its scholars, the North for its generals, and Shaangxi for imperial mausoleums. China has discovered over 100 imperial tombs, more than 70 of which are located in Shaanxi, including such internationally famous tombs as the Qinshihuang Mausoleum, the Maoling Mausoleum, the Yangling Mausoleum, the Zhaoling Mausoleum, and the Qianling Mausoleum. They sit around Xi’an, manifesting themselves to all ages.

摄影：尚洪涛

摄影：王幼健

**包容的城市**
An Inclusive City

今天的西安人已不再由纯粹的关中人组成，近百年来，西安的人口结构发生了很大变化。一是1949年前河南人逃荒涌入，二是1950年代中期建设大量兵工厂，以上海人和东北人为主的技术工人移民至此。陈忠实回忆读书时班上有三分之二的同学是外地口音。他强调西安是一个非常包容的城市，一点都不排外。

Today Xi'an is no longer populated by the Guanzhong natives alone. Over the past century, great demographic changes have taken place in Xi'an, with many fleeing into Xi'an from the famine in Henan before 1949 and many skilled workers migrating to the newly-built arsenals in Xi'an from either the northeast or Shanghai in the mid-1950s. Chen Zhongshi recalls that when he was in school, two thirds of his classmates spoke with other accents. He emphasizes that Xi'an is very inclusive, not xenophobic at all.

**真实的“夜宴”**
A Dangerous Feast

公元前206年，中国历史上最著名的饭局——鸿门宴，影响了秦末农民战争和楚汉战争。如今走进临潼区新丰镇鸿门堡村，站在两千多年前的古遗址上，遥想当年项羽与刘邦的命运纠缠，“项庄舞剑，意在沛公”的历史时刻，教人如何不感怀。

In 206 B.C., the most famous dinner party in Chinese history—"The Hongmen Feast"—influenced the peasant revolutions at the end of the Qin Dynasty (221 - 206 B.C.) and the Chu-Han Contention (206 - 202 B.C.). Now, walking into the Hongmenbao Village in Xinfeng Town, Lintong District, standing on the historic site of a battle 2,000 years ago, thinking of the legend between Xiang Yu and Liu Bang, and imagining the historic moment when "Xiang Zhuang (Xiang Yu's uncle) performed the sword dance as a cover for his attempt on Liu Bang's life", how can one not be overwhelmed with mixed feelings.

**半坡人**
The Banpo People

到西安半坡，可以回味人类的童年时期。6000多年前在此生活的半坡人，将夭折的孩子埋葬在陶制顶瓮棺里，然后用绘有人面鱼纹的小盆扣住瓮口，在小盆顶底部挖出一个小小顶孔，供孩子的灵魂自由地出入，这体现着他们朦胧的灵魂不死的宗教观念。这里出土的人面鱼纹陶盆如今收藏在中国国家博物馆。

The Xi'an Banpo Museum brings us back to the childhood of mankind. Over 6,000 years ago, the villagers here had the tradition of burying a deceased child in an urn, whose cover was usually a small basin decorated with the pattern of a human-faced fish. There was often a hole through the bottom of the basin so that the child's soul could enter and leave freely. This tradition shows the villergers' early belief in the eternal and undying soul. Such a basin unearthed in Banpo is currently housed at the National Museum of China.

## 中国美女
## Chinese Beauties

唐代长安，是中国女人最美的时间和地点。如日中天的国力、八面来风的宏大气度，让美恣意绽放。一切时尚审美标准都从这里出发，然后迅速辐射全国波及海外。要知彼时彼地女人有多美，去博物馆看看西安出土的女俑、仕女图和墓道壁画中的女人，造型多变，自信大胆，未必输于今日之 Lady Gaga。

Chang'an, the name for Xi'an during the Tang Dynasty, had the most beautiful women in Chinese history. The national strength then brought China to its zenith in influence around the world, allowing free rein to beauty. All aesthetic criteria then in vogue originated from here, and spread nationwide, even beyond. To catch a glimpse of how beautiful women were at that time, you need to visit the museums in Xi'an, where the unearthed clay figurines of maids, the paintings of court ladies, and the portraits of women on tombs' murals all have a diverse, confident, and bold styling, putting Lady Gaga to shame.

摄影：尚洪涛

**方言与雅言**
**The Dialect and the Elegant Language**

从西周开始，关中话就以大雅清丽被称为“雅言”，历经秦汉成为一统天下的语言典范，相当于今天的普通话。现在，陕西方言里面还留存着一些值得玩味的“雅言”，比如外地人最爱学的一句陕西方言“嫽咋咧”（太棒了），其中“嫽”字，形容美妙至极，出自《诗经·陈风·月出》：“月出皎兮，佼人嫽兮”。

Ever since the Western Zhou Dynasty, the language spoken in Guanzhong has been called “elegant language”. Modeled after elegance and aesthetics, it became the national standard tongue after the Qin and Han dynasties, serving as the exemplary language across China. Modern Shaanxi dialect still maintains some traits of classic Chinese, such as the phrase “嫽咋咧” (amazing) that non-locals love the most. The character “嫽”, literally, “utmost loveliness”, comes from “Moonlight”, the “Odes of Chen” in the *Book of Odes*: “The moon comes forth in her brightness; how lovely is that beautiful lady.”

**“印度”的由来**
**The Origin of “India”**

《西游记》里的唐僧原型玄奘。他在游历西域回到长安后，本人口述，弟子整理了一本著作，名叫《大唐西域记》。这本书十多万字，记录了128个国家和地区的疆域、地理、文化、风俗以及信仰等。其中，“印度”这个中文名字，就是玄奘起的。

The character Tang Seng in *Journey to the West* is based on Xuanzang, a famed monk in the Tang Dynasty. On his return to Chang’an from India, his disciples, following his dictation, compiled a book titled *Great Tang Records on the Western Regions*. Over 10,000 characters in length, the book records the geography, culture, customs and religions in over 128 countries and regions. The Chinese name for India, 印度, was coined by Xuanzang in this book.

**史上最大王陵**
**The Largest Mausoleum**

平定六国统一天下的秦始皇，即位后就开始倾全国之力修建自己往生后的安息之所。据史书记载，陵园由丞相李斯主持规划设计，大将章邯监工。这座被称为史上规模最大的帝王陵墓，耗时39年，动用劳力72万人次，人力物力是埃及胡夫金字塔的八倍。另据考古证明，秦陵地宫几千年来未被盗掘。

Hardly had Qinshihuang united China by conquering the six kingdoms and taken the throne when he mobilized the whole nation’s resources to build his final resting place. It is recorded that the mausoleum was designed by Prime Minister Li Si (284 - 208 B.C.), and its construction overseen by General Zhang Han (? - 205 B.C.). It took 720,000 laborers 39 years to complete the largest imperial mausoleum, which cost eight times more than the Great Pyramid of Giza. This underground palace, as modern archeology proves, has escaped robbery over several thousands of years.

**大明宫**
The Daming Palace

电视剧《大明宫词》风靡一时，陈忠实也被剧情吸引，称在追剧过程中陷入“一个纯粹的西安人的癖好”，在心里追问：这些人和这些曲折故事，就发生在我生活着的西安吗？她们拖地的长裙和高贵的软靴，就拖在踩在西安北郊的那片被荒草掩遮着础石的大明宫遗址里吗？西安在千余年前那么风光那么神气过？

*Palace of Desire* was a hit TV drama in China. Writer Chen Zhongshi, engrossed in the plot, fell into the habit of being a pure Xi'anese. He wondered if these stories really happened in Xi'an, a city where he lives. Did the trains of their skirts and those luxurious soft boots really appear in the Daming Palace, which lies in ruins and buried amid wild grass now? Was Xi'an really that glamorous several centuries ago?

**金花路与金花落**
Gold Flower Road and Empress Dowager

话说八国联军攻打北京，慈禧太后仓皇西逃，行至西安东郊一带，忽听锣鼓喧天、杀声阵阵，吓得老佛爷连头上的金花都抖掉在地，最后才发现原来是艺人在街头舞枪弄棒。当地居民编出顺口溜：“金花落，金花落，金花落在黄土窝，百姓看得乐呵呵。”从此这里就叫金花落，即今天的金花路。

When the Eight-Nation Alliance invaded Beijing in the summer of 1900, Empress Dowager Cixi fled west. In the east suburbs of Xi'an, suddenly emerged deafening sounds of gongs, drums and roars of soldiers. Cixi was so frightened that even the gold flowers on her head fell to the ground. It turned out to be a martial performance on the street. Locals made up a limerick about this anecdote, “The gold flowers fall, the gold flowers fall, the gold flowers fall onto the yellow dirt, and the onlookers laugh to their heart's content.” From then on, this place had been called “Gold Flowers Fall”. Later on it became known as Gold Flower Road.

**寻找蓝田人**
In Search of Lantian Man

蓝田人生活在距今 110 万年到 115 万年之前，其化石 1964 年被发现于蓝田境内公王岭。当时发现的化石为一 30 多岁女性的头骨，她是目前亚洲北部所发现的最古老的直立人。现在的公王岭空旷而宁静，已经寻找不到蓝田人的痕迹，但台原的断层之中残留的动物化石，印证着这里曾经的繁荣。

Lantian Man lived 1.1 million years to 1.15 million years ago, and its fossils were discovered in Mt. Gongwang of Lantian County in 1964. The fossils are believed to be the skull of a female in her 30s. She was the most ancient Homo erectus discovered in northern Asia. Mt. Gongwang is now desolate and quiet, the trace of the Lantian Man is nowhere to be found. The remnants of animal fossils in the fault zone, however, still serve as the imprint of past prosperity.

### 百年前，西方人看陕西
### How Westerners Viewed Shaanxi a Century Ago

1901 年 11 月，美国纽约《基督教先驱报》记者尼科尔斯到西安调查大旱灾情，在临潼、三原等县赈款，使得基督教和美国的影响力在西北内陆大为提升。尼科尔斯将赈灾之旅写成了一本《穿越神秘的陕西》，详记关于西安城与西安人的所见所闻，堪称近代西方人近距离观察和描述西安的第一本全景之作。

In November 1901, American journalist Francis Nichols from the New York-based *Christian Herald* journeyed to Xi'an to investigate a severe drought. He raised funds in counties like Lintong, Sanyuan, and so on, significantly increasing the influence of Christianity and the United States in the northwest China. Based on this trip, Nichols wrote *Through Hidden Shensi*, recording his experience around Xi'an. The book provided the first panorama of Xi'an from a Westerner's perspective in modern times.

### 唐长安的最高建筑
### The Tallest Architecture in Chang'an of the Tang Dynasty

大慈恩寺建于贞观二十二年（公元 648 年），是太子李治为追念亡母长孙皇后而建。李治即位后，在寺内建造佛塔，用来保存玄奘法师从印度取回的经像舍利，由于样式仿照印度雁塔，故名雁塔。武则天在位时期，翻建为七层。在当时，雁塔是长安城中最高的建筑，供人瞻仰。如今虽过千年，它依然是西安的象征。

Da Ci'en Temple was built in the year 648 upon the order of crown prince Li Zhi (628 - 683) in commemoration of his deceased mother Empress Zhangsun (601 - 636). After Li Zhi took the throne, he built a pagoda in the temple to preserve the Buddhist figurines and sultras Xuanzang brought back from India. Since the architecture was styled after the Mahayana temple (wild-goose pagoda) in India, it was called the Pagoda of Wild Goose. During the reign of Empress Wu Zetian, the pagoda was renovated into a seven–storied one, the tallest building then in Chang'an. Throughout history it has remained the symbol of Xi'an.

摄影：窦翊明

**释"秦"**

Deciphering "Qin"

"秦"是一个会意字。甲骨文的"秦"，上部中间是一株谷穗，左右是两只手，下部用两株禾谷象征成熟了的庄稼，整个字形表示两手掐取谷穗，故其本义是粮食丰收。"秦"还有收获和勤劳之意。古代的关中是中国农业最发达的地区之一，占据此地的诸侯国取"秦"为国名，寓意着这里的丰厚与富庶。

Qin ( 秦 ) is an associative compound character. In its oracle bone script, there is a pictogram of millet ear in the middle of the upper part, with two hands on both sides, and in the lower part, there are two straws, which symbolize ripe crops. With two hands picking millet ears, the character 秦 itself means a bumper crop. Meanwhile it connotes harvest and hardworking. In ancient times, Guanzhong was one of the most advanced agricultural regions. The vassal state occupying the land chose 秦 as its name to wish for abundance and prosperity.

**李白与稠酒**

Li Bai and the Osmanthus Wine

杜甫诗说："李白斗酒诗百篇，长安市上酒家眠，天子呼来不上船，自称臣是酒中仙。"这里提到的酒便是当时长安名饮——黄桂稠酒。《旧唐书·文苑传》记载，李白在长乐坊喝多了稠酒，到了玄宗的殿上，戏弄高力士为他脱鞋换履，这段历史趣闻与黄桂稠酒一起流传至今。今天，稠酒仍是传统西安人待客的佳品。

Du Fu wrote in his poem, "Li Bai, with a jugful of liquor, will write one hundred poems. He drowses in a wine-shop on a street of Chang-an; And though his sovereign calls, He will not board the imperial barge. 'Please your Majesty,' says he, 'I am a god of wine.'" The wine mentioned in the poem was the famed drink in Chang'an at the time: osmanthus wine. As recorded in the *Old Book of Tang*, Li Bai drank too much wine in Changlefang (a bar), went to the palace of Emperor Xuanzong, and teased Gao Lishi (an eunuch) to take off his shoes for him. This anecdote has passed down along with osmanthus wine. Today, the wine remains the traditional treat the Xi'anese give their guests.

**锅盔**

Signature Round Baked Cake

在中国历史上，秦能一统天下，除了秦军能征善战之外，有一种干粮也功不可没，这就是至今依然被陕西人所钟爱的锅盔。锅盔的保质期比较长，适合较长时间的存放和携带，放上十天半个月也不会起霉变质，适合长距离作战食用。

In Chinese history, the unification of China by the Qin state is not only attributed to the Qin army's excellency in war, but also to a kind of dried food the people of Shaanxi still love: guokui, a large round baked cake. Guokui has a relatively long shelf life, allowing it to be stored for a long time and making it suitable to bring to war. It will not spoil for a span of 10 to 15 days; hence the ideal food supply for battles far away.

## 陕博里的低调文物

### The Low-key Artifacts in the Shaanxi History Museum

作为中国第一座大型现代化国家级博物馆，陕西历史博物馆被誉为“古都明珠，华夏宝库”。在陕西历史博物馆门前的水池里有一块长条状的石头很不起眼，其实这个低调的文物大有来头，它就是当年汉武帝修建太液池时雕刻的石鲸鱼，代表了汉代雕刻的最高工艺水平，堪比霍去病墓前的马踏匈奴。

The first modern national museum in China, Shaanxi History Museum is hailed as “the pearl of the ancient city and the treasure vault of China”. In the pond in front of the museum lies a rectangular stone. Seemingly insignificant, this stone has a glorious past. It was the stone whale carved for Emperor Wu of Han’s Taiye Pond, and stands for the Han Dynasty’s highest level of craftsmanship along with the statue “Horse Treads on the Hun” in front of the Mausoleum of Huo Qubing.

摄影：翟小雪

**骷髅头文物**
Scary Artifacts

西北大学有个鲜为人知的人体标本库，里面存放着上千具古人遗骸，从四千多年前的史前时期到数百年前的都有。在考古学家眼里，这些收集的“骷髅头”全是珍贵文物，其价值远高于出土的金银珠宝。一个出土自唐墓的老年头骨被证实是古欧洲人，这也从一个侧面证明唐代长安城是一个名副其实的国际化大都市。

In Northwest University in Xi'an, there is a little known bank of human specimens, housing over a thousand remains of ancient people who lived from four thousand years ago to several hundred years ago. To archeologists, these “skulls” are all precious artifacts, more valuable than other unearthed treasures. The skull of an old man from a Tang tomb was identified as that of an ancient European, giving fresh evidence for the fact that Chang'an was a metropolitan city in the Tang Dynasty.

**天坛**
The Temple of Heaven

说起天坛，很少会把它和西安联系起来。其实西安不仅有天坛，而且它还被专家称为“天下第一坛”。安坐在西安南郊一隅的西安天坛，是现存年代最久远、级别最高的唐代天坛遗址。一千多年前的史书把西安天坛叫作圜丘，它沿用了 314 年，隋文帝以及唐代的 21 位皇帝都曾在此举行过隆重的祭天仪式。

Speaking of the Temple of Heaven, few would think of Xi'an. Actually there is one and it is regarded as “the best temple in the world” by experts. Situated in a corner in the southern suburbs, the Temple of Heaven is the oldest and most prestigious one in the Tang Dynasty. A history book over a thousand years ago referred to this temple as the “Circular Mound Altar”, which remained in use for 314 years. Emperor Wen of Sui (reigned 581 - 604) and 21 emperors of the Tang Dynasty all held grand ceremonies to worship heaven here.

摄影：尚洪涛

**古城都有"西安门"**

**Every Ancient City Has a "Xi'an Gate"**

两千多年前，汉朝定都长安时，有一座城门看似不起眼，它的名字却在后世广泛留存，这就是"西安门"。因为它离皇宫很近，所以一般百姓不能通行。在南京，也有一座西安门，是明朝皇帝出入最多的城门之一，级别很高，留存至今。在北京，也有一座西安门，不过现在只剩下宽阔的马路了。

More than two thousand years ago, when the Han Dynasty decided to make Chang'an the capital, there was a nondescript city gate that has served as a bridge between the present and the past. That was "Xi'an Gate", which was very close to the imperial palace and inaccessible to the common people. Nanjing, too, has a Xi'an Gate, the passageway that the emperors of the Ming Dynasty used the most. And it has been preserved to this day. Although Bejing had a Xi'an gate, too, it has turned into a wide road now.

**"穷骨头"最坚强**

**"Poor Men's Bones" Are the Strongest**

有家考古研究院称挖到西周芮国国君家族墓，请西北大学文博学院的陈靓副教授做人骨鉴定，却被客气地拒绝。据"古墓派"学者的经验：能穿越几千年而保存较好的只有穷人的骨头。道理很简单：穷人墓浅，少有墓室，富人墓深，墓室也大，空气和湿度都利于细菌繁衍，所以越是富人，越早早地尸骨无存。

After the strenuous excavation of the royal mausoleum of the Rui state during the Western Zhou Dynasty, an archaeology institute asked associate professor Chen Liang from the School of Cultural Heritage of Northwest University to identify the human remains. Chen declined the request. According to experts in this field, only poor people's bones can be well-preserved through thousands of years. The reason is simple: poor people's tombs are shallow with few chambers, and rich people are buried deep with large chambers, which provides air and humidity for bacteria. So the richer the tomb owners are, the earlier their remains disappear.

**康熙阅兵**

**The Kangxi Emperor Reviewed His Army**

在西安城内西北角，有一个凝聚着清代西安城"武"元素的地方——习武园，这里曾是清代的一处阅兵练武场所。康熙四十二年，为安定西北，康熙皇帝西巡陕西。在西安期间，康熙皇帝在此检阅了西安驻军。对检阅十分满意的康熙作诗曰："大阅三军训甲士，来朝诸部趋藩王。"

Located in the northwest of Xi'an is a parade ground called Xiwu Square, a venue for military review in the Qing Dynasty. In 1704, the Kangxi Emperor visited Shaanxi to stabilize the northwest boarders. During his stay in Xi'an, he inspected the local troops in this square. Very satisfied with the review, Kangxi Emperor wrote a poem, in which he spoke highly of the soldiers and expressed his confidence in winning the war against invasions.

## 西汉美酒

## The Liquor of the Western Han Dynasty

2003 年 6 月，文景路的一处汉代高级贵族墓葬出土了一个西汉早期的凤首青铜钟，里面盛着 26 公斤美酒。这壶青绿色酒液是自建国以来我国第一次出土的保存完好的古代美酒。为何是绿色？墓主人是谁？是哪种粮食发酵？至今还有一个个谜团待解。现在这壶 2000 年前的美酒就存放在西安博物院地下一层。

An early Western Han phoenix-headed bronze jar was excavated from a tomb of a noble in the Han Dynasty on Wenjing Road in June 2003. The jar was filled with 26 kilograms of liquor. This vessel of green liquid is the best-preserved and the largest amount of ancient liquor that China has unearthed since the founding of the PRC. Why is it green? Who was the owner of the tomb? What was used to ferment? Many mysteries remain unsolved. The 2,000-year-old vessel of liquor is on display on the B1 floor at the Xi'an Museum.

摄影：尚洪涛

### 迷你长安城
### Miniature Chang'an

唐长安城始建于隋文帝二年（公元 582 年），东西 9721 米，南北 8651 米，面积 84 平方公里，城市人口约百万，是当时世界上规模最大的城市，至唐天复四年（公元 904 年）毁于军阀朱温的兵乱之灾。如今您可以在西安博物院看到以 1 ∶ 1500 比例复制的 1300 年前长安城原貌，一览宫城、皇城、外郭城的盛唐格局。

Construction of the Tang Chang'an began in 582 when Emperor Wen of Sui reigned. The city stretches for 9,721 meters from the east to the west and 8,651 meters from the north to the south, It boasted an area of 84 square kilometers and a population of over a million. The then largest city in the world was, however, destroyed by during warlord Zhu Wen's armed rebellion in 904. At the Xi'an History Museum, you can see a 1:1,500 scale model of Chang'an 1,300 years ago, showcasing the layout of the city, including the gated palaces, imperial palaces, and outer city walls, during the heyday of the Tang Dynasty.

### “西漂”的乡愁菜
### The Flavors of Home for the Migrants West

新中国成立之初，为支援西北建设，上海有大批工程师和技术工人“西迁”，西安西郊的工厂区成为他们的第二个家。今天在丰登南路上，经营最久的是一家上海菜馆，门面不大，像极了上海弄堂里普通小馆。常来的食客操一口吴侬软语。几十年工厂繁荣凋敝，生活起起落落，只有那不变的家常滋味慰藉着怀乡人的胃。

Shortly after the founding of the PRC, a lot of engineers and technicians from Shanghai migrated west, and made the factory district in the western suburbs of Xi'an their second home. Now, the oldest restaurant on Fengdeng South Road is a Shanghainese one. Small as it is, the restaurant looks very much like those in an alley in Shanghai. Frequent customers all speak Shanghainese. The past few decades have witnessed the ups and downs of the factories and these migrants. The Shanghai cuisine remains the only consolation to those migrants.

### 穿越千年的宝剑
### An Ancient Sword

兵马俑二号坑展示着一把青铜剑，出土时被一尊百余斤的陶俑压着，呈弯曲状。当陶俑被移开时，奇迹发生，这把剑竟自然反弹，还原平直。现在仍可一剑穿过 30 张报纸。经检测，这把剑表面有一层薄薄的铬盐氧化层，可防腐抗锈。以往认为这种工艺在近代德国才出现，这把剑证实秦代中国已有这样的工艺。

In Pit 2 of the Terracotta Army Museum there is a bronze sword on display. When it was unearthed, it was bent beneath a clay warrior over 50 kg in weight. By a miracle the sword sprung back into its original shape when the statue was removed. Now, it can still easily pierce through a stack of 30 pieces of newspaper. Test results show that the surface of the sword is a thin chromate oxidized layer that protects it from erosion and rusting. It was believed that this technique didn't appear in Germany until modern times, yet this sword proves that China already had it in the Qin Dynasty.

**武则天与感业寺**
Wu Zetian and the Ganye Temple

只有资深的武则天粉丝才能找得到她出家为尼的感业寺。就是在这块宝地，唐高宗祭日行香时遇见了她。现寺院遗址位于西安市西北六村堡的感业寺小学内，仅存部分殿宇基座与几通石碑，其中明朝万历年间竖立的《重修感业寺碑记》石碑，宛然记述着当年的宫廷旧事。

After visiting the Qianling Mausoleum, only dedicated fans of Wu Zetian would look further for the Ganye Temple, where Wu was converted to Buddhism and encountered Emperor Gaozong (reign 649 - 683). The ruins of the temple can be found in Ganye Temple Elementary School in Liucunbu, Xi'an. Only parts of the temple's foundation and several steles survive. One of the steles erected during the Wanli period of the Ming Dynasty records the romance in the Tang palaces.

**墙上的流水槽**
The Rain Gutters on the Wall

清乾隆年间，陕西巡抚毕沅对西安城墙进行了一次大规模的维修，这工程的最大贡献之一就是改造了全城的排水系统，修筑了流水槽。流水槽为砖石结构，附贴于城墙内壁，从城顶直达城基，每隔 40—60 米设一个，全城共 167 个。正是这些流水槽防止了城墙墙体受雨水浸泡而塌毁，对城墙起到重要的保护作用。

During the Qianlong period (1736 - 1795) in the Qing Dynasty, Bi Yuan, Governor of Shaanxi Province, carried out an extensive renovation of Xi'an's city wall. The largest contribution of this project was the revamping of the city's irrigation system and the construction of rain gutters. Made of bricks and stones, the gutters were attached to the inner side of the city wall from the top to the base, set at intervals of 40 to 60 meters, totaling 167. It was these gutters that played an important role in preventing the city wall from collapsing due to rain erosion.

摄影：翟小雪

**八百壮士跳黄河**
**Eight Hundred Heroes Jumped into the Yellow River**

传说70多年前的中条山战役中，抗日部队被日军围困在黄河边的悬崖上，弹尽粮绝，三面绝壁。八百余名十七八岁的“陕西冷娃”不愿投降，他们面朝家乡，先跪天，再跪爹娘，高吼秦腔，扑向了滚滚黄河。

It is said that during the Battle of South Shaanxi (1941), the anti-Japanese army would rather die than become captives. They knelt first to heaven, then to their parents. Finally they roared the Qingqiang opera and jumped into the raging Yellow River. Most of the 800 martyrs were 17 and 18-year-olds from Shaanxi.

**一把火烧掉的城门**
**The City Gate That Went Up in Flames**

西安城墙的东门叫长乐门，随明城墙一起构筑，以前是东侧出入西安的唯一门户。现城楼、箭楼均保存完好，唯闸楼已毁。据说，当年李自成攻入西安时，看到“长乐门”三个字，就对身边的将士说：“若让皇帝长乐，百姓就要长苦了。”将士们一听此言，群情激愤，点火烧毁了这座城楼，直到清代才得以重建。

Constructed along with the city wall of the Ming Dynasty, Changle (endless happiness) Gate was the only entrance into the city from the east. The main tower and the arrow tower remain intact; but the gate tower with a suspension bridge has been virtually destroyed. It is said that when Li Zicheng (1606 - 1645), the leader of a peasant revolt, conquered Xi'an and found the name of the gate, he said to his soldiers, “if the emperor enjoys endless happiness, we, the common people, will be in endless pain.” Highly indignant, his followers set fire to the gate tower, which was not to be rebuilt until the Qing Dynasty.

**“皇帝”的由来**
**The Origin of the Word “Emperor”**

今天，我们站在秦始皇陵的地下军阵前，似乎依然能感受到两千多年前秦始皇横扫六合的气势。秦统一中国后，嬴政将传说中的三皇五帝各取一字，合并成“皇帝”一词，意味着自己功过三皇，德超五帝。从此，皇帝代替了国王的称号，成为历代君主的称谓。而嬴政作为秦朝的第一位皇帝，就是“始皇帝”。

Standing in front of Emperor Qinshihuang's underground army today, we are still swept over by his military might when he defeated the six states that divided the nation. After Qin united China, Yingzheng (Qinshihuang's name) took two characters from the phrase 三皇五帝 (Three August Ones and Five Lords) to coin the term 皇帝 (emperor), implying that his victories and virtues surpassed all previous kings. From then on, 皇帝 replaced the title for king, and became the term for the monarch. As the founding father of the Qin Dynasty, Yingzheng proclaimed himself “Shi Huangdi”, i.e. the First Emperor.

摄影：尚洪涛

文化·传承
Civilization and Heritage

**城门是地标**

**The City Gate as the Landmark**

西安城墙保护得很好，堪称中国现存最完整的古代城垣建筑。有城墙必有城门，18 个城门自然就成为辨识方位的重要地标。到西安无论去哪儿，你只要说清在哪个城门处或附近，总能轻易找到。于是，在西安的公交站牌上，你最常见到的站名便是“某某门”。

So well preserved is the city wall of Xi'an that it is considered the best existing rampart of its kind in China. With the city wall come 18 city gates, which have been the most distinct landmarks to tell directions. Therefore it is easy to get anywhere in Xi'an as long as you know which gate is your destination or close to it. No wonder the bus stop in this city is often called "Blah Blah Gate".

**长安永安**

**Chang'an in Eternal Peace**

外地人来西安必会前往西安城墙一游，西安人每天也都在城墙下穿梭，但却甚少有人留意过：西安城墙的四个城门，东门长乐门、西门安定门、南门永宁门、北门安远门，每个城门各取头一个字，合起来恰为“长安永安”。

Even though tourists always go to see the city wall when visiting Xi'an, and the locals pass by the city wall every day, few people have ever noticed that if you take the first character of the four gate names, "Chang Le" Gate in the east, "An Ding" Gate in the west, "Yong Ning" Gate in the south, and "An Yuan" Gate in the north, you would find "Chang An Yong An", which means Chang'an will be in eternal peace.

摄影：王幼健

摄影：王幼健

## 棋盘式格局
## Grid Layout

从飞机上看，西安是个不折不扣的四方城，出奇齐整。《周礼·考工记》载："匠人营国，方九里，旁三国。国中九经九纬，经途九轨，左祖右社，前朝后市。"是西安古城的标准模式。从周秦开始，西安提供了中国传统城区的模式，而现在的西安城，仍以这种棋盘式格局作为总基础。

Overlooked from a plane, Xi'an is exactly a square city in extraordinary order. *The Records of Trades from Rites of Zhou* reads, "Craftsmen constructed the capital nine *li* square, with three gates on each side. Within the gates are nine horizontal and nine vertical main roads. On the left of the palace lies the ancestral temple, on the right the Temple of Earth and Harvests, in the front the assembly palace and in the back the market." Today's Xi'an is based on this model grid.

## 民族融合的熔炉
## A Melting Pot of Ethnicities

西安是民族融合的熔炉。曾经在北部的匈奴族、鲜卑族和羯族，在西部的氐族和羌族，为了生存，从汉到魏晋南北朝，不断向西安及其周边迁移。五胡与汉族的杂居，促进了民族融合。7 世纪之后，又有经商的波斯人和阿拉伯人以西安为家。那些人的后裔今天仍在西安，他们早就完全是中国人了。

Xi'an is a melting pot where ethnicities live in harmony. From the Han Dynasty to the Wei (220 - 265), Jin (265 - 420), Southern and Northern Dynasties (420 - 589), the people of Huns, Xianbei, and Jie in the north, and Di and Qiang in the west, all migrated to Xi'an and its vicinity for survival. Their living together with the Han Chinese accelerated the integration of ethnicities. Since the 7th Century, Persian and Arabian businessmen began to make Xi'an their new home. Their descendants still reside in Xi'an today, but they are already part of the Chinese people.

摄影：王幼健

### 晨钟暮鼓
### The Dawn Bell and Dusk Drum

许多城市都有钟鼓楼，但在贾平凹看来，“中国的任何地方的钟鼓楼皆不如西安的雄伟。晨钟暮鼓已经变成了一句成语，这里还依然是事实，至今许多外地人一早一晚聚于钟鼓楼广场，要看的是一队古装打扮的人神色庄严地去钟楼鼓楼鸣钟敲鼓，恍惚到了远古的时代。”

Bell Towers and Drum Towers are found in many cities. However, Jia Pingwa noted, “No Bell towers and Drum Towers across China are as grand as those in Xi’an. The idiom ‘dawn bell and dusk drum’ is still a common practice here. Many nonlocals gather at the square between the two structures in due course to watch a group of men in traditional costumes solemnly mount the towers to strike the bell and the drum, feeling as if they had traveled back to ancient times.”

### 古城墙新游法
### New Ways to Enjoy the Ancient Wall

现存的西安城墙是明洪武年间为军事防御而建，如今西安城墙已是游览胜地。春登城墙放风筝；秋上城墙赛国际马拉松；好天气就骑自行车绕城墙一周，感受 13.9 公里的全貌；农历新年的城墙灯会另有一番盛世景象；城墙脚下外侧的环城公园亦是市民晨练、遛弯、谈恋爱、吼秦腔的最佳场所。

The remaining city wall of Xi’an was built for military defense during the Hongwu period (1368 - 1398). Now the fortifications are a popular tourist destination. While spring sees people fly kites on the wall, autumn witnesses the City Wall International Marathon. Nice days often find people cycle around the 13.9 km-long rampart for a panoramic view. During the Lunar New Year, the lantern fair on the city wall presents a festive scene. The Huancheng Park at the outer foot of the city wall is an ideal place for the locals to take exercise in the morning, walk, date, or sing Qinqiang opera.

### 穿越之城
### The City of Time Travel

吃着泡馍听着秦腔，在西安城墙上骑行。白天穿行在高新繁华街市，晚上游走在德福巷、大唐不夜城享受小资和穿越。你所走的每一寸土地都有可能是帝王将相曾经踏过的。行走在西安就像穿越时空，你可以亲眼目睹、亲手触摸、亲身体验的东西太多了。

You may eat *paomo* (cake stew) while listening to Qinqiang opera or cruise on top of the city wall. To enjoy the petty bourgeoisie lifestyle, you may walk amongst the prosperous modern districts by day and wander through Defu Alley and the Great Tang Ever-bright City at night to travel back in time. Wherever you go, every inch of earth beneath your feet may have been stepped on by former emperors and aristocrats. Walking in Xi’an is just like traveling through time, there are so many things for you to witness, feel, and experience.

### 侥幸存活的城墙
### The Wall That Luckily Survived

1958 年，西安市做出拆除城墙的决定，也得到了省上“原则同意”的复函。弱势的文物工作者为了保护城墙，越过省上，以省文管会的名义向国务院发报。很快，时任国务院副总理的习仲勋同志办公室发来电报，坚决制止拆除城墙，西安城墙这才得以保留下来。

In 1958, the municipal government of Xi'an decided to tear down the city wall and got the approval from the provincial government. Some marginalized antiquarians reported the issue to the State Council in the name of the Cultural Protection Association. Soon came a telegram from the office of Vice Premier Xi Zhongxun, denouncing the decision. Hence the city wall survived.

### 用埙聆听西安
### Listening to Xi'an via the Xun

西安书院门除了卖文房四宝外，还卖一种古老的乐器——埙。西安半坡村仰韶文化遗址的陶哨就是埙的原始形态之一，距今约 6000 年。贾平凹说埙的声响最能表达中华民族的性格，最能与西安这座古城氛围相融。埙音色古朴醇厚，在古城墙下听一曲埙乐，时间仿佛在那一刻停滞，而你也与这座千年古城更亲近了。

Aside from the four traditional treasures of the study, an ancient instrument called *xun* is also available at the stalls around Xi'an Academy. One of the *xun*'s predecessors is a 6,000-year-old ceramic whistle unearthed at the archaeological site of Yangshao culture at Banpo Village. The sound of the *xun* is symbolic of the Chinese nation and harmonious with the atmosphere of the ancient city, according to Jia Pingwa. Listening to a tune of the *xun* by the city wall, one feels as if time were still and the ancient city more intimate.

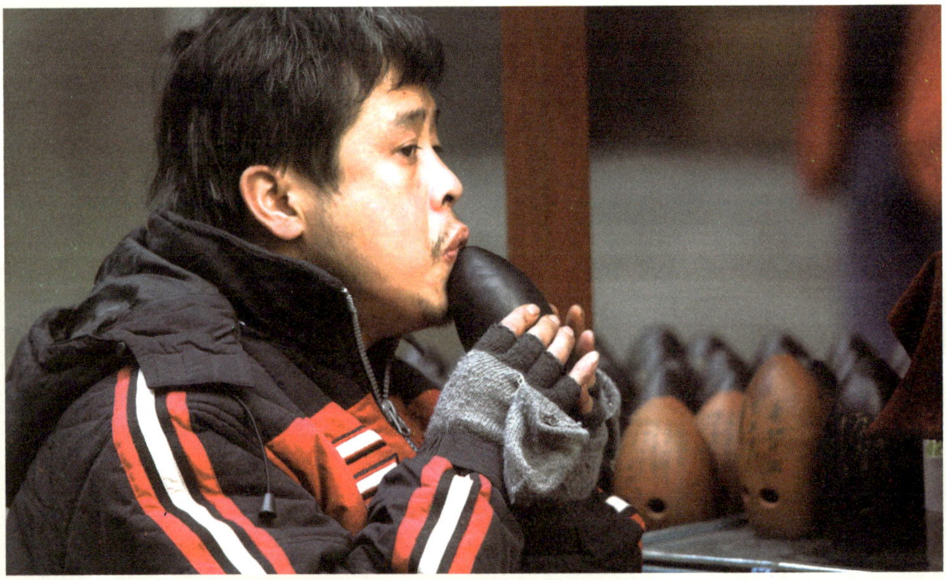

摄影：尚洪涛

摄影：翟小雪

**华阴老腔**
Laoqiang Opera

电影《白鹿原》中的老腔表演惊艳了许多人。其实早在上世纪90年代，老腔就因为张艺谋的影片《活着》征服了世界。产生于明末清初的老腔最大的特色在于原生态，被称为“中国戏曲的活化石”。一人唱、满台吼，声嘶力竭中包含满腔热血。在西安，听一曲老腔，绝对会让你热泪盈眶。

The performance of Laoqiang opera in the film *White Deer Plain* astonished many. Actually it had already won hearts around the globe in Zhang Yimou's *To Live* in the 1990s. This opera emerged at the end of the Ming Dynasty. Distinguished by its primitive nature, the opera has established itself as "the living fossil of Chinese opera". With one performer singing and others howling on the stage, Laoqiang displays its passion through desperate roaring. Listening to Laoqing in Xi'an, probably you will be moved to tears.

**西安安慰了孔子的心**
Xi'an Consoled Confucius

作家朱鸿说：“秦始皇在西安坑过儒，烧过儒之书，使儒学陷入了惨淡之境。不过汉武帝又在西安接受董仲舒的建议，把儒学变成了正宗和主流。从那时候开始，儒学作为一种意识形态，一种思想，一种文化，就一直弥漫于中国。西安荣幸地安慰了孔子的心。”

Zhu Hong, a writer, once said that it was in Xi'an that Qinshihuang buried Confucian scholars alive, burned Confucian books into ashes, and put Confucianism into a doomed state. Yet it was also in Xi'an that the Emperor Wu of Han accepted Dong Zhongshu's (a Confucius philosopher) suggestion and made Confucianism mainstream. From then on, Confucianism as an ideology, a thinking and a culture has permeated all levels of Chinese society. Xi'an is honored to be a great consolation to Confucius.

摄影：王健

**灯笼村**
**The Village of Lanterns**

三兆花灯照九州，精工细作传千古。西安雁塔区的三兆村做灯笼已经有上千年的历史，由于村里几乎家家户户都会做灯，因此成了远近闻名的“灯笼村”。每到农历新年前，这里是一派红红火火的景象。村民院落摆满各式各样的花灯，村路上车来车往，成百上千的灯笼被南来北往的汽车送往全国，甚至送出国门。

Sanzhou Village is well-known for its lanterns around China and the superb craftsmanship is a permanent heritage. Sanzhao Village, Yanta District, Xi'an, has been engaged in lantern making for over a thousand years. Almost every family here knows how to make lanterns, so the village is known as "the Lantern Village". Before each Chinese New Year, this village becomes a sea of red lanterns. All courtyards are filled with lanterns in varying forms. Trucks come and go on the country road, and hundreds and thousands of lanterns are delivered to different places around China, even overseas.

**菊花、古剑和酒**
**Chrysanthemum, Ancient Sword, and Alcohol**

研究区域文化的学者常感慨：为什么代表中国先锋文化的“摇滚乐标志人物”大多都与西安有密切的关系。郑钧、张楚、许巍……即便是成员没有一个陕西人的“唐朝乐队”，他们的成名曲、代表作也全部与西安有关。“菊花、古剑和酒”，也许都曾在长安的古街区中秘密潜藏。

Scholars in regional culture often wonder why so many Chinese rock'n'roll icons like Zheng Jun, Zhang Chu, Xu Wei etc., all come from Xi'an, Shaanxi Province. Although the Tang Dynasty Band has no member from Shaanxi, their most famous songs are all about Xi'an. "Chrysanthemum, ancient sword, and alcohol", as mentioned in their lyrics, may have hidden amid the ancient districts of Chang'an.

**推崇唐诗**
**Esteem for Tang Poetry**

如果从文学作品里了解陕西，唐诗大概是最好的教材。许多耳熟能详的唐诗名作都是写陕西的。秦岭里一个极偏僻的古庙和山林，都有不少名家的吟咏，而这些诗作都必须用陕西话来念才押韵。现代西安，无论古迹或民居，随处可见对唐诗的推崇，连餐馆茶室的对联都很讲究。

The poetry of the Tang Dynasty is the best material for one to get a glimpse of Shaanxi from literary works since a lot of well-known Tang poems are about Shaanxi. Even a remote temple or forest in the Qinling Mountains could be the subject of many famous poems. These poems only rhyme when read out loud in the Shaanxi dialect. In modern Xi'an, either historic sites or ordinary houses might bear traces of esteem for Tang poetry. Even couplets in restaurants and tea houses would be written in strict rhyming schemes.

**长安情结**

**The Obsession with Chang'an**

中国文人有“长安情结”，无论是辛弃疾的“西北望长安，可怜无数山”，还是李白的“长安不见使人愁”，都说明“长安”已是文化符号。郑钧笔下“繁华的都市”是《长安长安》，世园会的主题曲也唱《送你一个长安》。有人建议将西安改回长安，还在网上发起投票。

Chinese literati have an obsession with Chang'an. Poet Xin Qiji's (1140 - 1207) "I look into the lost Chang'an, northwestward, alas, countless mountains stand in my view", and Li Bai's "With Chang'an out of my sight, I'm upset" both show that "Chang'an" has become a cultural symbol. The "prosperous city" in rock singer Zheng Jun's song was "Chang'an, Chang'an", and the theme song of Xi'an China International Horticultural Exposition was "A Chang'an for You". Some people even suggested changing Xi'an back to Chang'an, and started a poll online. However, the idea was cast off as lacking confidence in contemporary culture.

**女人的路**

**The Journey of Women**

人类历史有多长，女人的路就有多长。西安有座妇女文化博物馆，位于陕西师范大学内。在这里，你可以清晰地看到一条“女人的路”：带鞋码的“三寸金莲”，只在女人之间使用的文字——江永女书，来自全国 56 个民族的嫁衣……这些由女性编织的历史充满着温度与色彩，鲜活地呈现在每一位观者的面前。

The journey of women is as long as human history. The Women's Culture Museum in Shaanxi Normal University, Xi'an, reveals the clear "journey of women": lotus shoes in different sizes for women with bound feet in feudal age, the Nüshu script—characters used exclusively among women, wedding gowns from all 56 ethnicities in China, and so on. Colorful and warm, women's history is fascinatingly displayed in the museum. .

**鲜活的历史课**

**A Lively History Lesson**

2012 年底，网友 @ 小鱼水中游的爸爸 带着女儿小鱼与另外几位网友一起穿越关中，寻访十八座唐代帝陵。刚上小学的小鱼不是第一次随爸爸踏上追寻历史和文明的旅程，感受文化。寻找唐帝陵也好，探访古寺院也罢，想必只有西安能给孩子上一堂如此鲜活的历史课。

At the end of 2012, netizen "Dad of a Swimming Fish" traveled across Guanzhong with his daughter and several other online friends to visit the eighteen imperial mausoleums of the Tang Dynasty. It wasn't the first time that his daughter had joined him on a journey to explore history, civilization and culture. Their trips to the imperial mausoleums of the Tang Dynasty and the ancient temples in Xi'an are the liveliest lesson in history.

## 变与不变
## The Changing and the Constant

有600年历史的明城墙是西安城市建筑的一部分，更是老百姓生活的一部分。每日穿梭于城门内外，延续着细水长流的生活。古老城墙的亘古不变与市井生活的潮流更迭，一静一动，形成西安特有的风景。

The 600-year-old city wall of the Ming Dynasty is not just an important architecture in Xi'an but also a part of local residents' life. Every day, they bustle in and out of the city, carrying on their lives. The stillness of the ancient city wall makes a sharp contrast to the ever-changing tide of daily life. This is distinctive of Xi'an.

## 中国古代音乐的活化石
## The Living Fossil of Ancient Chinese Music

西安鼓乐是流传在西安及周边地区的民间大型鼓乐，起源于隋唐，至今仍保持着相当完整的曲目、谱式、结构、乐器及演奏形式，是迄今为止在我国境内发现并保存最完整的大型民间乐种之一。2009年西安鼓乐入选“世界非物质文化遗产”，被音乐界和史学界誉为“中国古代音乐活化石”。

Xi'an drum music, a type of percussion music originated in the Sui and Tang dynasties, is popular in the vicinity of Xi'an. Its repertoire, style, structure, instruments, and performing methods have all survived. It is one of the best preserved and the most complete large-scale folk music forms in China. In 2009, Xi'an drum music was listed as a World Intangible Cultural Heritage, and praised as the "living fossil of ancient Chinese music" by the music industry and historians.

摄影：尚洪涛

摄影：翟小雪

## 博物馆人气高
## Museum's Popularity

“不到西安等于没到中国，而不去秦始皇陵兵马俑则等于没到西安。”这是秦始皇陵兵马俑博物馆在世人眼中的地位；而陕西历史博物馆内，则会让您感受到“给我一天，还您万年”的震撼。悠久的历史赋予西安丰厚的文化积淀和文物遗存，有媒体调查显示，西安各类博物馆的人气在全国居于首位。

"Don't say you've been to China if you didn't go to Xi'an, and don't say you've been to Xi'an if you didn't visit the Terracotta Army." These words reveal the immense significance of the Emperor Qinshihuang's Mausoleum Site Museum. The Shaanxi History Museum will offer you an overwhelming experience of "one day for ten thousand years". Ancient history has gifted Xi'an rich cultural heritage and historical relics. Media surveys indicate that the museums in Xi'an enjoy a greater popularity than those in other parts of China.

## 庙会穿越两千年
## 2,000-Year-Old Temple Fairs

体验一个地方的年味，最具特色要数庙会了。陕西省民间文艺家协会主席傅功振说，中国“庙”的源头就在陕西，从两千年前起，西安就有了“庙会”。如今，在小雁塔新年祈福庙会、大唐西市唐风文化庙会、西安城墙元宵灯会，您依然可以领略古时庙会的热闹场面，体味西安人逛庙会的老传统。

The temple fair is usually the best place to taste the local tradition of the Spring Festival. Fu Gongzhen, chairman of Shaanxi Folk Literature and Art Society, says that all Chinese temples owe their origin to Shaanxi. As early as two thousand years ago, there had been "temple fairs" in Xi'an. Now, the New Year Temple Fair near the Small Wild Goose Pagoda, the Temple Fair of Tang's Culture in the West Market, and the Lantern Festival on top of the city wall could all remind us of those thriving ancient temple fairs and showcase the age-old tradition of roaming around the temple fairs.

### 不舍"秦、汉、唐"
### All About "Qin, Han, and Tang"

西安成为政治经济文化顶峰的时代是在唐朝，而这里作为政权核心的中央地位，却是在汉代建立的，而西安被外界关注最多的无疑是秦始皇陵兵马俑。所以，"秦、汉、唐"这三个字在这片土地上出现频率最高。宾馆、饭店、企业名称乃至产品品牌，都舍不得这三个字。

It was during the Tang Dynasty that Xi'an reached its zenith in politics, economy and culture. Actually, it was already the center of politics in the Han Dynasty. Xi'an is best known for its Terracotta Army from the Qin Dynasty. Therefore, the three characters Qin, Han, and Tang are the most familiar sight on this land. You can always find these words in the names of hotels, restaurants, companies and brands.

### 豆村大蜡
### The Giant Candles of Dou Village

秦岭脚下的周至县终南镇豆村，自唐朝起每年四月初八都有"大蜡会"，庙会时特制的大蜡一旦点燃就能长明一年。如今，灌制大蜡的秘方传承到第四十二代传人赵立功，他做的一米多高的大蜡遇高温不熔不化，放置时间再长也不变形、不褪色。老人说："我做过一对 500 斤重的大蜡，带着 3 个徒弟用了一个多月。"

Giant Candle Fair ( 大蜡会 ) is held every year on the eighth of the fourth lunar month since the Tang Dynasty in Dou Village, Zhongnan town, Zhouzhi County, at the foot of the Qinling Mountains. Once lit, the grand candle specially made for the fair will last a whole year. Zhao Ligong is the 42nd successor to the secret knowhow of candle making. The one-meter-tall candle he makes neither melts in warm temperature nor deforms or fades over time. The old man said, "I once made a pair of giant candles that weighed 250 kg. It took me and three apprentices over a month to finish".

摄影：尚洪涛

## 北张村的手工造纸
## The Handmade Paper of Beizhang Village

75 岁的张逢学造了一辈子纸，是长安区北张村公认的造纸手艺最高的纸匠。老人说："我用古法造纸造出的白麻纸韧性好，耐保存，书画作品百十年后拿出来仍然跟刚画的时候一样。"像北张村这样还延续着古代蔡伦造纸法的地方很少见，世界造纸历史学会的李仿赞叹："世界纸根在中国，中国纸根在古长安。"

Regarded as the best papermaker in Beizhang Village, Chang'an District, Zhang Fengxue, aged 75, has produced papers throughout his life. "I adopt an ancient method for making white hemp paper, so the paper is strong and can be stored for a long time. After 100 years, the calligraphy or painting on this kind of paper still looks as fresh as before," said the old man. Rare are the places where the papermaking process devised by Cai Lun (63 - 121), the inventor of paper, has survived. Li Fang from the Association of Paper History praised, "The world owes papermaking to China, and China owes it to Chang'an."

摄影：尚洪涛

摄影：尚洪涛、翟小雪

## 影子的舞蹈
## Dancing Shadow Puppots

皮影戏如今虽然遍布全国很多城市，但它最早诞生却是在两千年前的陕西。如今，这里的皮影戏仍非常有名，西安人爱把这种利用“影子”舞蹈叙事的表演叫“影子戏”，在灯光照射与艺人的手指挥动间，这些用兽皮或纸板做成的“人影”仿若有了生命，灵动活泼。

Shadow puppetry is now popular in many cities across China, but it was initiated in Shaanxi two thousand years ago. A well-known ancient form of storytelling and entertainment, shadow puppetry is called shadow play by the Xi'anese. By moving either the figures or the source light, an artist can breathe life to the puppets made of leather or cardboard.

摄影：王幼健

摄影：翟小雪

**陶罐**
**Pottery**

“江南瓷器江北陶”，江北主要指长江支流汉江北面，即秦岭北麓。陕西的文物藏家大都偏爱陶器。古玩鉴赏家范炳南家中，陶罐都摆在书架案头，瓷器尽在厨房与楼道，他说：“眼前摆个瓷器，浑身拘得很”。画家邢庆仁的话更狠：“哦，我年轻时也喜欢瓷器那矫揉造作的劲儿。”

In the saying “Fine porcelain is from south of the river and fine pottery from north of the river”, north of the river refers to areas on the north of the Han River, a tributary of the Yangtze River, to be more specific, the north foot of the Qinling Mountains. Most antique collectors in Shaanxi favor pottery. In the house of Fan Bingnan, a connoisseur of Chinese antiques, pottery wares are all placed on bookshelves and desks while porcelains are in the kitchen and the doorway. He explained, “The sight of a porcelain makes me uneasy.” Painter Xing Qingren’s words were even harsher, “Oh, I used to like the pretentiousness of porcelain when I was young as well.”

**给央视配音的大钟**
**The Bell That Dubbed for CCTV**

在碑林中，还有一处与碑无关的景致，那便是原本悬在钟楼内的景云钟。景云钟造于唐景云二年（公元 711 年），故得名景云。最初挂在唐长安城内的景龙观钟楼，明初移至现西安钟楼用以报时。1953 年移藏至西安碑林博物馆。每年除夕，中央电视台辞旧迎新的“新年钟声”，就是景云钟的实地录音。

In the Beilin (Stele Forest) Museum locates the only item that has nothing to do with the steles is the Jingyun Bell, originally hung in the Bell Tower in the Jingyun Taoist Temple. Jingyun Bell was cast in 711, the 2nd year of the Jingyun reign during the Tang Dynasty, hence the name Jingyun. In early Ming Dynasty, it was moved to the Bell Tower to tell the time. And in 1953, it was moved to its current location. On every lunar year’s eve, it is the live sound of Jingyun Bell that, via CCTV, ushers in the new year.

摄影：尚洪涛

## 百年剧社 易俗社

## The Century-Old Theatre Yisushe

入夜，西一路上店铺纷纷打烊，易俗社的灯笼却高高亮起。这家追随辛亥革命而建的戏院，一出生便与众不同。不为江湖卖艺，只为移风易俗。西安事变时，杨虎成坐镇于此，明里是陪南京来人看戏，暗里却运筹兵谏，演出一幕历史大戏。100 年过去了，这方寸舞台从烽火连天唱到太平盛世，不变的是那秦人秦腔。

When the night falls, the stores on Lane One to the west of Jiefang Road close one by one, but the lanterns of Yisushe Theatre still shine brightly. Since its establishment after the revolution of 1911, the theater has distinguished itself from others. It was not intended to make money through performance but to right the wrong. During the Xi'an Incident, General Yang Hucheng sat here, pretending to watch an opera with the senior officers of KMT but maneuvering his army seceretly. He staged a great historic drama. Over last century, the small theater has been insisted on staging Qin opera either in war years or the peace time.

## 窖藏汉唐

## The Cellar of History

藏窖是北方农村特有的储物洞穴，从地面挖直径一米五左右的直井，至底下两丈左右深，扩大一圈，冬暖夏凉，主要储藏薯类。西安的一位作家诺思，在他文章中这样写道：西安就是个巨大的藏窖，窖藏着的是中华文化的精华——汉唐。

In the countryside of northern China, pit-like cellars are very common. Dig a well of 1.5 meters in diameter and expand the underground space when it is 6 or 7 meters deep. Warm in winter and cool in summer, the cellar is mainly used for storing potatoes. Nuo Si, a writer from Xi'an, wrote in his article: Xi'an itself is a gigantic cellar which stores the essence of Chinese civilization—the legacy of the Han and Tang dynasties.

**佛教祖庭**

The Ancestral Temples of Mahayana

大乘佛教八大祖庭，六个都在西安。古时的长安更是佛教翻译和传播中心，历代4700余部汉译佛典中，在长安译出者占多半。可以说，佛教花开于印度，结果在中国，而中国大乘佛教根系尽在长安。

Six of the eight ancestral temples of Mahayana are located in Xi'an. Ancient Chang'an was the center for scripture translation and dissemination. More than half of the 4,700 Buddhist texts have been rendered into Chinese in Chang'an. Buddhism blossomed in India, but bore fruits in China. Mahayana Buddhism in China originated from Chang'an.

摄影：尚洪涛

**以碑为镜**

A Maxim on a Stele

“吏不畏吾严而畏吾廉，民不服吾能而服吾公，公则民不敢慢，廉则吏不敢欺，公生明，廉生威。”西安碑林馆藏清代官箴碑上的“官场箴言”，今天仍值得为官者借鉴。细数西安碑林大大小小的石碑，内容无一例外是人们向往的社会生活准则。一块块碑文像一面面镜子，时隔百年，面碑深思，仍能触动心灵。

“While my subordinates fear my integrity more than my power, my people admire my fairness more than my talents. Fairness pre-empts contempt from the people. Integrity pre-empts deception from the officials. Fairness ensures a brilliant judgment and integrity breeds an awesome power.” This maxim inscribed on a stele from the Qing Dynasty is still valuable for present officials. A careful scrutiny of the steles will reveal that they are all about ideal norms of behaviour. Old as they are, each of them illuminates the soul of the visitor standing solemnly in front of it.

**中国人都该练书法**

Every Chinese Should Practice Calligraphy

书法已被现代生活渐渐疏离，但在西安碑林工作几十年的陈根远研究员仍坚定地认为：每个中国人都应该学习一点书法。这既是了解传统文化的好途径，也能带来心灵的满足。不需要大张旗鼓地找名师，只需买几本字帖。在繁忙的生活中静下心来，摆砚磨墨铺纸落笔，不知不觉就成为传承文化的一分子，何乐而不为?

Calligraphy seems estranged from our daily life, but Chen Genyuan, a senior researcher at the Xi’an Beilin Museum, contends that every Chinese should learn calligraphy. It is not only an effective way to learn traditional culture, but also an intellectual fulfillment. There is no need to strain every sinew to find a prestigious teacher; just buy a couple of copybooks. Let your soul take a rest from the busy life by taking out the ink stone, grinding some ink, laying out a piece of paper, and pressing down the brush. In this process, you are also inheriting traditional Chinese culture. Why not go ahead and do it?

**拓印历史**

Stone Rubbing History

拓片制作始于东汉，时至今日，拓印不但是一种行业，也是一门绝活儿手艺。众所周知的是，碑林博物馆拥有浩瀚的石刻藏品、卓越的书法作品，而“众所不知”的是，打拓片也是碑林博物馆内一道别致的风景线。浸纸、压紧、刷扫，在拓片师傅娴熟利落的拓印动作中，捕捉历史的痕迹。

Initiated in the Eastern Han Dynasty (25 - 220), stone rubbing is both an industry and a great craftsmanship. It is widely known that the Beilin Museum houses a vast collection of stone inscriptions and extraordinary calligraphy works, yet few know that stone rubbing is also a unique form of art to appreciate. Those craftsmen wet the paper, tamp it into the engravings, and brush gently. Their deft skills reveal a trace of history.

摄影：张宇明

## 水陆庵泥塑

### The Statues at Shuilu Nunnery

蓝田县王顺山下的水陆庵，是六朝名刹，唐朝时僧侣达千人。现庵内保存有壁塑3700多尊，是目前发现的中国最大的壁塑群。其中除一组为五代时期作品外，其余均为明代著名雕塑家乔仲超等人所塑。塑像内容为佛陀画传与经变，塑像个体或一掌大小，或一人之高，纵横罗列，布局精妙，气势恢宏。

Shuilu Nunnery at the foot of Mt. Wangshun in Lantian County is an ancient temple that housed over a thousand monks in the Tang Dynasty. The 3,700 painted sculptures here are the largest group of its kind so far discovered in China. All the statues were sculpted by famous sculptors like Qiao Zhognchao during the Ming Dynasty except one set of works from the Five Dynasties period (907 - 960). Based on the Buddha's life and sutra, the sculptures range from palm-sized to man-sized, stacked in marvelous ways with an air of grandeur.

摄影：尚洪涛

**属于城墙的节日**
**A Festival in Honor of the City Wall**

一年 365 天，有数不清的节日和纪念日，而在西安，更比其他城市都多了一个特别的节日——“西安城墙亲近日”。从 2009 年起，西安市政府将每年的 11 月 1 日设立为“西安城墙亲近日”，一个只属于城墙的节日。对于西安人而言，城墙不仅是这座城市的地标，是可以触摸的历史，更是他们的精神家园。

There are numerous holidays and memorial days in a year. The Xi'anese celebrate yet one more special holiday than people in other cities. In 2009, Xi'an Municipal Government proclaimed November 1 to be the "Xi'an City Wall Ascending Day", a holiday exclusively in honor of the city wall. To the Xi'anese, the city wall is more than a landmark. It is their tangible history and their spiritual home.

**《华严经》与华严宗祖庭**
**The *Flower Garland Sutra* and the Ancestral Temple of the Huayan School**

明代高僧憨山大师曾言：“不读《华严》，不知佛家之富贵。”《华严经》是佛陀成道后，对文殊菩萨、普贤菩萨等大乘菩萨解释无尽法界时所讲，也是佛教华严宗最重要的根本典籍之一，被誉为“经中之王”。现长安区少陵原的华严寺尚存有华严宗初祖杜顺禅师与华严四祖清凉国师的墓塔。

Master Hanshan in the Ming Dynasty remarked, "One wouldn't know the richness of Buddhism without reading the *Flower Garland Sutra* (*Avataṃsaka Sūtra*)." The *Avataṃsaka Sūtra* contains the teachings about infinite Dharma Realm, from the Buddha, after his awakening, to mahāyāna bodhisattvas such as Manjusri and Samantabhadra. Crowned "the king of sutras", it is one of the most fundamental scriptures for the Huayan School of Chinese Buddhism. Huayan Temple in Chang'an District on Shaolingyuan still houses the stupas of Dushun, founder of the School, and Pure-minded preceptor of the State, the Fourth Patriarch of the School.

**文物书库**
**The Library of Cultural Relics**

中国首座以文物图书为主题的图书馆——陕西文物图书中心坐落在碑林博物馆两座 20 世纪初建成的小楼内，其中南楼是由梁思成设计的歇山式建筑。馆藏古籍图书、平装图书、过报过刊 15 余万册，其中古籍图书 4199 种，珍贵古善本 54 部。经、史、子、集、丛五类齐全。它们既是记录时光的书籍，也是承载历史的文物。

China's first library on the theme of cultural relics includes two early-20th century buildings in the Beilin Museum. The south building is designed by Liang Sicheng (1901 - 1972), a famous architect. The library holds over 150,000 volumes of ancient books, paperbacks, and dated issues of newspapers and magazines, including 4,199 ancient titles and 54 volumes of rare and highly valuable ancient texts. They are not only history books but historical relics as well.

摄影：王幼健

人文 · 西安
Culture and Lifestyle

**排队推广日**

Queue Promotion Day

11 月 11 日是光棍节。可是在西安，从 2009 年起，这一天还有另外一个名字——“排队推广日”，意在倡导市民自觉排队、规范行路。一个城市的秩序如果能够像这四个 1 一样整整齐齐排成一排，难道不是一道亮丽的城市风景吗？在许多西安人眼里，“双十一”是比光棍节更重要的公共责任日。

Singles' Day falls on November 11, but in Xi'an, this day has had another title since 2009, Queue Promotion Day, advocating queuing and order in transportation. If things in a city can be lined up as orderly as the four "1"s, wouldn't that make for a beautiful city scene? Many people in Xi'an regard "Double Eleven" as a Public Responsibility Day rather than a mere Singles' Day.

**一元钱的温暖**

The Benevolence of One Yuan

家住西安柏树林的 92 岁孤寡老人崔玉英最喜欢到家门口的一家私房菜馆吃饭。三年来，只要老人来吃饭，不论吃多少，老板何卓远都只收一元钱，既让老人吃饱，又不伤老人尊严。何卓远的善举感动了西安，上百家店铺加入“1 元关爱计划”，为年满 80 岁的孤寡老人提供一元就餐、一元买药等服务。

Cui Yuying, a 92-year-old heirless widow in Xi'an, frequents a nearby restaurant, whose owner, He Zhuoyuan, charges the senior patron only one *yuan* every time she comes over the past three years, no matter how much she eats. With dignity, Cui eats to her fill. He Zhuoyuan's benevolence is so touching that over 100 stores have joined the "One *Yuan* Project", providing the over-80s with meals or medicines for one *yuan* only.

**翰墨雅俗**

Elegant Customs

西安人一直尊崇逢年过节、婚丧嫁娶送字画的雅俗。因此，不少人家里都藏有字画。西安街头出自名家之手的牌匾随处可见，被称为又一“碑林”。很多人还是能写善画的高手，平时隐身在机关乡野，一遇群贤盛会，便真人露峥嵘。难怪西安的书画店很多，且不管春夏秋冬，生意始终红火。

The Xi'anese have always observed the elegant tradition of presenting calligraphy and painting scrolls as gifts at festivals, weddings and funerals. Consequently, many families collect calligraphy and painting scrolls. On the streets, plaques inscribed by famous calligraphers are very common, so they are called an alternate "Beilin" (Forest of Stone Steles). Many locals, skilled at calligraphy and painting, would usually maintain a low profile. Yet when they encounter other masters of the arts, they would reveal their true talents. No wonder calligraphy and painting shops, though great in number, enjoy good business all year round in Xi'an.

**同一种味道**
**The Same Kind of Taste**

餐饮文化大师张振楣先生，一到西安就听人介绍说，来西安如果不去兵马俑，就等于没来西安；又有人说，来西安如果不尝羊肉泡馍，就白来一趟西安。于是他先吃泡馍，再去兵马俑。结果吃过、去过之后，张振楣突然悟到，西安这两样东西其实是一回事，都是“历史 + 文化”。

As soon as cuisine connoisseur Mr. Zhang Zhenmei arrived in Xi’an, he was told that a tour to Xi’an would be a vain one if the tourist missed the Terracotta Army or a taste of the mutton stew with cake shreds, known as *yangrou paomo* in Chinese. So Zhang tried *yangrou paomo* first, and then visited the Terracotta Army. After that, it suddenly dawned on him: the two specialties of Xi’an are in fact the same thing: the combination of history and culture.

**挖地三尺就见宝**
**Treasures Are Easy to Dig Up**

1973 年，陈家桥村一名学生用铁锨平整土地时，挖出一件铜器。两年后，铜器经过把玩露出金色文字。经过专家鉴定，这是一枚罕见的战国虎符。这枚虎符，也是目前我国现存最早的虎符实物，距今已有 2000 多年。挖地三尺就见宝，在西安，类似这样神奇的故事比比皆是。

In 1973, a student in Chenjiaqiao Village dug out a copper artifact when leveling the field with a shovel. After two years of wear, the artifact revealed golden writings. After examination, experts concluded that this was a rare *hufu* (tiger-shaped tally) from the Warring States era (475 - 221 B.C.) over 2,000 years ago, the most ancient of its kind discovered so far. Effortless but amazing, such discoveries are legion Xi’an.

**重阳宫碑林**
**The Stele Forest at Chongyang Temple**

重阳宫是道教全真派的祖庭。因为全真派祖师王重阳与元代皇帝的关系，建于户县重阳宫内的碑林以收藏元代石刻著称。目前发现的二十余通八思巴蒙古文字碑中，此碑林存有六通；且形制高大，雕刻精美，多为皇帝玺书，是国内研究古代蒙古语言的珍贵资料。碑林中还有两通石刻出自赵孟頫之手。

Chongyang Temple is the ancestral temple of the Complete Perfection School of Taoism. The stele forest at Chongyang Temple is also known for the stone carvings of the Yuan Dynasty, thanks to the close relations between Wang Chongyang (1113 - 1170), founder of the Complete Perfection School, and the emperors of the Yuan Dynasty. Among the 20-strong stone steles with the Mongolian Phags-pa script discovered this far, six are housed here, of grand magnitude with intricate carvings, most of whom are imperial edicts and precious resources for studying ancient Mongolian languages. In addition, two epigraphs are calligraphy works of the great painter and calligrapher Zhao Mengfu (1254 - 1322).

**满眼文化**

**Omnipresent Culture**

西安人重文化，很多农村人家的中堂都挂有“一等人忠臣孝子，两件事读书耕田”的条幅。贾平凹说：即便那些流动于街头巷尾叫卖的小吃担，如甑糕、笼笼肉、蜂蜜凉粽，担头上晃悠晃悠的一个小木板招牌，也常是集了颜真卿的字或于右任的字。

Culture is prized in Xi'an. In the main hall of many rural houses hangs a scroll which reads “Live up to the ideal of loyalty and filial piety; attach importance to farming and studying.” Jia Pingwa recounts: even the street stands that roam the alleyways selling various snacks have their wooden signs inscribed with the works of Yan Zhenqin or Yu Youren, two greatest calligraphers in Chinese history.

**天然历史博物馆**

**The Natural History Museum**

西安文物甲天下，深厚的历史文化积淀和浩瀚的文物古迹遗存使西安享有“天然历史博物馆”的美称。秦始皇陵兵马俑被誉为“世界第八大奇迹”，明代古城墙遗址是至今世界上保存最完整、规模最宏大的古城墙遗址。近年，汉阳陵的开发又一次轰动了世界，其出土的裸体彩俑被誉为“东方维纳斯”。

Xi'an's artifacts top the world. Its profound history, rich culture, along with its vast reserve of archeological treasures have earned Xi'an the title of “Natural History Museum”. Qinshihuang's Terracotta Army is hailed as “the Eighth Wonder of the Ancient World”. The ancient city wall from the Ming Dynasty remains the best-preserved and grandest rampart of its kind in the world. In recent years, the excavation of the Hanyangling Mausoleum has amazed the world once again, and the naked color figurine unearthed is crowned as the “Eastern Venus”.

摄影：王幼健

**昭陵六骏**
**The Six Steeds of the Zhaoling Mausoleum**

为了纪念昔日骑过的六匹战马，李世民令工艺家阎立德和画家阎立本，用浮雕描绘六匹战马列置于自己陵前。六骏中有两件作品，于 1918 年被盗卖到国外，现藏于美国。其余四件作品，在盗卖时被发现制止，现存于碑林博物馆。

To commemorate his six warhorses, Li Shimin (Emperor Taizong of Tang, reigned 627 - 649) commissioned craftsman Yan Lide and painter Yan Liben to make carvings of the six steeds to put in front of his mausoleum. Two of the sculptures were stolen and sold to the Unites States. The selling of the other four was halted, and they are now stored in the Beilin Museum.

**槐树之城**
**The City of Pagoda Trees**

西安槐树特别多，既高又翠，槐花开时香满城。事实上，西安正是槐树文化的主要发祥地。三千多年前，西周在这里植槐棘分列官员；两千多年前，王莽在这里设槐市供儒生交易；一千多年前，韦孝宽在这里首创以槐树作为行道树。正源于这千百年的槐树因缘，西安将槐树定为市树。

The numerous pagoda trees in Xi'an stand tall and green, spreading the fragrance of their blossoming flowers throughout the city. Xi'an is in fact the birthplace of the culture of pagoda trees. Over 3,000 years ago, the court of Western Zhou Dynasty lined up and ranked officials under the pagoda trees. Over 2,000 years ago, Wang Mang (an official in the Han Dynasty who seized the throne and founded Xin Dynasty, reign 9 - 23) set up the Pagoda Tree Market for the trading of Confucian books. 1,000 years ago, General Wei Xiaokuan (509 - 580) made pagoda trees boulevard trees the first time in history. And out of this long-lasting love, the Xi'anese make the pagoda tree their city tree.

**财神赵公明**
**The God of Wealth Zhao Gongming**

财神赵公明故里在周至县集贤镇赵大村。在民间，如果是合伙生意，一定要拜关公，同时也要拜祭赵公明财神。《道藏》图谱里，财神形象为一手执鞭，一手托元宝，是武财神的样子；意为他法力无穷，率领招宝、纳珍、招财、利市等天尊，统管人世间一切金银财宝。每年正月初五，财神故里热闹非凡。

The hometown of the Zhao Gongming, the God of Wealth, is in Zhaoda Village, Jixian Town, Zhouzhi County. In Chinese culture, to run a venture capital, you must pay your respect to Lord Guan and the God of Wealth. In the *Taoist Canon*, the God of Wealth is described as a typical Martial God of Wealth: holding a whip in one hand and a gold ingot in the other, indicating his unlimited power. With the assistance of deities like Zhaobao (who brings in treasure), Nazhen (who collects treasures), Zhaocai (who brings in wealth), and Lishi (who is in charge of the lucky money), the God of Wealth manages all the treasures and wealth in the world. The hometown of the God of Wealth becomes bustling with life on the fifth day of every first lunar month.

**唐钱团团**

The "Gold Coins" Leaves

西安市区东去蓝田40分钟车程，有诗人王维亲手种植的银杏树。如今树龄有1300多岁，四人合围也难抱得过来。立秋之后，小雪之前，满树金黄的银杏叶，当地人称“唐钱团团”，为图一个好彩头，往来瞻顾的游人络绎不绝。

A short forty-minute drive east from Xi'an to Lantian, there stands a ginkgo tree planted by poet Wang Wei. Over 1,300 years old, the tree trunk is so wide that four people can barely hug it together. In autumn, the tree is in full leaf. Locals call the yellow leaves "gold coins" and tourists flock here to wish for good fortune.

**美国老人的西安情结**

An Elderly American's Love for Xi'an

古时长安吸引大批外国使节常驻，现在的西安也让许多过客变为常客。80岁的美国老人史蒂夫，2003年首次来到西安，之后的7年，每个春天他都来这里。在城墙根下晒太阳，跟来来往往的人聊天。“这里的人们很善良，我喜欢这里的一切，这里就是我的家。”史蒂夫说。

So amazing was the ancient Chang'an that many foreign emissaries couldn't tear themselves away from the capital. Nowadays Xi'an also turns numerous passersby into regular visitors. Steve, an 80-year-old American who first visited Xi'an in 2003, spent all the following seven springs here. He enjoyed the sunshine at the foot of the city wall, and chatted with people around. "People here are really kind. I like everything about this place. It is my second home," said Steve.

**文物“论资排辈”**

The Hierarchy of Artifacts

有游客问陕西历史博物馆工作人员，为何这里少见明清展品？工作人员语出惊人：夏商西周与春秋战国分庭抗礼，两晋和隋唐互争地盘，宋元只能占据少量展室，哪儿还有明清立足之地？此言不虚，西安地铁2号线修建过程中，发现并清理古墓130余座，出土器物200余件，前后跨越2000多年历史。

When asked why artifacts of the Ming and Qing dynasties are rarely on display, a staff member at the Shaanxi History Museum gave a great answer, "Xia (c. 2070 - 1600 B.C.), Shang (1600 - 1046 B.C.), Western Zhou, the Spring and Autumn Period (770 - 476 B.C.), and the Warring States Period are so important as to have their own exhibition space; the Jin (1115 - 1234), Sui and Tang dynasties are no less competitive. Even the Song and Yuan dynasties can only occupy a small space, where would we have left for the Ming and Qing dynasties?" Indeed, during the construction of subway Line 2 in Xi'an, over 130 ancient tombs and more than 200 artifacts that crossed over 2,000 years were excavated.

## 坊上人
## The Residents on Muslim Street

回民街，西安人称之为“坊上”，是西安主要的穆斯林聚居地，位于市中心繁华区域。高鼻深目的坊上人大多是中西亚古老移民的后裔，勤劳富足，信念虔诚。饮食生意是坊上人安身立命的根本，为食材锦上添花的本事，让他们少了很多生意上的应酬话，也使回民街成为大批游客来西安的必到之处。

Muslim Street, called "Fangshang" by the locals, is in downtown Xi'an. The dominant residents here are Muslims. With large nose and big eyes, these people are descendants of migrants from central and west Asia. Hardworking and devout, they live on the catering industry. Their ability to turn ingredients into tasty treats speaks for itself, which has made Muslim Street a must-visit destination for tourists to Xi'an.

摄影：翟小雪

## 西安的“名片”
## Name Cards of Xi'an

西安有许多“城市名片”。由“武士”和“仕女”构成的“仿古入城仪式”便是其中一张。重大活动和贵客到西安，参照古代官方和民间礼仪礼规，在700多年历史的明城墙南城门放下吊桥迎宾入城。当年欢迎美国总统克林顿的入城式最热烈，影响最大。如果你到西安旅游，能得到这张“名片”，那将是莫大的荣幸。

The welcome ceremony in the ancient style with the full cast of “imperial soldiers” and “court ladies” is one of the many “name cards” of Xi’an. When a distinguished guest arrives, the drawbridge at the 700-year-old south gate is lowered over the moat to welcome the guest. On these important occasions, ancient rituals are strictly performed. The welcome ceremony for former American President Bill Clinton was the most magnificent and impressive. If you get to receive this “name card” while visiting Xi’an, it shall be the greatest honor.

摄影：翟小雪　王健

**蓝田玉**
Lantian Jade

西安东南的蓝田县以出产美玉而闻名于世，唐代诗人李商隐在《锦瑟》中的名句“沧海月明珠有泪，蓝田日暖玉生烟”正是来源于此。蓝田玉以绿、白、天青、赭红、玄黑为主要色泽，色彩斑斓，光泽温润，纹理细密，质地坚硬。位于今天蓝田县大寨乡文刘坡的仰韶龙山文化遗址中，已有先民们制作的玉璧、玉戈等。

Lantian County in southeast Xi'an is known around the world for its gorgeous jade. It inspired Li Shangyin, a poet in the Tang Dynasty, to write a famous stanza, "A pearl fisher wept in the deep under the moonlight, and a craftsman looked for Lantian jade with his misty eyes bathing sunshine." Mostly green, white, blue, red, and black, Lantian jade is colorful, hard, and fine-grained with a soft glow. At the Yangshao and Longshan Cultural Site in today's Lantian County, there already have been excavated jade items such as jade emblems and jade daggers made by early settlers.

**长安画派**
The Painters of Chang'an Style

20世纪60年代，以赵望云、石鲁为代表的西安美术团体在北京等地组织了一次巡展。这些表现黄土高原古朴倔强的山水画和表现陕北农民勤劳淳朴的人物画引起轰动，他们被称为“长安画派”。他们的绘画题材以山水、人物为主，兼及花鸟，作品多描绘西北，特别是陕西地区的自然风光和风土人情。

In the 1960s, led by Zhao Wangyun and Shi Lu, the Xi'an art circle organized a touring exhibition in cities including Beijing. Their landscape paintings about the primitiveness of Loess Plateau and the hardworking farmers in northern Shaanxi rocked the art world. Their style has been called the "Chang'an Style" henceforth. Their subjects range from landscapes and portraits to flowers and birds. Their works usually depict the landscapes and customs of northwestern China, and Shaanxi in particular.

**伊斯兰文化**
Muslim Culture

西安城市中心保留着完整的伊斯兰文化街区，就在钟楼以西。除了人们熟知的回族风味小吃，弯弯曲曲的古巷内还藏着不少令人赞叹的伊斯兰建筑。化觉巷和大学习巷的两座清真大寺，融合伊斯兰文化和中国传统建筑的精髓，是不可错过的经典。

An Islamic culture block is wholesomely preserved in downtown Xi'an, just west of the Bell Tower. Aside from the well-known Hui ethnic cuisine, many spectacular Islamic structures are hidden in the ancient winding lanes. The two great mosques on Huajue Alley and Daxuexi Alley are two classical buildings that are not to be missed; both combine the essences of Islamic culture and traditional Chinese architecture.

### 处处皆是文化遗产
### Cultural Relics Everywhere

“西安到处都是文化遗产。”作家朱鸿说，“周之器，秦之砖，汉之瓦，唐之塔，是其典型。西安周围耸立着近乎八十个帝陵和近乎八百个陪葬之墓，其中誉满天下者有秦陵、汉武帝茂陵、唐高宗与武则天乾陵，当然还有人文初祖黄帝陵。”

“There are cultural relics everywhere in Xi’an,” writer Zhu Hong claimed, “Typical are the wares of Zhou, bricks of Qin, tiles of Han, and pagodas of Tang. Xi’an is surrounded by nearly 80 imperial mausoleums and 800 subordinate tombs. Among the most famous ones are the Mausoleum of Emperor Qinshihuang, the Maoling Mausoleum of Emperor Wu of Han, the Qianling Mausoleum of Emperor Gaozong of Tang and Wu Zetian, not to mention the Mausoleum of the Yellow Emperor (c. early 30th century - 21st century B. C.), the initiator of Chinese civilization.”

### 古城雾景
### Ancient City amid Mist

阴天走在古城的街道上也不必懊恼，灰蒙蒙的雾气反倒给古楼青砖增添了一份神秘感和厚重感，拿起相机，定格一个画面，这时带有浓重历史气息的古城景色就如水墨画一般。

If you happen to encounter a cloudy weather when walking along the streets in this ancient town, don’t be upset. The mist would make the ancient architectures and the old roof tiles more mysterious and solemn. Take a picture of the city with rich history, you will get a framed scenery, which looks like a Chinese ink and wash painting.

摄影：翟小雪

**三石纪唐**
**Three Remarkable Stones in the Tang Dynasty**

说到西安，“大唐盛世”是必然绕不过去的一段历史，作家朱鸿认为：唐有三石，琢而为器，遂蕴深意，探之可以得智慧，测变化。从这三石，即可回望浩渺盛世的一世烟尘。这三石为：李世民昭陵六骏石雕；乾陵武则天的无字碑；临潼华清宫青石拼砌而成的杨贵妃的海棠汤。

“The Golden Age of the Tang Dynasty” is an era that has to be mentioned when talking about Xi’an. Writer Zhu Hong believes that there are three stones that turned valuable after carved with profound meanings in the Tang Dynasty. One can attain wisdom and predict future change by exploring the beauty of them. These “three stones” offer a full view of the incomprehensibly long history. They are the stone sculpture Six Steeds of Zhaoling in honor of Li Shimin, the Wordless Stele in the Qianling Mausoleum of Wu Zetian and Consort Yang’s Crabapple Pool made of cobblestones at the Huaqing Palace in Lintong County.

**只游西安**
**Touring Xi’an Only**

若去云南旅游，只去昆明显然是不能尽兴的，游客大多还会去大理、丽江、西双版纳等地。而到陕西，西安一地的入境游客占到全省的 95% 以上，国内游客则占到全省的 85%。对于媒体这一报道，有人笑谈，西安可看可玩的实在太多，无暇顾及其他地方了。

When traveling in Yunnan, tourists won’t content themselves with Kunming alone. Their destinations will also include other cities like Dali, Lijiang and Xishuangbanna. However, this is not the case with Shaanxi, in which Xi’an alone receives 95 percent of foreign tourists and 85 percent of domestic tourists to this province. These figures are attributed, in a bantering manner, to a great number of attractions in Xi’an, so great that the tourists here can barely find any time for other cities in Shaanxi.

**第五代导演崛起的土壤**
**Home to the Fifth Generation Filmmakers**

陈凯歌、田壮壮、吴子牛、张艺谋、黄建新、周晓文、李少红等被称作“第五代导演”，他们的出现给中国影坛带来了巨大的冲击与荣耀。而这些人，都曾与西安发生过密切的关系。《红高粱》《盗马贼》《霸王别姬》等“第五代”的代表作都产生于西安电影制片厂，厂长吴天明更被称为“第五代导演的教父”。

Chen Kaige, Tian Zhuangzhuang, Wu Ziniu, Zhang Yimou, Huang Jianxin, Zhou Xiaowen, and Li Shaohong among others are called “the Fifth Generation Filmmakers”. Their appearance had huge impact and reflected great credit on China’s film industry. These filmmakers were somehow related to Xi’an, for their representative works such as *Red Sorghum, The Horse Thief*, and *Farewell My Concubine*, were all produced by the Xi’an Film Studio. Wu Tianming, the former manager, is praised as “the Godfather of the Fifth Generation”.

## 灞河倒着流
## The Ba River Flows Backwards

灞河原名滋水，春秋时改名霸水，后改“霸”为“灞”。“涌出石门归无路，反向西倒着流。杨柳别岸风香透，鹿原峙左骊山踞右，夹得一线瘦。倒着走便倒着走，独开水道也风流，自古青山遮不住，过了灞桥昂然调头，东去一拂袖。”陈忠实的这首词，表达了对灞河所承载的厚重历史文化的敬重。

Originally called Zi River, the Ba River was renamed “Bashui (霸水)” in the Spring and Autumn Period. Later, the character 霸 was changed to 灞. “Flowing out of the stone gate where there’s no return, yet flows west and rewinds backwards. Willows wave goodbye on the banks and the wind carries fragrances. The Deer Plain stands on the left and Mt. Li loom large on the right. Only a thin gap is left in between. If you are willing to run backwards, then run backwards. Starting a new waterway is free-spirited anyway. The green mountains have never been able to hide since ancient times, as soon as we pass the Ba Bridge the boat returns. Going eastward, with a gentle flick of the sleeves.” This poem by Chen Zhongshi expresses his great respect for the Ba River’s long history and rich culture.

## 八仙庵古玩市场
## The Antique Market at the Temple of Eight Immortals

西安的古玩市场有四五个，不过文化人一般喜欢到八仙庵古玩市场去。星期天是交易日，尤其热闹。当然，如同这个行当一样，这里的古玩也是真中掺假，假的像真。于是文化人就常常在这里上当，反复“交学费”。不过古玩爱好者既好之则乐之，是不怕上当的。

There are four or five antique markets in Xi’an, but pros prefer the one at the Temple of Eight Immortals Antique Market. The trading on Sundays is very intense. Of course, just like everywhere else, the antiques here are mixed. Hidden among the real ones, fake wares often look authentic. Even insiders are often swindled here, and pay for their “tuition” repeatedly. But, antique lovers will always be antique lovers. They are not afraid of being tricked.

## 古代史博物馆众多
## A Multitude of Ancient History Museums

在西安人看来，宋元之后的历史都太“新”了，五代以前的文物才值得进入古代史博物馆。从西周青铜器博物馆到唐朝的永泰公主墓博物馆，从国家级的陕西历史博物馆到省级的临潼博物馆，分布朝代、范围之密集，居世界首位。连冠名“西安”的西安博物院也是国家级的。

To the Xi’anese, history after the Song and Yuan dynasties is too “recent”, only artifacts before the Five Dynasties are museum-level. From the Western Zhou Bronze Ware Museum, to the Qianling Museum of the Tang Dynasty, from the state-level Shaanxi History Museum, to the provincial-level Lintong Museum, the density and periods included and are the top in the world. Even the Xi’an Museum, named after the city, is a state-level museum.

## 耍社火

## Celebrating *Shehuo*

社火是陕西尤其是关中一带的民间娱乐活动，是芯子、高跷、竹马、旱船、狮子、龙灯等的通称。每年春节，尤其是在农村，群众自发组织，抬芯子、跑竹马、踩高跷、耍狮子、走村串户，十分热闹。

*Shehuo* is a type of traditional festival entertainment in Shaanxi, especially the Guanzhong area. It is a collective term. Carrying floats, riding on bamboo horses, walking on stilts, and doing the lion dances, every year around the Spring Festival, especially in the countryside, the villagers volunteered to hold these activities from village to village. A festive mood reigns.

摄影：尚洪涛

摄影：尚洪涛

**戏曲“活化石”**

The “Living Fossil” of Opera

在戏曲界有这么一种说法，秦腔是中国戏曲的“活化石”，是国内多个戏种的鼻祖。西路秦腔入川后成为弹戏，东路在山西为晋剧，在河南为豫剧，在河北成为梆子。另外，拿今天的标准看，秦腔也算得上中国最早的摇滚。或声嘶力竭，或悲愤沉郁……现代摇滚的精神似乎能在秦腔里找到。

Some in the opera realm call Qinqiang opera the “living fossil” of Chinese opera, the forefather of several operas in China. Spreading west to Sichuan, it developed into Sichuan *tanxi*. The genre in the east evolved respectively into Jin opera in Shanxi, Yu opera in Henan, and Hebei *bangzi* in Hebei. Judging even by today’s standards, Qinqiang opera counts as the earliest Chinese rock music. The spirit of modern rock’n’roll, be it horse roaring or melancholy mood, seems to originate from the Qinqiang opera.

**嫦娥的“西安眼”**

The “Xi’an Eye” of Chang’e

2012年2月，我国发布当时全世界最清晰的全月图——“嫦娥二号”获得的7米分辨率、100%覆盖全月球的影像图。而拍下全月图的“眼睛”来自西安，即由中科院西安光机所研制的CCD立体相机，它也被亲切地称为“西安眼”。

In February 2012, China released a full coverage map of the moon in the highest resolution around the world. It was a 100 percent coverage map of the moon with a resolution of seven meters that Chang’e-2 obtained. The “eye” that took the image came from Xi’an. Affectionately called “Xi’an eye”, it was a CCD stereo camera made by the Xi’an Institute of Optics and Precision Mechanics of Chinese Academy of Sciences.

## 陕西风土与文学 The Land and Its Literature

"有什么样的风土，就有什么样的文章"。在作家朱鸿看来，陕北，粗犷、浩茫，山丘起伏，久唱信天游，从而有路遥的《平凡的世界》；关中，处四塞之内，内敛、精密、深厚，久唱秦腔，遵循儒家传统，遂有陈忠实的《白鹿原》；而陕南，纤细、阴柔、机巧、灵动，层峦叠嶂、青葱翠绿，自然出贾平凹的小说系列。

"The writing style originates from local customs." In the eyes of Zhu Hong, a famous writer, Shanbei is rough, boundless, mountainous, with the singing of *Xintianyou* (a Shaanxi folk melody) lingering around, and that's where Lu Yao's *Ordinary World* comes from; with the singing of Qinqiang opera lingering around. Guanzhong is located within four fortifications with restraint, precise, and profound people, following the Confucian traditions, and so there is Chen Zhongshi's *White Deer Plain*; and People in Shaannan are complicated, feminine, adept, spirited, living in the mountain area covered by emerald forests, from where of course originated Jia Wingwa's fictions.

## 诗歌之城 The City of Poetry

国学大师季羡林曾撰文说："今天到了西安，只要稍一留意，就会（发现）到处都是唐诗的遗迹。谁到了灞桥，到了渭水，到了那一些什么'原'，不会立刻就联想到唐代许多脍炙人口的诗句呢？西安简直是一座诗歌的城市，一座历史传说的城市，一座立即让人发思古之幽情的城市。"

Sinologist Ji Xianlin (1911 - 2009) once wrote, "Just looking around in today's Xi'an, you will find traces of Tang poetry everywhere. Passing by the Ba Bridge, the Wei River, and those plateaus, one would immediately think of some famous lines from Tang Poetry. Xi'an is like a city of poetry, a city in historical legend, and a city that arouses one's nostalgia for the ancient eras."

## 徘徊的当代艺术 The Confounded Contemporary Art

在西安，书画当道的传统艺术市场繁荣，当代艺术生长艰难。独立艺术家岳路平曾感叹：西安历史很厚，文化的地层像黄土层一样多；当代艺术很薄，薄得像黄土高原上的一层沙。往地下挖，考古学家可发现一个又一个有形的文化证据；在地面上徘徊，艺术家们不断打造的无形的新文化地基薄弱得只能靠文字来构建。

In Xi'an, the traditional art market dominated by calligraphy and paintings is booming, but the market for contemporary art has been struggling. Independent artist Yue Luping once remarked, "With a rich history, the layers of culture is as many as the layers of the yellow earth; yet contemporary art is weak, like a thin layer of sand on the Loess Plateau. When digging underground, archeologists find physical evidence of civilization one piece after another; yet on the surface, the intangible foundation for the new culture laid strenuously by artists is so weak that it can only be constructed with writing."

**《刀马旦》**
"Female Warrior"

"明明早上人还在香港，还在九龙茶馆喝煲汤，怎么场景一下跳到西安，我在护城河的堤岸，站在古老神秘的城墙，月光摇又晃……"这首风靡一时的《刀马旦》由周杰伦作曲、方文山作词，将东方美感融入西方 R&B 曲风，加上李玟的绝妙演唱，展现出流行音乐人对古老文化的致敬。

"Just this morning I was in Hong Kong, drinking soup in a Kowlong teahouse. Suddenly the scene changed to Xi'an, and I'm at the bank of the moat, standing by the mysterious ancient city wall, with the undulating moonlight..." The song "Female Warrior", composed by Jay Chou and lyricist Vincent Fang, adds oriental artistry to Western R&B melody. Combined with the marvelous singing by pop diva Coco Lee, it is a tribute from pop musicians to ancient culture.

**阅读之城**
The City of Reading

西安是一座崇尚阅读的城市，"省图"前排队入馆已成清晨一景。有读者这样描绘：这里走出来的不会是吃得红光满面的政客商人，也不会是喝得相互搀扶、趺趺撞撞的失意白领。夜色降临时，鱼贯而出的，是一个个挎着巨大的布袋子，行色匆匆的学生。他们在此处，收获的不仅仅是知识，还有友情，还有未来。

Xi'an is a city that prizes reading. The queue in front of the Shaanxi Library has become a regular scene in the morning. A reader described, "It won't be politicians or businessmen with a full belly walking out of the door, nor drunk and staggering depressed white collar workers. When the night falls, hurriedly filing out of the library are students with giant bags over their shoulders. Here, not only do they harvest knowledge, but also friendships and their future.

摄影：王旭东

## 中国诗歌节
## China Poetry Festival

诗歌是国家气质的最佳展示，西安几乎是一个诗人遍地的城市。翻开《中国诗歌节·诗歌专刊》就会发现，西安的诗人遍布社会各领域。从省部级官员到寂寂无名的小学生，汉唐之世的诗意血脉依然延续至今。遍览世界各国的同类节日，只有西安有此"胜景"。

Poetry is the best display of a nation's soul. Xi'an is a city filled with poets. Flip open *China Poetry Festival: Poetry Edition*, and you'll discover that Xi'an's poets come from all walks of life. From provincial-level officials to regular pupils, the poetic tradition of the Han and Tang dynasties has been passed down. Of the similar festivities around the world, none is a poetry event as spectacular as that in Xi'an.

## 户县农民画
## The Farmer Paintings of Hu County

户县居西安西南40公里，是闻名中外的农民画乡。户县农民画采用白描形式，构图简洁饱满，想象大胆丰富，注重色彩对比，以大红大紫的颜色为主。农民们一手拿着锄头，一手拿着画笔，画土地、画庄稼，画他们的猪狗牛羊，还有他们的农家小院。目前，户县农民画作者队伍已发展到2000多人。

Hu County, located 40 kilometers southwest of Xi'an, is world famous for farmer paintings. These works are usually of line drawing in traditional ink and brush style, with a simple but full composition, a bold imagination, and vivid, bright colors, mostly red and purple. Holding the hoe in one hand and paintbrush in the other, farmers draw the farmlands, the crops, their pigs, dogs, cows, sheep, and their farmyards. The number of peasant painters in Hu County has exceeded 2,000 already.

摄影：尚洪涛

### 钟楼今昔
### The Bell Tower's Past and Present

你能想象吗？钟楼曾经是西安最早的电影院，播放着西安最早的无声电影，后来又曾作为天文馆，甚至一度成了茶馆，大批的饮茶客在这里消磨睡前的闲暇。如今，钟楼依旧是西安的中心和标志，它和鼓楼相聚百米，如爱侣厮守，形影相随，晨暮响应，扮演着这个古老城市的地面遗存的名片角色。

Do you find it hard to imagine that the Bell Tower was the first movie theater in Xi'an, and screened the earliest silent films? Later it became a planetarium, and then even a tea house for a while where flocks of tea drinkers came to kill their leisurely hours before bed time. Now, the Bell Tower is still the center and the symbol of the city. Just a hundred meters west stands the Drum Tower. The two accompany each other like lovers, respond to each other at dawn and dusk, and play the role of landmarks in this ancient city.

### 街头书法家
### Street Calligraphers

西安的街头书法家是这样练字的：他们用的毛笔大得像小拖把，纸是地上铺着的方砖，没有墨汁，每人脚边都放一个塑料桶，桶里是清水，用毛笔蘸着清水，一笔一画写着行书或楷书。一句唐诗，写到最后一个字的时候，第一个已经风干了，字迹消隐，从头再来，如此循环往复。这样的场景，在西安很常见。

This is how street calligraphers practice calligraphy in Xi'an: the brush they use is as large as a mop; the paper is the street tiles; there is no ink, just a bucket of water by their feet; they dab the brush in water, and usually write a stanza of Tang poetry in the semi-cursive script or regular script. By the time they reach the last character, the first character has already dried up and faded away. So they start from the beginning and repeat the whole process. This is a common sight in Xi'an.

摄影：翟小雪　李念

**历史课代表**
**Representing History Class**

不知是哪位网友把中国比喻为一个班级，各大城市担任班干部，像西安这样的城市最适合它的角色就是历史课代表。

姓名：西安；

性别：男；

职务：西北小组组长兼历史课代表；

特点：班里最年长，能力不错，影响力较大，穿着比较古典，性格稳重，精通历史。

A netizen compared China to a class with major cities as the leaders. For a city like Xi'an, the most appropriate position for it would be the representative for history class.

Name: Xi'an

Gender: Male

Position: Leader of the Northwestern Team and representative for history class Characteristics: As the oldest in the class, he is capable, influential, mature and good at history, and always in vintage clothes."

**现代"飞天城"**
**A Modern "Space City"**

从天宫一号的天线控制中枢，到拍下天宫第一眼的"天眼"，再到神九的火箭动力系统，都有"西安造"的印记。中国的"飞天城"正在西安成形——这是全国唯一拥有完整卫星产业链的地区，拥有完整的科研、试验、生产、教育体系。以此为依托的西安国家民用航天产业基地，是国内产业门类最全的航天产业基地。

From the satellite control center of Tiangong-1, to the "Space Eye" that took the first photo of Tiangong, to the launch vehicle propulsion system of Shenzhou 9… they are all marked "Made in Xi'an". China's "Space City" is taking shape in Xi'an. This is the only region in China with a complete satellite production line, and complete research, testing, production, and education systems. Thanks to these facilities, Xi'an National Civil Aerospace Industrial Base enjoys the most complete aerospace industries in China.

**民间收藏**
**Private Collectors**

许多人都知道，作家贾平凹的一大爱好是收藏汉陶罐。有一次，他去了一个民间收藏家的工作室，面对满屋子的陶罐、陶谷仓，连贾平凹也得用"惊奇"来形容自己的感受。而同去的人说，像这样规模的收藏家，在这个城市不会少于 100 人。

Many know that a great hobby of writer Jia Pingwa is collecting potteries of the Han Dynasty. Once, he went to a collector's studio. Seeing a roomful of pottery vessels, even Jia had to use "amazed" to describe his feeling. It is said that Xi'an boasts more than 100 collectors whose collections are as stunning.

**灞柳**

The Willows by the Ba River

早在秦汉时期，灞水两岸已经广植柳树，流水与烟柳相依，构成一道美丽的风景。隋唐时，灞柳频频出现在诗人笔下，折柳送别成为唐诗题咏的主题之一。如今，在灞河两岸，西安人又种下两万多株柳树，重现了当年的灞柳风情。阳春三月去灞桥湿地公园吟诗折柳，很容易就体会到古人的那份情怀。

In as early as the Qin and Han dynasties, along the banks of the Ba River, there were willow trees rustling by the gurgling water. What a delightful scenery! In the Sui and Tang dynasties, these willow trees were often mentioned in poetry, and breaking a willow twig as a token of farewell became one of the themes. Now, the Xi'anese have once again planted over 20,000 willow trees on the banks of the Ba River, thereby recreating the past romanticism. Visiting the Ba Bridge Ecology Wetland Park in March and reciting poems under the willows, you will understand the soul of those ancient poems.

**深埋的树根**

Roots Deep into the Ground

有人曾这样比喻：如果把中国比作一棵参天大树，到了北京看见的是大树的树冠，到了西安看到的是深埋在地下的树根。作为世界四大文明古都之一，西安把中国五千年历史的根须从过去延伸到现在，还将延伸到未来。

Someone once made such a comparison that if China is a towering tree, what you see in Beijing is the tree's top, and what you see in Xi'an is the deep roots. As one of the four ancient capitals of civilization in the world, as the roots of China's 5,000 years of history, Xi'an not only extends its root from the past to the present, but to the future as well.

**曲江流饮**

Drinks Floating Along Qujiang

唐代中后期，新科进士们揭榜后会齐聚曲江，举行声势浩大的宴会活动。他们置杯酒于流水之上任其漂流，流至谁前则由谁饮酒作诗，众人再进行评比，这种优雅的文人酒会活动即为“曲江流饮”。“曲江流饮”与“杏园探花”“雁塔题名”一同被后人誉为“第一流人物的第一等风流事”。

In the second half of the Tang Dynasty, new Jinshi—successful candidates in the highest imperial examination—would gather at Qujiang after the release of the results, and hold a grand feast. They placed a glass of alcohol in a flowing stream. When the floating glass stopped in front of someone, the person was supposed to drink it up and compose a poem. The poems would then be reviewed. This kind of scholarly salon for literati is "曲江流饮" (drinks floating along Qujiang). Along with "picking flowers in the apricot garden" and "having the name inscribed on the Giant Wild Goose Pagoda", the three are crowned "the most romantic deeds for the most tasteful men".

摄影：翟小雪

**西安画廊**
**Galleries in Xi'an**

西安画廊有多少？回答是数量和银行分理处差不多。尤其是在书院门、西安美院周边，各种画廊比比皆是。但在西安人心目中印象最深的是东大街的美术家画廊，它在很长一段时间内记录下了青年人追逐艺术的浪漫足迹。眼下最有名气的是亮宝楼，但凡“有点身份”的人，几乎都接到过他们举办展览的短信。

How many galleries are there in Xi'an? There are as many galleries as bank branches. Around the Academy Gate and Xi'an Academy of Fine Arts especially, galleries are everywhere. The one that has left the Xi'annese with the deepest impression however, is the "Artists' Gallery" on the East Street. For a long time, it has witnessed a lot of young people's pursuit of art. The most famous gallery right now is Liangbao Lou. Almost everyone in a certain position has received messages about their prospective exhibitions.

**平和从容的汉俑**
**Gentle and Elegant Han Figures**

比起秦始皇兵马俑的肃穆与刚烈，阳陵汉俑则显得平和而从容，而且汉俑中有一部分是稀罕美女，更添几分温婉。来西安旅游，如果是中午 12 点以后的飞机离开西安，那一定别错过位于西安到咸阳机场途中的汉阳陵博物馆。它建立在考古现场之上，可踩着玻璃近距离透视文物，感受历史从脚下走过。

Compared with the solemnity and masculinity of Emperor Qinshihuang's Terracotta Army, pottery figures at the Hanyangling Mausoleum are gentler and calmer. Among them are also some rare beauties, adding a touch of grace to the figurines overall. On your trip to Xi'an, if your plane leaves after noon, you are advised not to miss the Hanyangling Museum on your way to Xianyang International Airport. Built on top of the archaeological site, the museum allows a close view of the artifacts through the toughened glass over site. History seems to pass by under your feet.

## 声音的 DNA
The DNA of Sound

今天的秦腔里还留有千年前秦风的调。戏曲研究的学者陈彦把它形容为西安声音的 DNA：“大的辉煌、大的历史都逝去了，骨子里的那种悲凉是一层底色，这才使得这里的人，这座城，有了厚度和底蕴。正因为本体上和秦人相附，这种艺术才会在经历了那么长久的历史之后仍然保持着一种鲜活的生命力。”

Today's Qinqiang opera still retains traces of the "Odes of Qin" which dates back to thousands of years ago. Chen Yan, an opera researcher, described such traces as the DNA of Xi'an's voice, "All the grandeur and all the history have passed, leaving a deep-rooted sorrow that gives depth and culture to the city and its people. Intrinsically typical of the Qin people, this art form is still bursting with enormous vitality despite its long history."

## 女皇帝之墓
The Empress' Mausoleum

乾陵位于距西安 2 小时车程的梁山之上，是唐高宗李治与中国历史上唯一的女皇帝武则天的合葬墓，也是世界上唯一的夫妻两位皇帝的合葬墓。史料记载，陵区仿长安城建制，有内外两重城墙，仅内城面积就有 240 万平方米。以唐朝的鼎盛之势，一代女皇的墓内定藏有无数罕世珍宝，而它历经千年，至今都未遭到盗掘。

Qianling Mausoleum, the only one for a couple of monarchs in history, is located on Mt. Liang, two-hour's dive away from Xi'an. It includes the tombs of Li Zhi, Emperor Gaozong of Tang and the only female emperor in Chinese history, Wu Zetian. According to documents, the mausoleum was modeled after Chang'an, with inner and outer city walls. The inner city covers 2,400 thousand square meters. It is hard to imagine how many treasures were buried in the royal tomb constructed in the prime of the Tang Dynasty. More amazingly, the tomb has escaped theft and robbery throughout centuries.

## 贩卖“历史”的小街
History Available in the Alley

走进鼓楼脚下的化觉巷古玩街，铺天盖地满眼的古旧物件，着实令怀古的人们痴迷，慈眉善目的菩萨像身上黄铜泥锈，似刚从土中翻出。手法犀利的剪纸，做工逼真的唐三彩，朴实简单的农民画，针脚密实、样式复古的绣靴，荷花浅浮的青瓷花瓶……这条街上的每一件物品，都像是从各个朝代穿越而来汇聚至此。

Walking through the antique Huajue Alley at the foot of the Drum Tower, history lovers would be amazed by the numerous antiques filling every inch of the view. The bodhisattva statues with benevolent expressions are covered with rust and mud as if they'd just been unearthed. The skillful paper cuts, lifelike Tang tri-colored glazed pottery, simple farmer paintings, embroidered shoes with extricate stitching in vintage styles, porcelain vase with lotus flowers... Every item on this street seems to have arrived here from its own time.

摄影：王旭东

## 撕纸作画还原老西安

## A Collage That Brings Back Old Xi'an

凉皮担子、拉拉车、南山樵夫、卖水人、剃头挑子……这些影响过大多数老西安人的街头技艺已经消失多年，很多年轻人并未亲眼见过。年过七旬、擅长油画和版画创作的西安市民李运正用撕碎的纸片作画，创作了一系列独具匠心的《老西安》撕纸画，还原了那些久违的老西安街景和老手艺。

Cold noodle carts, little carriages, woodmen in the south mountain, water vendors, barber's shouldering poles... These sights that had influenced most of the locals have disappeared for years, so they are unfamiliar to many young people. Li Yunzheng, a Xi'anese, over 70 years old and good at oil painting and printmaking, made a magnificent series of collages titled "Old Xi'an", which brought back the dearly-missed street scenes and old craftsmanship of Xi'an.

 摄影：翟小雪

**贾平凹的“古文功底”**
Jia Pingwa and Classic Chinese

贾平凹的文学语言让许多人赞叹他古文功底深厚，但他却解释说这是得益于对西安土话的研究。西安土话中遗存着许多上古语言的词汇，特别是动词，它们生动的表意令贾平凹的写作受益匪浅。比如西安人常用的“咥”就是古语遗存，是吃的意思，但吃得凶猛。

Jia Pingwa's amazing diction in his works prompts a popular assumption that he is well-versed in classic Chinese. Jia, however, insists that he benefits from his study of the Xi'an dialect. Many classic Chinese words have survived in the local dialect, and those vivid verbs, in particular, are conducive to his writing. An ancient word still in use today, the character咥, for instance, means “to bolt or devour food”.

**汉阳陵里“挖宝”**
Digging Up Treasures in the Hanyangling Mausoleum

汉阳陵是中国占地面积最大的博物馆，但最值得一提的还是这里的模拟考古基地，有外葬坑、建筑遗址、墓葬三大类五种共八个探方，每个探方都“埋着”瓦当、陶猪、陶羊、陶鸡、陶俑等文物复制品，体验者戴上手套，俯下身子，拿着小铲子、小刷子，一点点剥开土层，慢慢“挖宝”。

Hanyangling Mausoleum is the most spacious museum in China, yet the most interesting part is that visitors can explore in a make-believe archaeological base, which is divided into eight archaeological units, and falls into five types and three categories with pits, architectural ruins, and tombs. In each pit, there are duplicates of relics such as eaves tiles, clay pigs, clay sheep, clay chicken, and clay figurines buried in the earth. Wearing gloves, visitors crouch down, and slowly dig a hole and dust away the earth with small shovels and brushes to “unearth buried treasures”.

**秦腔自乐班**
Qinqiang Amateur Clubs

西安的秦腔自乐班到底有多少，没人说得清。环城公园、南门、柏树林、下马陵、小雁塔……随处可见那些为了纯粹的喜好和快乐而聚在一起的人们。不管是谁，认识不认识，只要是喜欢秦腔，谁想唱便出来唱，不想唱便坐下来听，唱者声情并茂，听者如痴如醉……站在他们中间，你能够感觉到这个城市的底蕴。

The number of Qinqiang opera amateur clubs in Xi'an is uncertain. At places like the City Wall Park, the south gate, Baishulin, Xiamaling, the Small Wild Goose Pagoda, etc., you could spot groups of people in pursuit of their interests and entertainment. Known or unknown to the group, any Qinqiang lover is welcome to sing a piece or just sit down and listen. The singer presents remarkable voice and emotions while the audiences get intoxicated by the tunes... Standing amongst them, you could feel the cultural pulse of this city.

摄影：王健

# 秦岭 · 秦川
Mountains and Plains

**不同凡响的横线**

A Significant Line Across China

上世纪 50 年代以前的很长一段时间内，人们一直把中国南方和北方，笼统地归结为长江流域和黄河流域。而后来，科学家们一致认定，以秦岭为界，在中国版图上画出一道东西向的横线，作为南北大陆地理分界线，这条不同凡响的横线，就是位于中国大陆南北中轴线上的秦岭和淮河。

Prior to the 1950s, Southern China had long been vaguely referred to as the Yangtze River basin and the northern China as the Yellow River basin. Later, scientists decided to make the Qinling Mountains the dividing line. Hence a horizontal (east-west) line has been drawn on the map of China to mark the geographical border of Southern and Northern China. This extraordinary line of demarcation consists of the Qinling Mountains and the Huai River on China's medial axis.

**"秦岭"由来是个谜**

The Mysterious Origin of the "Qinling Mountains"

自古以来，秦岭就一直充满着神秘色彩，就连它名字的由来到如今都还是个谜。究竟出自谁人之口，得于何时，史学界至今仍莫衷一是。只有一种观点被普遍认可，那就是它源于古代秦人和秦帝国的威名。司马迁在《史记》中写下的"秦岭，天下之大阻"这句话，也让秦岭正式开始有了文字记载。

The Qinling Mountains has always been mysterious since ancient times. Even the origin of its name remains a mystery. Historians today still disagree about who first named it and when it was first named. The only theory that has been widely accepted is that the name is attributed to the mighty Qin Empire and its people. *Records of the Grand Historian* by Sima Qian (145 B.C. - ?) reads "the Qinling Mountains is a great barrier in the world." This marks the first official record of the Qinling Mountains.

**华夏龙脉**

The Sacred Soul of Cathay

"试登秦岭望秦川，遥忆青门春可怜。"在古代诗歌中，秦岭出现频率很高；在地理学家眼里，秦岭是中国南方和北方的分界线，是长江黄河的分水岭；在气候学家眼里，秦岭是北亚热带和暖温带的过渡地带；在文学家眼里，秦岭和黄河并称为中华民族的父亲山、母亲河，被尊为华夏文明的龙脉。

"When ascending the Qinling Mountains to gaze upon the plains, I recalled the gorgeous spring of the Green Gate." The Qinling Mountains comes up frequently in ancient poetry. In the eyes of geographers, the Qinling Mountains divides Northern and Southern China, and separates the Yangtze and the Yellow River. In the eyes of climatologists, it marks the transitory zone between the north subtropical and warm temperate climate. In the eyes of writers, the Qinling Mountains and the Yellow River are regarded not only as the Father Mountain and Mother River of China but also as the sacred soul of Cathay Civilization.

摄影：宋艳刚

**空谷幽兰**

*Road to Heaven*

美国著名汉学家比尔·波特在上个世纪80年代亲身探访隐居在终南山等地的中国隐士，并出版《空谷幽兰》一书，在海外掀起了学习中国传统文化的热潮。陕西媒体寻访得知，目前有来自全国各地的五千多位隐士藏身终南山，过着千年以前的生活。

In the 1980s, famous American sinologist Bill Porter visited hermits in the Zhongnan Mountains, and published a book titled *Road to Heaven*, which prompted a wave of learning traditional Chinese culture overseas. Shaanxi media found that more than 5,000 hermits from all over China were hiding in the Zhongnan Mountains, living a life that was centuries old.

**中央国家公园**

*The Central National Park*

横亘华夏腹地的秦岭，滋养了“八百里秦川”——关中平原。2005年，《中国国家地理》杂志率先提出“秦岭中央国家公园”的概念，主编单之蔷说：“假如没有秦岭，中国将不成其为中国。”

The Qinling Mountains across the center of Cathay has nurtured the vast Qin Valley—the Guanzhong Plain. In 2005, *China National Geography* initiated the concept of “the Qinling Mountains Central National Park”. Its editor-in-chief Shan Zhiqiang said, “Without the Qinling Mountains, China wouldn't have taken its present form”.

## 男人山和女人山

### The Mountain of Masculinity and the Mountain of Femininity

以西安市为界，关中东部有华山，关中西部有太白山。“华山是一块完整的巨石形成的，坚硬、挺拔、险峭”，著名作家贾平凹把它认作是阳山、男人山，认为“它是纯粹的山，没有附加的东西，上华山就是体现着真正上山的意义。”而太白山“峰峦浑然，终年积雪，神秘莫测”，贾平凹把它认作女人山。

With Xi'an in the center, the Guanzhong plain is guarded by Mt. Hua in the east and Mt. Taibai in the west. “Mt. Hua is formed out of one wholesome block of giant rock; it is tough, tall, and steep.” Jia Pingwa considers it to be a masculine mountain because “it is a pure mountain with nothing attached. Climbing Mt. Hua is mountaineering in its true sense.” Mt. Taibai, on the other hand, is “covered with snow year-round, mysterious, unpredictable, but harmonious”, which Jia considers to be a feminine mountain.

## 秦岭深处的老县城

### An Old Town in the Mountains

隐匿在秦岭深处的周至老县城见证了关中匪事的盛衰。由于地处傥骆古道重要驿关，这里曾繁盛一时，清朝时土匪猖獗，县太爷弃城而逃，只剩 20 余户村民与秦岭异兽共同守着这座颓败城池，老县城成为山中隐秘传说。近年来，由于作家叶广芩的推广，老县城再度为人关注，吸引无数人跋山涉水而来。

The ancient town of Zhouzhi, hidden deep in the Qinling Mountains, had witnessed the rise and fall of Guanzhong's bandits. An important pass on the ancient Tangluo Road, the county once enjoyed great prosperity. When bandits ransacked the area during the Qing Dynasty, the magistrate fled, abandoning the town, leaving 20 households and animals in the Qinling Mountains to defend it, which befell to mythical legend. In recent years, thanks to writer Ye Guangqin's promotion, this ancient town has returned to the spotlight and attracted flocks of people near and far.

摄影：刘珂

摄影：王健

**拔仙台**
**The Baxiantai**

3767米高的拔仙台是秦岭主峰太白山的最高顶，也是陕西的最高点。8月份，站在石海一般的拔仙台上，即使穿着最厚的羽绒服还是感觉很冷，风大得能把人吹倒。住在这里的道姑杨侠十几年来默默守护着拔仙台上的庙宇，忍受寒冷、孤独和寂寞，却豁达地给攀登到这里的人们送上最真诚的祝福。

3,767 meters above sea level, Baxiantai is the summit of Mt. Taibai in the Qinling Mountains. It is also the highest point in Shaanxi Province. Even in August, a visitor with the warmest down jacket standing amongst the sea of stones on Baxiantai would still feel chilly. The wind blows so strong that men could barely stand. Yang Xia, a Taoist nun, has guarded the temple on Baxiantai for a dozen of years, enduring coldness, loneliness, and solitude. Amazingly she gives her sincere and generous wishes to visitors who climb all the way here.

**自来水如同矿泉水**
**Tap Water Like Natural Mineral Water**

西安饮用水源来自于秦岭深处的黑河水。根据国家标准，三类水质就可作为饮用水源。而监测数据显示，黑河引水工程的水质常年99%以上是一类，也就是最好的水质。有报道说：“西安的自来水味道略甜，和天然矿泉水一个味。”

The source of the drinking water in Xi’an is the Hei River in the Qinling Mountains. According to national standards, the water of Class III quality qualifies as drinking water. Monitoring data shows that the water quality of the Hei River Water-induction Project meets Class I standards, the highest water quality, 99 percent of the time. It is reported that the tap water in Xi’an tastes a little sweet, with the same flavor as natural mineral water.

**终南山的茅棚学堂**
A School Hut in the Zhongnan Mountains

一对夫妇带着女儿在终南山中居住多年，用诵读经典的方式教育女儿，希望培养出他们心目中人格完整的现代“君子”。“我们不担心，都是别人在替我们担心。”面对社会上沸沸扬扬的争议，夫妇俩充满信心，称这不是对现行教育体制的抗争，也不是拿孩子做“实验”，只是认为居住山林更适于对孩子“格物”教育。

A couple who have lived in the Zhongnan Mountains with their daughter for years are educating the child with ancient classics in the hope that they could raise a modern day "junzi"—a superior person—with ideal characteristics and virtues. "We don't worry; others have been worrying about us." Despite the raging controversy about their lifestyle, the couple are very confident by saying that they are neither defying the current educational system, nor performing an "experiment" on their child. They simply believe that living in the mountains and forests is better for their daughter to learn the nature of things.

**《秦岭七十二峪考》**
*Study of the 72 Valley Mouths of the Qinling Mountains*

长安身为“十三朝帝都”，帝气如此“兴旺”，据说均与著名的“八水绕长安”息息相关。这“八水”又多与黄河和秦岭之间的峪口有关。清朝学者毛奇龄所著《秦岭七十二峪考》是考证国内著名山系峪口的少见的经典作品，现在早已经成为国内资深驴友攀越秦岭的必备“法典”。

As the capital of 13 dynasties, Chang'an owes its powerful imperial aura to the eight famous rivers around Chang'an. Most of these rivers are related to the valley mouth between the Yellow River and the Qinling Mountains. *Study of the 72 Valley Mouths of the Qinling Mountains* by Mao Qiling (1623 - 1716)—a scholar in the Qing Dynasty—is a rare classic about the valley mouths of famous mountain ranges in China. The book has become Chinese backpackers' bible when climbing the Qinling Mountains.

**佛坪大熊猫保护区**
The Pandas in Foping

位于秦岭中段南坡的陕西佛坪国家级自然保护区，52 万亩保存完好的原始森林里，生活着 110—130 只野生大熊猫，核心地带平均每 0.48 平方千米就有一只，自然分布密度和野外可遇见率居全国之首。与四川大熊猫形态不同，四川大熊猫像熊，秦岭大熊猫看上去更像猫，更憨态可掬，被誉为“国宝中的美人”。

Shaanxi Foping National Nature Reserve is located on the southern slope of the middle section of the Qinling Mountains. In the well-preserved primeval forest that covers 35 thousand hectares live 110 to 130 wild giant pandas. In the central region, there is one panda every 0.48 square kilometer approximately. The density and likelihood of encountering one in the wild are top in the country. These giant pandas look different from those in Sichuan. The latter look more like bears while the former look more like cats. Therefore, Qinling pandas, much cuter, are called "the beauty in the world of pandas".

摄影：翟小雪　尚洪涛　雍严格

## 秦岭四宝
## The Four Treasures

生活在秦岭中的朱鹮、大熊猫、金丝猴和羚牛被誉为“秦岭四宝”。朱鹮一度被认为已在野外绝灭，直至 1981 年夏才在陕西洋县重新发现；秦岭大熊猫目前仅有 300 只左右；羚牛通体白色间泛金黄，长相极为威武，但数量不足 5000 头；秦岭金丝猴属于川金丝猴，估计有 3000—5000 只。

Crested ibis, giant panda, golden monkey, and takin are crowned the “Four Treasures of the Qinling Mountains”. Crested ibises were thought to have been extinct until 1981 when they were rediscovered in Yang County, Shaanxi. There are only about 300 pandas now in the Qinling Mountains. Creamy-white with a little of gold, takins look mighty but their number dwindles to less than 5,000. The number of Qinling golden monkeys, a sub species of the Sichuan golden monkeys, is estimated to be between 3,000 and 5,000.

## 冒险者的天堂
### Heaven for Adventurers

外地游客来西安大都会走街串巷寻找秦风古韵，但也有一群人一来就往山里钻，因为在岩友看来，西安的魅力在秦岭。有着“中国蜘蛛侠”之称的刘永邦就多次来秦岭攀岩，在他看来，秦岭有国内最好的攀岩条件。秦岭山中 400 多条各级别的登山路线也诱惑着城里人每逢周末就进山“撒野”。

When tourists come to Xi'an, they usually search the alleys, big or small, for traces of the Qin Dynasty, but some of them go straight into the mountains. In the eyes of rock climbers, the charm of Xi'an lies in the Qinling Mountains. "China's Spider Man" Liu Yongbang has come here for rock climbing several times because he deems that Qinling has the best condition for rock climbing in China. Over 400 climbing routes of varying difficulty in the mountains also "seduce" urban residents to "go wild" here on weekends.

## 婚纱外景地
### A Natural Location for Wedding Photos

青山绿水的秦岭，是西安人拍摄婚纱照的天然外景地。就这样，婚纱公司还嫌单调呢，干脆在山中包地种花田，种一片薰衣草，这就成“普罗旺斯”了。想要黄色花海的效果可以到长安区杨庄老美院门前，春天，绿油油的麦田和金灿灿的油菜花，还有那碧波荡漾的河水，就是一幅天然秀美的画卷。

With gorgeous peaks and winding rivers, the Qinling Mountains are regarded as a natural location for wedding photos by Xi'anese. Some wedding companies that think it's too plain take troubles to rent lands in the mountains to plant flowers and grow lavender, thereby creating a Provence of their own. While a field of yellow flowers is not that hard to get. In front of the old Academy of Fine Arts in Yangzhuang, Chang'an District, the extensive green wheat fields, golden rape flowers, and the rippling river in springtime make a scenery, natural but breathtaking.

## 写生村
### A Village for Sketching

距西安市区 50 公里的蓝田焦岱镇鲍旗寨村，三面环山，沟壑林立，洋峪河从村边缓缓流过。秋末冬初时节，绿的田、棕的土，金色的玉米、火红的柿子……漫步村间小道，整个人就像进入一幅优美的油画中。因为非常适合写生，这里成为西安美院学生的写生村。村民既是学生的房东，也是他们笔下的风景。

Baoqizhai Village, located 50 kilometers from Xi'an, in Jiaodai Town, Lantian County, is enclosed by mountains on three sides and numerous steep ravines. The Yangyu River flows gently by the village. In late fall and early winter, strolling along the paths in the village, you would feel like stepping into a beautiful oil painting full of green fields, brown earth, golden corn, and orange persimmon. Since this is an ideal place for sketching, it has become the base for students at Xi'an Academy of Fine Arts. Villagers are landlords as well as part of the landscape.

## 骑行去南山
Biking to the South Mountain

靠山吃山，靠水吃水。靠着我国南北分界线的秦岭，西安人怎能不充分利用？一到周末，骑行去南山成了西安人的最爱之一。大学生、上班族，三三两两相约，春看山花，秋看红叶，好不惬意。政府还规划在那里开辟专门的自行车道呢。

One has to live on the natural environment, be it a mountain or a river. The Xi'anese, who live right next to the Qinling Mountains, opt to take advantage of it fully. Biking to the South Mountain, another term for the Qingling Mountains, is one of the Xi'anese favorite sports. College students and professionals bike there in twos and threes. Either the flowers in spring or the red leaves in autumn will make the trip an enjoyable one. The municipal government has planned to pave a bicycle lane there.

## 山脚下的漫游
Roaming the Mountain Foot

来西安游玩，永远都不用担心会单调，光秦岭脚下就够你游走了。春季去王莽乡看粉嫩桃花，去杨庄赏遍野油菜花；夏季随便钻进一个峪口避暑，山涧嬉戏，踏足乡下，采摘新鲜的葡萄、西瓜；秋季五台山登高，赏满山红叶；冬季进沣峪口体验精彩刺激的高山滑雪，泡在天然的温泉水中享受温润。

You never need to worry about being bored when visiting Xi'an. The foot of Qinling Mountains alone is a wonderland for you. In the spring, you can immerse yourself in the pink peach blossoms in Wangmang Town or in the wild rape flowers around Yangzhuang. In the summer, you may get into a valley resort to avoid the heat, play in a stream, and pick fresh grapes and watermelons in the countryside. In the fall, you may hike in Mt. Wutai and enjoy the beauty of red leaves. In the winter, you can go to Yangyukou Valley to experience the thrill of skiing on a high mountain and soak in the rejuvenating warmth of natural hot springs.

摄影：翟小雪

## 水源地保护神
## The Guardian of a Water Source

上世纪 80 年代，对于日渐缺水的西安市来说，距市区 80 公里外的黑河水越来越显得弥足珍贵。黑河引水工程完工，水源安全问题受到了高度重视。2003 年 5 月，西安市公安局黑河分局正式组建成立，这也是全国首家专门为保护水源地而设立的公安分局，民警远离都市，扎根大山，担负着守护黑河安全的重任。

In the 1980s, to a city like Xi'an with increasing water scarcity, the Hei River, 80 kilometers from the urban district, seemed utmost precious. When the Hei River Diversion Project was carried out, much importance was attached to water safety. In May, 2003, the Hei River branch of Xi'an Public Security Bureau was established. This was the first one of its kind in China to protect the water source. Based deep in the mountains away from the city, the officers assumed the weighty responsibility for water safety.

## 净水鸟
## A Water-Cleaning Bird

净水鸟黑背、红腹、红尾、白顶，学名叫白顶溪鸲，生活在太白山的二爷海和大爷海水边。当它看见水面有污物时，就会飞快俯身，用长长的嘴将脏东西衔走， 因此被人们称为“净水鸟”。在西安，有一群以“净水鸟”命名的志愿者团队，他们每年去太白山捡拾垃圾，维护太白山的自然环境。

The "water-cleaning bird", whose formal name is white-capped redstart, has a black back, red stomach, red tail and white cap. They dwell by Daye Lake and Erye Lake in Mt. Taibai. When they spot garbage floating on the water, they quickly dash over to pick it up with their long beak. Hence, they are called "water-cleaning birds". A volunteer group named after these birds in Xi'an goes to Mt. Taibai every year to pick up trash and protect the environment.

## 人人都有一座山
## Everyone Has His Own Mountain

从高空俯瞰，秦岭是由千山万岭组成的一片山地。最早它并不叫“秦岭”，只有当地人给眼前的某一座山起一个名字。西安人叫“终南山”，蓝田人叫“王顺山”，周至和眉县人叫“太白山”，华阴人叫“华山”……每个县、每个镇、甚至每个庄稼人，都给他面对的山起一个名字。清代的地理志里，秦岭中有名称的山就有几百座。

Overlooking the Qinling Mountains, you will find that it is a mountain range of numerous mountains and valleys. It wasn't called the "Qinling Mountains" at first, since locals only gave names to individual mountains nearby. The Xi'anese, for instance, called it the "Zhongnan Mountains", the people in Lantian called it "Mt. Wangshun", the people in Zhouzhi and the Mei County called it "Mt. Taibai", and the people of Huayin called it "Mt. Hua"... Every county, every town, and every farmer gave a name to the mountain in front of him. According to a geographical record of the Qin Dynasty, hundreds of mountains along the Qinling range had their own names.

## 楼观台

### Louguan Terrace

位于秦岭山中的楼观台，因为有了与老子的联系，自古至今一直声名远扬。2500 年前老子在楼观著《道德经》五千言，并在此筑台授经。直到今天，从四面八方来到这里的游人，还是要虔诚恭敬地给老子——这位和西方的苏格拉底一样，为人类思想夜空带来耀眼光芒的圣贤，点上一炷感恩的香火。

Thanks to Lao Zi, Louguan Terrace in the Qinling Mountains, has enjoyed great fame for 2,500 years. It was the venue where Lao Zi composed his 5,000-character *Tao Te Ching* and gave lectures. To this day, tourists from all over still pay their respect to Lao Zi, a sage, who, like Socrates in the West, illuminated the intellectual dark ages of humanity.

摄影：王旭东

**南水北调**

**The South-to-North Water Diversion Project**

渭河和汉江这两条旱涝两极分化的河流，都出于秦岭。秦岭南麓和北麓分别流淌着上百条河流。其中，北麓河流最终被渭河一网收尽送给了黄河，南麓的河流被汉江总揽一身交给了长江。1953 年 2 月，毛泽东视察长江时提出一个大胆的设想——把南方的水调一部分到北方，这也就是南水北调工程蓝图的基本框架。

Both the Wei River and the Han River originate from the Qinling Mountains, but are in drastic contrast—the former suffers from drought and the latter from flood. Both to the south and the north of the Qinling Mountains, over a hundred rivers flow, either into the Wei River, a tributary to the Yellow River; or into the Han River, a tributary to the Yangtze River. In February, 1953, Mao Zedong (1893 - 1976) raised a bold proposal when he inspected the Yangtze River: transfer some of the water from the South to the North. That was the basic frame of the blueprint for the South-to-north Water Diversion Project.

**朱鹮营巢地**

**Crested Ibis Habitat**

朱鹮是古老的鸟类，它比人类历史还要久远得多，但在 20 世纪短短的几十年内，它由一个庞大繁盛的种群骤减到灭绝的边缘，在主要分布国家相继消失。1964 年，我国林业部门也表示无任何朱鹮的野外消息。从此，专家开始了多年的找鸟任务，直到 1981 年，在秦岭南麓的洋县，找到了当时地球上唯一的朱鹮营巢地。

Crested ibis is one of the oldest bird species in the world, much more ancient than humankind. However, within last few decades of the 20th century, this large and populous species was driven to the verge of extinction, and disappeared from many major habitats. In 1964, China's forestry department also confirmed that no Crested ibis was found in the wild. From then on, experts started a search for these birds. Finally in 1981, in Yang County, Shaanxi Province, on the south side of the Qinling Mountains, they found the only surviving habitat of the Crested ibis.

摄影：尚洪涛

摄影：尚洪涛

摄影：王幼健

**献给地球的礼物**
Gift to the Earth

2003 年 4 月，世界自然基金会宣布，秦岭是全球第 83 份“献给地球的礼物”，这也是中国境内继湿地之后第二份“献给地球的礼物”。中国工程院院士王浩认为，欧洲的阿尔卑斯山、美洲的落基山以及中国的秦岭，是地球上的“三姐妹”。刘昌明院士则表示，秦岭不仅是中国的宝山，也是世界的宝山。

In April 2013, the World Wide Fund for Nature announced that the Qinling Mountains were listed as the world's 83rd “Gift to the Earth”, and it is the second “Gift to the Earth” chosen in China following the wetland. Wang Hao, an academician of Chinese Academy of Engineering, holds that the Alps in Europe, the Rocky Mountains in America and the Qinling Mountains in China are “Three Sisters” on the Earth. Academician Liu Changming adds that the Qinling Mountain range is a treasure not only of China but also of the world.

**生命守护者**
Guards of Life

在西安，一群热爱公益事业的户外运动爱好者组建了专门从事紧急救援的民间公益团体“曙光救援”。每当有驴友在秦岭山中遇到危险需要救援时，总有他们相助。虽然这样的营救没有报酬甚至要自掏腰包，但这些救援队员却乐在其中。

In Xi'an, a group of outdoor sports lovers dedicated to public good established an NGO, named Shuguang (Twilight) Rescue, which specializes in emergency rescues. Whenever travelers confront dangers in the Qinling Mountains and need help, they will always rush to the site. Though they are not paid and very often have to carry out the rescue at their own cost, all the members take pleasure in helping those in need.

**太白积雪**

Eternal Snow on Mt. Taibai

太白山是我国南北分水岭——秦岭山脉的主峰，横卧于陕西省眉县、太白县、周至县三县境内。“太白积雪”作为关中八景之一，早在北魏郦道元的《水经注》里就有记载：“冬夏积雪，望之皑然。”这里的胜景被历代文人所赞美，李白就曾诗曰：“西上太白峰，夕阳穷登攀。”

Mt. Taibai, the main peak of the Qinling Mountains, which is the divide of the northern and southern China, stretches across three counties in Shaanxi, namely Meixian, Taibai and Zhouzhi. “The eternal snow on Mt. Taibai”, regarded as one of the “top eight scenic spots in Guanzhong”, was noted by Li Daoyuan (c. 470 - 527), a geographer during the Northern Wei Dynasty (386 - 534), in the Annotation on the Water Classic, “Mt. Taibai is covered by snow all year long and it is pure white everywhere”. This spectacular view inspired many poets including Li Bai who noted down his journey in a line, “I climbed Mt. Taibai from its west, only to reach the top when the sun sets”.

**太白山上无闲草**

Medicinal Herbs on Mt. Taibai

秦岭自古就有“药山”之称。“去天三百浮云间，积雪捧海壮奇观。举目云海贯宏图，俯首满山尽灵丹。”唐代名医孙思邈、王焘均在太白山钻研中草药。秦岭药用植物十分丰富，共有药用植物 2271 种，其中太白山中草药有 640 多种。有人说，游一次太白山，就等于读了半部《本草纲目》。

The Qinling Mountains have been called the “mountain of medical herbs” since ancient times. “Rising into the floating clouds, the Qingling Mountains offer a spectacular scene as the sea of clouds extends far beyond and precious medical herbs spread all over the slopes.” Sun Simiao (581 - 682) and Wang Tao (670 - 755), two famous doctors in the Tang Dynasty (618 - 907), both studied herbal medicine in Mt. Taibai. There is a rich variety of medicinal herbs in the Qinling Mountains, 2,271 species to be exact, of which over 640 have been found in Mt. Taibai. It is said that a trip to Mt. Taibai equals reading half of the *Compendium of Materia Medica*.

摄影：张宇明

**诗意的指路牌**
Poetic Road Sign

与绝大多数森林公园里常见的“仙人指路”“一线天”之类的景点介绍不同，西安朱雀森林公园里木牌上写的都是此处是什么地质现象、如何形成之类。其中有一处牌子的文字写得甚至很有诗意：“万古开天地，冰川覆山岳。时来封冰解，堆石巨如海。”

Different from introduction to scenic spots like “the Immortal Points out the Way” and “A Glimpse of the Sky” in most forest parks, the wooden signs in the Zhuque National Forest Park in Xi’an introduce geological phenomena and their formation. The words on one sign in particular were rather poetic: “Millions years ago, the earth and sky were made, ice caps covered all the mountains. When the ice melted, stacks of huge rocks accumulated in the vast place looking like a surging sea.”

**鳌太穿越**
Crossing the Mt. Taibai

在驴友中流传着这样一句话：“能否证明你是真正的‘强驴’，就看你有没有胆量去穿越太白山”。从鳌山到太白山的“鳌太穿越”是秦岭穿越的顶级线路，被驴友誉为国内强度最大、风景最美、耗时最长同时也是最危险的线路。两山之间直线距离约 40 公里，徒步距离约 120 公里，大多数穿越路线在海拔 3000 米以上。

There is a saying popular amoung travelers: “A trip through Mt. Taibai proves if you are a hardcore backpacker.” The route from Mr. Ao to Mt. Taibai is the number one route to cut across the Qinling Mountains, which has been praised as the most strenuous, the most beautiful, the most time-consuming, and the most dangerous route in China. The linear distance between the two mountains is only about 40 km, but on foot, you have to walk around 120 km to get through, not to mention that a majority of the route is 3000 meters above sea level.

**隐居生活**
Living in Seclusion

久居北京 30 年的媒体人姜军托朋友帮忙联系在秦岭小住，虽然只在沣峪口观音山里住了 4 天，但回到北京一年多后，他对秦岭的隐居生活仍念念不忘。他说在山里不管看到什么，想到的都是人世间的事情。怎么才能把脑子洗干净？后来想明白了：出去后，在人世间遇到什么事，想到的都是山里的事，就达到目的了。

Jiang Jun, a media person who had lived in Beijing for 30 years, managed to reside in the Qinling Mountains for a while with his friend’s help. Although he only spent four days in the Guanyin Mountains of the Fengyu Pass, he still cherished the memory of his hermit experience more than a year after he returned to Beijing. When he was staying in the mountains, he said, whatever he saw he wouldn’t drive away his earthly cares. He pondered how to free his mind. He was finally enlightened: his worldly concerns would be put out of his mind when he gets back to the mortal world. Isn’t it a kind of fulfillment?

**一洞贯南北**

**A Tunnel Linking the South and the North**

西安到汉中的高速公路从秦岭腹地“穿堂而过”。全线有136座隧道，集中在户县到洋县间18公里的隧道群，穿越了中国地理的南北分界线。在秦岭一号隧道北口时，还是北方的天，北方的人，而只需经过十多分钟到达秦岭三号隧道南口时，看见的便是南方的天、南方的花草，连居民都操着川音了。

The expressway from Xi'an to Hanzhong runs across the heartland of the Qinling Mountains. Along the route there are 136 tunnels, which are concentrated in the 18-km-long section between Hu County and Yang County crossing the geographic division of Southern and Northern China. At the north entrance of tunnel Number One of the Qinling Mountains, you can still see the sky of northern China and its people. A little more than 10 minutes later, when you reach the south entrance of tunnel Number Three, you will see the sky of southern China and the plants growing there. It is even with the Sichuan accent that the local residents there speak to you.

**紫荆花海**

**The Sea of Bauhinia**

秦岭太平峪由隋、唐皇室建太平宫而得名，是观花避暑的山水乐园。每年春季，景区内的天然花海万亩紫荆花齐齐盛放，可谓是隐藏在秦岭山地中一处瑰丽的景象。

The Taiping Valley in the Qinling Mountains was named after the Taiping Palace built by the royal families in the Sui and Tang dynasties. It is a haven for visitors to enjoy the beauty of flowers and to keep away from the summer heat. Every spring, the vast rose-purple sea of bauhinia in full bloom is a spectacle hidden deep in the Qinling Mountains.

**天然健身房**

**A Natural Gym**

西安人拥有的真正花园是巨大的秦岭。十年前对秦岭感兴趣的还只有背包客，近些年城市直通秦岭的道路一条条贯通，西安人开始成群结队进山徒步体验，这些“山友”自己开发线路，以去过更多峪口为荣。年轻人会发现，自己的脚步往往赶不上“老爸老妈级山友”，不由地羡慕他们能在这天然健身房里自由锻炼。

The Xi'anese find a real garden in the enormous Qinling Mountains. Ten years ago, only backpackers were interested in the Qinling Mountains. In recent years, however, as roads linking the city to Qinling were completed one after another, more and more Xi'anese are teaming up for hiking in the mountains. These "mountain friends" devise their own routes and take pride in exploring more ravines and valleys. Young men often find that they cannot catch up with some "mountain friends" who are of their parents' age, and envy their ability to exercise in this natural gym at will.

**最美的山路**

**The Most Beautiful Mountain Trails**

秦岭观音山的路都是由碎石、细草、沙砾、断枝、苔藓、落叶和更早时的落叶共同铺就的，媒体人@姜军 说，这里“堪称世界上最美的山路”，草是直立的，落叶是横铺的，一层一层，色彩斑斓，又美又有弹性。而且一段路有一段路的花色图纹，因为树种不同，落叶的形状色彩都不一样，间或还有些核桃、黄楸等果实。

The paths in the Guanyin Mountains of the Qinling are “paved” with gravel, grass, sand, broken twigs, moss, and leaves fallen recently and a long time ago. Jiang Jun, a media person, claims the paths here are the most beautiful in the world. The grass stands straight and the fallen leaves blanket the ground one layer on top of another, displaying gorgeous colors, beautiful and elastic. Each section of the path has its unique pattern because various trees produce fallen leaves of different shapes and colors, and occasionally mix up with walnuts and rowans.

**秦岭之所赐**

**Gifts from the Qinling Mountains**

关中自古被誉为金城汤池，万世之业。而绵延千里的秦岭带给西安的，绝不仅仅是一座巨大要塞给予的安全屏障，还有一分山色的秀丽与深邃。终南山终年白云缭绕，“青霭入看无”“八水绕长安”也早就注定了这片沃土的生机……西安周围的山、原、河、湖，每一处都各有风光。八百里秦川，何其壮哉！

Since ancient times, Guanzhong has been praised as an impregnable basin for an everlasting reign. However, the long Qinling range not only offers Xi’an the strongest defense fortification but also beautiful mountainous landscapes. The Zhongnan Mountains are covered by white clouds all the year round. The clouds over the basin and the eight rivers around the city ensure the vitality of the fertile land. Each of the mountains, plains, rivers, and lakes around Xi’an offers a wondrous scenery. How grand is the vast!

摄影：王幼健

摄影 [illegible]小雪

# 秦人·秦风

People and Customs

### “额滴神”走向全国
### Outreach of Shaanxi Dialect in the country

从《有话好好说》中张艺谋的陕味台词“安红，额爱你”到《武林外传》中佟掌柜那脆声慢口的“额滴神啊”，陕西话已红遍全国。网易娱乐曾做过一项调查，陕西话成为最受欢迎的荧屏方言。有人说，语言的辐射和传播是一个自然过程，其背后必然隐含着经济和文化上的某种优势和吸引力。

Thanks to *Keep Cool* and *My Own Swordsman* respectively spiced up with “An Hong, I luve you!” and “*edi shen ah*” (Oh My God!) the Shaanxi dialect has gained popularity across China and, as a Netease survey shows, particularly in TV programs. Language dissemination is a natural process, so underscoring the dialect’s popularity are some economic and cultural advantages and appeal.

### 关西汉子出名早
### The Early Fame of the “West Men”

秦人因居于函谷关以西，所以被誉为关西大汉。当年，苏东坡以诗会友，问曰：“我与柳永何人词佳？”人对曰：“唱苏词需寻来八尺关西大汉，持铁绰板唱‘大江东去’；唱柳词则要请二八佳人，持红牙板唱‘晓风残月’。”东坡闻之抚掌大笑。可见，关西汉子说话高亢豪迈、阳刚气足在宋代就已经名闻天下。

The people in Shaanxi are nicknamed “West Men” because they live to the west of the Hangu Pass. Once, Su Dongpo, a famed poet in the Song Dynasty, asked in a poetry salon, “Who is the better poet, Liu Yong or I?” There came a clever response, “To sing Su’s pieces involves a towering ‘West Man’ with iron clappers, bellowing ‘the Great River flows eastward’; whereas to sing Liu’s pieces involves a 16-year-old rosebud with wooden clappers, crooning ‘the morning breeze and the waning moon’.” Su applauded and laughed. Obviously, by the Song Dynasty the West Men had gained the fame for their masculine speech and heroic manners.

### 斯文的北音
### A Refined Northern Dialect

有些外地人认为陕西话土，实际上陕西话古雅而充满内涵：“端走”即直走，“汤宽”就是汤多，“吃毕”则为吃完……细品起来，这些词哪一个不是极具文化内涵。正如作家王安忆听罢陕西乡音的评价：“这话好听，是北音，可却柔极了，字与字之间有舒缓的拖腔，用字又那么斯文。”

Construed as uncouth by some out-of-towners, the Shaanxi dialect is actually imbued with classic elegance. “*Duan zou*” (端走), for example, means “to walk straight”, “*tang kuan*” (汤宽) “abundant soup”, and “*chi bi*” (吃毕) “meal finished”. A scrutiny of these phrases reveals a cultural reserve of quaint senses. “This dialect sounds pleasant. Though spoken by the northerners, it is very soft and intervaled between the characters measured drawl and the diction is refined,” observed Wang Anyi, a renowned writer, upon savoring the Shaanxi dialect.

**嫽咋咧**
Slang for "Awesome"

四岁半的小男孩王仔仔在电视节目《饭没了秀》中大秀了一把陕西话。"呀，美得很！""那比美得很还美得很咋说？""嫽得太！""那比嫽得太还嫽得太咋说？""嫽咋咧（好到极致）！"仔仔和主持人一番令人捧腹的对话，也让这三句陕西话的语气程度在一个孩子口中有了"合理"的排位。

Wang Zaizai, a four-and-a-half-year-old Xi'an boy, once made a show of the Shaanxi dialect in the "Family Show" on TV. "*Ya, mei de hen*!" (Wow, so wonderful!) "Then what's more wonderful than '*mei de hen*'?" "*Liao de tai*!" (Awesome!) "And what's more '*liao de tai*' than '*liao de tai*'?" "*Liao za lie*!" (Extremely awesome!) The hilarious conversation between Zaizai and the host exemplified in a very interesting way the degrees of note underlining these pet phrases in the Shaanxi dialect.

**环境与"正大"文化**
The Environment and the Culture of "Righteousness"

西安的路大部分都是直东直西直南直北，路两边是国槐、松树和白杨。秦岭横贯城南，突兀而起。在陕西作家朱鸿看来，这种环境造就了西安文化的正大性。西安人绝不保守，在思想上追求上进，"包括辛亥革命等历史上很多改变社会的革命运动，西安人都是积极参与的"。

The grid of the streets in Xi'an resembles a chessboard. Lining the streets are Chinese scholar tress, pines, and white poplar trees. Imposing and magnificent, the Qingling Mountains rise high along the southern border of Xi'an. It is this environment that has helped nurture the distinctive righteousness in Xi'an culture, noted Zhu Hong, a Shaanxi writer. Never conservative, local people have tremendous drive. "They have taken active parts in a series of historic social movements like the Revolution of 1911."

**西安是"都派"**
Xi'anese "Capital Style"

中国有所谓京派和海派，作家朱鸿说，如果一定要给古都西安人一个简称，只能是"都派"。"也许西安人平稳，缺乏冒险的冲动，但它却蕴蓄、涌动着创造的激情，而且循蹈规律，善于创造，此乃地域的恩赐；也许西安人不够时髦和精灵，但它却言有其渊，行有其源，而且深谋远虑，厚道雍容，此乃历史的恩赐。"

Now that there are the so-called "Beijing Style" and "Shanghai Style" in China. The Xi'anese can be classified as the "Capital Style", since Xi'an has been the capital of the Zhou, Qin, Han and Tang dynasties, writer Zhu Hong suggests, "Presumably prizing stability and shying away from adventures, the Xi'anese boast a latent passion for creation. Blessed by their homeland, they abide by the natural laws and have a genius for creation. Perhaps they don't appear trendy or ingenious enough, but their words and deeds are well grounded, and they are reputed for their farsightedness, prudence, kindness and elegance as they are blessed by history."

摄影：尚洪涛

**关于秦腔的谬传**
**A Misreport About Qinqiang Opera**

一提到秦腔，人们总禁不住想到“三千万人民齐吼秦腔”，似乎陕西人唯嗜秦腔，其他剧种一概不好。作家朱鸿说，这是错觉，实际上，“秦腔的爱好者和演唱者，在陕西，主要集中于关中一带。在陕西南部的，主要喜欢山二簧和花鼓戏，在陕西北部的，主要喜欢信天游和二人台及道情。”

The mere mention of the Qinqiang opera will remind nonlocals of a spectacular scene of “all Shaanxi natives roaring out the Qingqiang opera”. The impression is that Shaanxi people take interest in no opera forms other than the Qinqiang. However, according to writer Zhu Hong, this is a misreport. The truth is, he says, that Qinqiang’s fans and singers are mainly concentrated in Guanzhong. In the southern part of Shaanxi, people mostly enjoy the Erhuang Hill opera and Huagu opera, whereas people in the northern part mainly enjoy Xintianyou, Er’rentai, and Daoqing operas.”

**西安人爱足球**
**Xi’anese Love Football**

西安人爱足球，尤爱陕西国力。尽管国力二字在足坛已消失多年，但在西安聊国力还是最能拉近彼此距离的方式。学者商子雍说，足球融入了西安这座城市的生活。此话不假，无论是生活在这里的男人还是女人，性格里都有一股球场上的豪迈劲。

Xi’anese love football, especially the team Shaanxi Guoli. Although its name has disappeared from the football world for many years, the Guoli team remains the most endearing topic. Football has become a part of the Xi’an life, says writer Shang Ziyong. He is right. Men or women, people in this city all share the heroic spirit displayed on the football ground.

**叫号式服务**
**A Number Calling Service**

西安的泡馍馆和面馆的普遍特点是叫号式服务。大概因为烹煮需要时间，无法立等即取，所以往往进门先点餐付款，然后店家发一个铜牌或纸片，上面有号。拿着号坐下，耳朵一定要灵。跑堂的端着东西，用陕西话高喊：“××号！××号！”你要迅速大声回应：“在这呢。”饭到眼前就可以放松神经，尽情享用了。

One special feature of the *paomo* and noodle restaurants in Xi’an is the number calling service. Since stewing takes time, customers cannot pick up their order right away. After entering the eatery, customers usually pay for their order first, and each of them is given a copper plate or a piece of paper with a number on it. After taking their seat, they need to be all ears. The waiter would carry the food while calling out loud in Shaanxi dialect, “Number xx! Number xx!” The customer would need to respond fast and loud, “Here.” When the food arrives, the customer can finally relax and enjoy the food to his heart’s content.

**秦国人**

**The Men of Qin**

陈凯歌写过一篇《秦国人》的文章这样描绘秦俑：与庙宇中的神像不同，他们既无狰狞的金刚相，也无慧目低垂的君临感……平和的面容和坦白直视的双目，并不使人想到他们是军人。只是无论将军、校尉或兵士，头上都不着盔，只以布巾束发，表示义无反顾的勇力。

This is how, Chen Kaige, a famous Chinese film director, described the terracotta warriors in an essay entitled “Men of Qin”: Unlike the divine statues in temples, their facial expressions are neither like hideous warrior attendants of Buddha nor like discerning Buddha himself in a condescending manner... Their calm and peaceful faces and their candid glances assume no sign of warriors. Whether generals, captains, or soldiers, none of them wears a helmet, only their hair tied up with a piece of cloth, demonstrating their boundless courage.

**陕西冷娃**

**The Cold Lads of Shaanxi**

“陕西冷娃”常用来形容关中地区的青年男性。“南方才子北方将，陕西冷娃排两行”——这是外地人对陕西关中人的总体评价。一个“冷”字，有惊叹、欣赏、赞许的含义，很少有贬责的意思。近代陕西才子、比较文学专家吴宓，曾将“陕西冷娃”这个群体性格概括为：生、冷、蹭、倔。

“Cold Lads of Shaanxi” is a term often used to describe young men in Guanzhong. “Gifted scholars in the south, generals in the north, cold lads of Shaanxi form two lines” – such is the overall comment that nonlocals give the Guanzhong people in Shaanxi. Here, the word “cold” embodies wonder, admiration, and appreciation rather than condemnation. Wu Mi (1894 - 1978), a contemporary scholar from Shaanxi and an expert on comparative literature, once summed up the characteristics of these Shaanxi “cold lads”: aloof, rash, irritable and stubborn.

**两种文化，一种表达**

**Two Cultures, One Wisdom**

关中民间有句谚语“狗狂一摊屎，人狂没好事”。“屎”与“死”关中方言发音相同。作家陈忠实回忆：儿时每每玩到癫狂状态，母亲就会掷出这句话警告。后来，他读到欧洲名谚“上帝欲让谁灭亡，必先使其疯狂”时非常欣喜，感慨欧洲民间和关中民间以谚语方式归结出的生活哲理竟如出一辙。

A proverb in Guanzhong reads: “A dog is doomed that is mad, so is a man when mad.” Well-known writer Chen Zhongshi recalls whenever he was mad and out of control in his childhood, his mother would warn him with the proverb. Later on, he was elated to find the English saying, “Those whom the gods wish to destroy they first make mad.” He was struck by the similar wisdom in Europe and Guanzhong expressed through proverbs.

摄影：刘珂 谢伟

**美男子**
**Handsome Men**

作家和谷：秦代留下的遗产中，最生动和完美的莫过于秦俑的脸。面对那一张张躲过 2200 多年岁月磨蚀的陶制面孔时，我们感到一个沉睡的意识被唤醒，正如我们面对一位可称为"美男子"的男人时，灵魂深处所感到的轻微跳动。朴素、宏阔、刚毅、俊朗，使一切浮浅、奢靡、卖乖、作秀的面孔相形见绌。

Writer He Gu noted: Of all the Qin heritages, nothing compares with the lively and perfect face of a terracotta warrior. Standing in front of the 2,200-year-old clay faces that have withstood the corrosion of time, we feel our sleeping souls awakened, which tremble as if confronting a handsome man. Alongside these simple, broad, strong, and good-looking faces, all superficial, polished, hypocritical and pretentious faces pale into insignificance.

**秦人不党**
**A Dislike for Cliques**

相比于吴宓总结的"生、冷、蹭、倔"，陈忠实更赞同用"秦人不党"形容关中人的性格。"不党"指做事光明正大，不结党营私。他多次说："我不敢说自己就是典型的西安人，但要是别人这么说，我愿意把这当成恭维。我就是喜欢在这块土地上生活，永远也不会离开，因为在这里心里感觉最踏实、自在。"

In contrast to Wu Mi's summary: "aloof, rash, irritable and stubborn", Chen Zhongshi, another famous writer from Shaanxi, prefers to describe the Guanzhong people as detesting cliques, indicating that they play fair and square and never gang up for selfish interests. He has said on several occasions: "I dare not say that I am a typical Xi'anese, but if someone calls me a Xi'anese, I'd take it as a compliment. I sincerely like to live on this land and never leave it, because I feel most at ease and carefree here."

## 摇滚的秦腔

## The Rock'n'Roll Qinqiang Opera

郑钧说秦腔在很多地方和现代摇滚非常像，摇滚就是现代的秦腔。而在西安城墙边，以老百姓为主角的摇滚演唱会每天都在上演。贾平凹说："那高亢激越的怒吼之中撕不断扯不尽的是幽怨沉缓的哭音慢板，就如冬日常见到的平原之上的粗桩和细枝组合的柿树一样，西风里，你感受到的是无尽的悲怆和凄凉。"

According to Zheng Jun, Qinqiang opera resembles rock'n'roll in many ways, and rock'n'roll is therefore the modern day Qinqiang. Rock concerts, tarring the common people, take place by the city wall on a daily basis. Jia Pingwa once said: "In this high spirited powerful singing lies the sorrowful and deliberate, mournful and heartbreaking tones, reminiscent of persimmon trees with their slim branches and heavy trunks seen on the moors in winter. Standing in the cold wind, you feel endless sorrow and desolation."

摄影：尚洪涛

### 宁给个好心，不给个好脸
### Give a Kind Heart Rather Than a Kind Face

西安人不太擅长表达和外露情感，尤其是西安男人。在不少老西安的家庭里，有个有趣的现象，男人对妻子儿女纵然有满腔的爱，却不会形诸脸上、挂在嘴上。挂在他们嘴边的一句话是“宁给个好心，不给个好脸”，对子女更是如此。

The Xi'anese, especially the men, are implicit in speech. It is interesting that in many traditional Xi'an families the husband's love for his wife and children seldom finds expressions in his face or utterance although his bosom is filled with love for them. The menfolk often say “we would rather give them a kind heart than a kind face.” This applies especially true towards children.

### 古乐的力量
### The Power of Ancient Tunes

贾平凹曾经同几个朋友带着埙夜里登城墙吹奏，城墙下涌集了许多人倾听，埙声是那样的浑厚、神秘、悲凄，有极强的穿透力，以致一些年幼的少女惊恐而哭。

Famous local writer Jia Pingwa once ascended the city wall with a couple of friends to play the *xun*, an egg-shaped ancient wind instrument made of pottery or clay, with one to six holes. The melody it produces is rich, mysterious, penetrating, and appealing to many, and might frighten teenage girls into tears.

### 话多惹人厌
### Contempt for Windbags

陕西人性格直率爽朗，说话做事干脆利落，无论男女，三言两语就把话说完了，最不喜人喋喋不休。对于那些不分时间、不分场合总是说个不停的长舌妇、长舌男，陕西人会斥责“话多得很”，正眼都不瞧。

Straightforward and open-hearted, people from Shaanxi always cut to the chase. Both men and women tend to get the point across in just a few words, and dislike constant chatter. Anyone who waffles at will is despised as a windbag.

### “屋里人”与“外头人”
### “Person in the House” and “Person Outside the House”

关中男人常把已婚妇人称“屋里人”。其渊源虽无从考证，但很大程度上与劳动分工、男耕女织的出现有关。过去农家，男的在田间劳作，女的在家纺线织布。久而久之，便有了把男人叫作“外头人”，把女人叫作“屋里人”的称谓。

Men in Guanzhong refer to a married woman as “*wu li ren*” (person in the house). The origin of the phrase is unknown, but by and large it had to do with the division of labor: the man labored in the fields while the woman stayed at home weaving. As time went on, the man came to be called “*wai tou ren*” (person outside the house), and the wife “*wu li ren*” (person in the house).

**关中麦客**

Guanzhong's Wheat Harvesters

就像新疆的摘棉大军一样，过去，每到夏初，关中道上就有从陇东、渭北台塬、商洛一带来的青壮年帮忙收麦，称为“麦客”。他们大多结伴而来，虽属有偿劳动，但也会受到热情款待，形成了关中平原上独一无二的现象。近年来，由于现代化收割机的普及，“麦客”已成为历史。

Just like large flocks of cotton-pickers pouring into Xinjiang to help harvest cotton, wheat harvesters gathered in Guanzhong every early summer. Young and strong, they came in groups from Longdong, Taiyuan and Shangluo to help harvest wheat. Though getting paid, these seasonal laborers are warmly received, posing a unique sight on the Guanzhong plain. However, with the popularization of harvesting machines, "wheat harvester" has become a historical term.

**方言中的人生观**

The Philosophy in Dialect

陕西话中把“我”读作“额”，据说西安人这种自称应该写作“厄”。“厄”这个字在汉语中多表达命运的曲折以及凶险，如此自称是表现在经历千年风霜和历史兴衰后的豁然开朗，因为在命运中暗含了很多凶险和难关，认清了这一点，才会这样自我称呼，对自己也是一种警醒。

In the dialect of Shaanxi, the word for "*wo*" ( 我 , meaning "I") is pronounced "*er*". Some linguists believe that this word should be written as " 厄 ", a character that signifies the winding paths and dangers down the road of life. This personal pronoun shows an open and clear view on life, which only comes after having witnessed thousands of years of history and the rise and fall of dynasties. People, who use this word as a personal pronoun, realize that there are many risks and hurdles in life. It serves as a self-reminder.

**主妇必备功课**

A Housewife's Must-know

在关中，面做得好不好，被视作一位家庭主妇是否称职的重要标准。油泼面、炸酱面、烩面、炒面、卤面、菠菜面、浆水面、旗花面、蒜蘸面、凉拌面、棍棍面、刀削面、揪面片……如果哪位姑娘出嫁前没有几样“拿手好面”，恐怕自己都会不好意思了。

In Guanzhong, the ability to make good noodles is an important criterion of a capable housewife. Oil sprinkled noodles, fried sauce noodles, braised noodles, fried noodles, noodles with gravy, spinach noodles, melted soup noodles, flag-shaped noodles, garlic dipped noodles, cold noodles, *gungunmian* (thick round noodles), shaved noodles, and flaked noodles... If a girl can't make some specialty noodles before she marries, she would feel embarrassed herself.

**海碗**

**The Sea of a Bowl**

贾平凹在作品《老西安》中曾提到：陕西是内陆省份，一般人是没有见过海的，陕北沙漠地带的人将小小湖泊就称作了“海”。当然，西安人也将“海”字理解为大，说到谁的官大就是“他把官做海咧”。大的碗也叫作“海碗”。所有的羊肉泡馍馆和面馆使用的都是海碗。

In *Old Xi'an*, Jia Pingwa described Shaanxi as an inland province, where most people have never seen the sea, and people from the barren northern Shaanxi would call a small lake a “sea”. In Xi'an, the character 海 (pronounced as *hai*, referring to “sea”) connotes “being large and gigantic”. If an official's rank is high, people will say his rank is *hai*. Likewise, a large bowl is referred to as a “sea-like bowl”, a term popular in all *paomo* and noodle restaurants.

摄影：尚洪涛

## 到西仓“逛档子”
### Shopping the Stalls in Xicang

位于西安庙后街一带的西仓，因明清时官府粮仓设于此地得名。让其真正进入老百姓心中的，却是后来这里形成的庞大又传统的花鸟集市。如今，西仓鸟市仍保持着百年前定期开市的传统，开市时来西仓“逛档子”不仅是西安鸟友的习惯，还吸引着大批外地粉丝。

As the name suggests, Xicang, i.e. the West Granary, used to be a large warehouse in the Miaohou Street in the Ming and Qing dynasties. What made it popular among people was the grand traditional flower and bird market that later came into being. To this day, this market still opens on a regular basis in time-honored tradition. Checking out the stalls in Xicang is not just a habit of local bird lovers but that of out-of-town fans as well.

摄影：王幼健

### 乡村筵席
### The Countryside Feast

西安乡下走亲访友，一般都是当天去当天回。主家待客以午餐为主，端上桌的菜品讲究“十三花碟子”，即五个肉碟、四个菜碟和四个干果碟子，主食一般为白面蒸馍。在农家院里支起圆桌摆上酒菜，红火的乡村筵席开咥（意：吃）了。

When visiting relatives or friends in the countryside, the Xi'anese usually leave and return within one day. The host treats the guests to a luncheon. Traditionally on the table are 13 dishes including five meat dishes, four vegetable dishes, and four plates of nuts. The staple is steamed bread made from wheat flour. Set up round tables in the yards, serve up drinks and food, and the festive country feast formally begins.

### 凳子不坐蹲起来
### A Preference for Squatting

形容关中男人吃面有这么一句话：“吃饭蹲在大门外，油泼辣子一道菜，碗和面盆分不开，凳子不坐蹲起来。”在农村，遇上饭口的时候，远远就看到男人们端着面盆大小的粗瓷老碗，蹲在家门口的树荫下，手中的筷子搅动着和裤带一样宽的扯面，围在一起边吃边聊。看见客来了，还会招呼你一声：“吃了么？”

When eating noodles, a guy in Guanzhong will squat in front of his gate with a large bowl in hand despite the stool nearby. At mealtime, you will see from afar men holding big porcelain bowls, squatting in the shades by their doors, stirring noodles as wide as belts with chopsticks, and chatting casually. When they see you, they will greet you with a question: "Have you eaten?"

### 爱管事的西安人
### Meddlesome Xi'anese

西安人喜欢管事，邻居吵架要管，邻居家的姑娘请假在家待着要管，邻居家的儿子不在家住也要管，还要打听清楚什么原因，然后再把自己的发现讲给周围人听。在大街上，但凡有个交通事故或者吵闹打架的，不出三分钟，看热闹的便会围成一圈，大家你一言我一语的，直到劝说得双方和解才散开。

The Xi'anese tend to meddle in others' affairs. They interfere in their neighbors' quarreling. Even their neighbor's daughter taking a day off to stay at home and their neighbor's son moving out of the house may attract their attention. Not only that, they also dig out the reasons behind, and tell their discoveries to others. In public, any traffic accident or fight will attract a large crowd of bystanders in less than three minutes. Each onlooker would provide his or her own input until the dispute is resolved.

**收藏大家**
A Big Collector

西安多文物，也便有了众多的收藏家，阎甘园算是其中的大家了。贾平凹去拜访时，阎家已搬到保吉巷的一个小院子里，小院的主人是阎甘园的儿子阎秉初。聊了许久，贾平凹才注意到，自己坐的是明代的红木椅子，端着吃茶的是清代的茶碗，看着桌旁一只猫食盘样子特别，一打听竟是乾隆年间的耀州老瓷。

Xi'an's great amount of historical relics has bred many collectors. Yan Ganyuan is one of the greatest barons. When Jia Pingwa visited, Yan's family had already moved to a little residence on Baoji Lane, owned by Yan Ganyuan's son, Yan Bingchu. They chatted for a long time before Jia Pingwa suddenly realized that he was sitting in a mahogany chair of the Ming Dynasty and drinking with a teacup of the Qing Dynasty. Even the unique food plate for the pet cat by the table, he learned, was a Yaozhou porcelain from the Qianlong reign.

**温情告示**
A Heartwarming Dissuasion

陕西历史博物馆门口，等候参观的队伍常常蜿蜒曲折四五百米。曾有一位头发花白的老大爷举着张纸在这人龙中穿梭，纸上写着："陕西乡党、西安人：别排了，让外地客人先看！"见此，许多人不禁感动得鼓起掌来。来自江苏徐州的 @ 尹二姑娘呵呵呵 感慨地说："西安是座充满人情味儿的城市。"

At the gate of the Shaanxi History Museum, the line of visitors waiting to get in often reaches 400 to 500 meters long. An old man with gray hair used to walk amongst the crowd, holding up a piece of paper that read, "Shaanxi fellows, Xi'an locals, don't queue anymore. Let the nonlocal tourists in first!" Many were so moved as to clap their hands. A netizen exclaimed, "Xi'an is a city with human touch."

**勺勺客**
Chefs

勺勺客，是关中方言中"厨师"的称号。陈忠实曾经撰文《一把铁勺走天下》，讲的就是蓝田县的厨师大军。63 万人口的县，当勺勺客的有 3 万多人。风味小吃名厨靳有成、"蒸锅王"王鸿儒、慈禧太后御厨李芹溪、酥饼大师薛志刚……一代又一代的勺勺客，创造了美食奇迹，也创出了"中国厨师之乡"的美誉。

In the Guanzhong dialect, "Shaoshaoke" means "chef". Chen Zhongshi's article "Travel the World with an Iron Spoon" is centered on the chefs of Lantian County. In a town with 630 thousand people, over 30 thousand are cooks. Among the famous ones: Chef Jin Youcheng specializing in snacks; the "King of Steamer" Wang Hongru, the imperial chef for Empress Dowager Cixi Li Qinxi; and pastry master Xue Zhigang, to name just a few. Generations of master chefs have not only created cuisine miracles but also established Lantian County's reputation as "the home of chefs" in China.

**“啊达”**

“*A Da*” Means Where

西安人在指路、问路时，“达”是最常用的一个拟声字。“啊达”意为“哪里”，“沃达”是指“那里”，“这达”自然是“这里”。想象一下，唐僧当年从长安出发去取经，恐怕一出门就要被问：“师傅，从啊达来，要往啊达去？”

When Xi'anese give or ask for directions, “*da*” is the most common onomatopoeia they use. “*A da*” means “where”, “*wo da*” means “there”, and “*zhe da*” means “here”. It is not difficult to picture that when Xuanzang started his journey to the West, people around would ask him: “Master, *a da* are you from, and *a da* are you going?”

**掰馍讲究大**

Specifics in Shredding Cakes

吃羊肉泡馍，掰馍的讲究太大了。小炒、口汤、干刨、水围城，每种吃法对馍要求的大小都不一样，不一定是掰得越小越好。据说，以前坊上的老吃家都是前一天晚上要两个馍拿回家，一边看新闻联播一边掰馍。等到睡觉前，就掰得差不多了，第二天一早，把盛着馍的碗一抱，讲究吃这头一锅汤。

There are a lot of specifics in tearing cakes into shreds when eating *yangrou paomo*. No matter stir-fried, soaked in broth, dry, or extra soup, the size of the cake shreds is the same, yet the smaller isn't always the better. It is said that in the old times, foodies would take two cakes home the night before, and tear them into pieces while watching CCTV news. The tearing would almost be finished by bedtime. Early next morning, they would take the cake shreds in a bowl and go for the very first pot of broth.

摄影：翟小雪

**为何称“乡党”**

The Etymology of “Countryman”

西安的方言土语，许多都与古代的语言文化有联系。例如“乡党”一词，据《周礼》记载，一万两千五百家为“乡”，五百家为“党”，“乡党”连用，就是本乡本土、乡里乡亲的意思。西安人在外，遇到乡党格外亲。就连回到故土的名人，也常用“乡党们好”来问候大家。

Many words in the Xi'an dialect are related to ancient language and culture. The word *xiangdang* (literally, “hometown party”, meaning “countrymen”), for example, refers to people from the same place. The Xi'anese away from home feel very close to a *xiangdang*. Even famous celebrities back to Xi'an would greet the locals with “hello, *xiangdang*.” As documented in the *Rites of Zhou*, 12,500 households constitute as “*xiang*”, and 500 households make up for a “*dang*”. With the two combined together, *xiangdang* means fellow men from the same area and the same neighborhood.

**掰馍大赛**

The Cake Shredding Competition

2012 年 12 月西安举办的掰馍大赛吸引了很多市民参加，两个小时后，这场靠指头拼实力的比赛有了结果，冠军得到了一件印有“馍”字样的文化衫。发起者说，之所以举办这样的活动，是因为泡馍掰馍绝对能代表西安饮食文化特点，再加上刚到冬天，正是吃泡馍的时候，一切正合适。

The cake shredding competition held in Xi'an in December 2012 attracted a lot of participants. After two hours, this competition, which is all about having the strongest fingers, had a winner who won a T-shirt with the character 馍 printed in the front. The host said the reason for this event was that tearing cakes was characteristic of Xi'an's culinary culture. And winter was the best time for having *paomo*, so it all fit perfectly.

**关中习俗“耍公婆”**

Tricking the In-laws

关中一些地区在儿女办喜事时有“耍公婆”习俗。就是在婚礼当天，亲朋好友将公婆乔装打扮一番，给他们穿上戏服或者更加怪异的服装，脸上也涂抹得五颜六色，在婚庆现场“粉墨登场”，给大家带来欢笑。现场越是热闹，参与的人越多，证明公婆人缘越好。

Some areas of Guanzhong follow the custom of tricking the in-laws on the wedding day. Specifically, friends and relatives do a makeover for the in-laws, make them wear opera costumes or something even weirder, and put all colors of makeup on their face. When the in-laws make their appearance at the wedding, everyone dissolves into fits of laughter. The noisier the wedding is, the more attendants there are, which in turn shows how popular the in-laws are.

摄影：翟小雪

**露天“理发店”**
**An Outdoor Barbershop**

一辆自行车、一张老旧的凳子，一张面盆，再加上电推子剃须刀等家什，就是一个简陋的露天“理发店”。在西安街头巷尾，不时还会见到这样装备的理发匠，他们每月或每周定时定点出现，理发一次三四元，往来的都是老人和熟客，一边理发一边聊天。有老人说，除了理发，这也是他们说笑找乐的地方。

With a bike, an old stool, a basin, and such items as clippers and razors, you'll get a simple outdoor barbershop. Such barbershops are still found somewhere on the streets in Xi'an. They open at a fixed spot on a monthly or weekly basis. A haircut costs three or four *yuan*, and customers are all elders and regulars who always chat over haircut. Some elders admit that they come here not only for a haircut but a chat as well.

**陕北民歌惊艳欧洲**
**Shaanbei Folk Music Amazed Europe**

2013年巴黎时装周上，设计师山本耀司采用《黄土高坡》作为时装秀的背景音乐。该视频一出，有网友感叹太惊艳了。这也再次印证了“民族的就是世界的”。导演、音乐制作人周小舟说，陕北民歌曾两次走进欧洲，这首歌都是保留曲目。它旋律激昂、欢快，富有感染力，所以接受度很高。

At the 2013 Paris Fashion Week, famous designer Yohji Yamamoto chose "Loess Plateau" as the music for the show. When the video came out, netizens were amazed. This once again proves that "what is ethnic is global". Famous director and movie producer Zhou Xiaozhou points out that when Shaanbei folk music was performed in Europe twice, this song was on the set list both times. Its melody is spirited, uplifting, and affecting, so it is highly acceptable.

**钟楼补衣女**

The Patching Girls Around the Bell Tower

“补衣服不？”西安钟楼开元商场门口，一声声浓重四川口音的吆喝此起彼伏。这群以织补衣服为生的“补衣女”，是古城存在了 20 多年的独特风景，她们手脚麻利技术娴熟。不过，在这里补衣服一定要讨价还价，开口要价 100 元，还价后 5 到 10 元就可成交。

"Want to patch your clothes?" At the gate of Kaiyuan Shopping Mall near the Bell Tower in Xi'an, you can hear shout-outs with heavy Sichuan accent. These girls that live on mending clothes have been a unique scene in this ancient city for over 20 years. Their hands are adept and their skills magnificent. But you would have to bargain when you patch your clothes here. Sometimes they ask for 100 *yuan*, yet you can get it down to 5 to 10 *yuan*.

**太与太太**

"Tai" and "Taitai"

陕西话中，“太”可用作副词做补语，修饰形容词；“太太”不是指老婆，只为加强语气。称心如意叫“好得太”，不讲道理叫“蛮得太”，穿戴时髦叫“洋得太”，长得漂亮叫“美得太”，多才多艺叫“能得太”，聪明伶俐叫“精得太”，调皮捣蛋叫“瞎得太”。重叠用法加重语气：“人家这手艺好得太太”，“我这蒜苗嫩得太太”。

In Shaanxi dialect, *tai* can be used as an adverb to modify an adjective. *Taitai* doesn't mean "wife" but "very" or "much". It is used simply as an emphatic complement. To express your great satisfaction, for instance, you may say "very good". To exaggerate someone's irrationality, you may say he is "very impervious". Other examples: very fashionable, very pretty, very capable, very smart, very naughty, etc. Of course a reiterative locution will help get the meaning across in a more emphatic way. "His skill is very, very great!" "My garlic sprouts are very, very tender."

**《爷们儿》**

"Menfolk"

尽管陕西浐灞足球队已经远走他乡，但陕西足协主席王军为球队写的那首队歌《爷们儿》仍深入人心。这首歌之所以能广为传唱，是因为歌词道出了关中男人的特点，特别是源自古突厥语的方言“科利马擦”把关中男人的直爽一语唱透，而生活在这里的爷们还会继续“不认铆，不低头，一直向前走”。

Although Shaanxi Chanba Football Club has left, the theme song "Menfolk" that president Wang Jun of the Football Association of Shaanxi Province wrote for the team is deeply rooted in people's heart. This song became so popular because the lyrics are spot on about Guanzhong men's characteristics. "Speed up", sung in a dialect that originated from ancient Turkic language, directly show the straightforwardness of Guanzhong men. The menfolk here will "never give up, always be brave, and carry on".

**很爷们儿的姑娘**
A Chivalrous Girl

“路见不平一声吼，该出手时就出手”，这可不只是武林中人才有的壮举。2013 年 3 月 10 日，西安一名女售票员在公交车上发现小偷偷学生的钱，她让司机靠边停车，打开车门一脚就把小偷踹了下去，还说：“你还是不是人，连学生都偷。”网友赞：“姑娘，你真爷们儿！”

“A true hero deems any vice intolerable and lends a hand to any victim he meets.” This is not only for martial arts heroes. On March 10, 2013, when a female bus conductor in Xi’an caught a thief stealing money from a student, she asked the driver to pull over, opened the door, and kicked the thief off. She shouted, “Are you even human? You even steal from a student.” Netizens gave her thumbs up: “Girl, you are awesome!”

**陕西明星嫽得很**
The Awesome Shaanxi Stars

有媒体做过调查发现，陕西导演大都是争奖型的，张艺谋、王全安堪称代表；陕西演员大都是大器晚成型，像张涵予、张嘉译、闫妮等；而陕西歌手，则大都个性鲜明，在乐坛独树一帜，像许巍、郑均、张楚。人杰地灵，厚积薄发，从“影帝”到“视帝”、“影后”，再到乐坛的领军人物，陕西人无一旁落。

According to a research by media, many Shaanxi directors are award winners, especially Zhang Yimou and Wang Quan’an. Shaanxi actors are mostly late boomers, Zhang Hanyu, Zhang Jiayi, and Yan Ni for instance. Shaanxi singers, on the other hand, with strong personality, are leaders in the music industry, such as Xu Wei, Zheng Jun and Zhang Chu. Ingenious people in a wonderful place, from the best actors to best musicians, Shaanxi has got all of them.

**西安女人**
Xi’anese Women

历史上的长安有最悠久的后宫，但今天生活在这里的女人却少有“宫心计”，看闫妮就知道。欧洲华文作家方丽娜表示与西安女人打交道无须设防，说错了话也不担心被误会。“祖上俯视天下，号令六宫，却没有把西安女人的心性熏染得飞扬跋扈，倒是半坡氏族的一脉相承，把母性的厚道与宽容赋予她们。”

The imperial harem with the longest history is located in Chang’an, but the women who live here don’t scheme like the conniving concubines, as exemplified by Yan Ni, a straightforward actress. European writer Fang Lina, who writes in Chinese, says that dealing with Xi’an women, there is no need to guard yourself, and you don’t have to worry about being misunderstood for saying something wrong. “The fact that their ancestors ruled the nation and kept a lot of concubines didn’t make the women domineering and arrogant. On the contrary, their Banpo ancestry passed down the kindness and tolerance of motherhood.”

### 从山水画到音乐的传承
### Fusing Landscapes into Music

长安画派奠基人赵望云的儿子、音乐家赵季平说，小时候他常跑到画案旁看父亲画画，觉得父亲作品中有节奏、有旋律、有配器，画面的搭配布局、墨色变化都和音乐的神韵有相通的地方。感受到国画山水中的各种“声响”，后来就不知不觉地把它们运用到音乐创作中了。

Artist Zhao Wangyun was the founder of the Chang'an school of painting. His son Zhao Jiping, a famous musician, said that in his childhood he often went to the painting desk to watch his father working. He sensed beats, rhythm, and the sound of different instruments in his father's works and realized that the layout of a painting and the change in the ink color share some similarities with music. Now that he had felt the varying "sounds" in the landscape paintings, he unconsciously integrated them into his music composition.

### 走亲戚四样礼
### Gifts for Relatives

过春节走亲戚，各地风俗各不同。西安讲究走亲戚要提“四样礼”：两瓶西凤酒、两斤腊牛肉、两斤水果、两斤白皮点心（特指陕西特产水晶饼）。随着时代的变化、物质的丰富，如今人们送礼的种类不再拘泥于这四样。四样礼的内容更新换代，依然蕴含着喜庆吉祥的节日浓情。

The custom of visiting relatives during the Spring Festival varies across China. The Xi'anese usually take "four kinds of gifts", namely two bottles of Xifeng liquor, a kilogram of curbed beef, a kilogram of fruits, and a kilogram of local crystal cakes. With the development of the society, the Xi'anese are living better lives and their gifts are not limited to these four kinds of gifts anymore. Yet the festive spirit lingers on.

### 黄土地上沧桑的脸
### Weathered Faces on the Yellow Earth

一方水土养一方人。就像历史的风雨把黄土地塑造成千沟万壑，艰辛的生活、沉重的文化使生活在黄土地上的人们大多脸上布满皱纹，紧锁眉头。这种脸体现着人的脾性、经历和思考。许多人说看到这种脸，就想到兵马俑，兵马俑的塑造者都是苦役。看看张艺谋、陈忠实那一张张沧桑的脸，就知道这是一个种群。

We are defined by where we come from. All the wind and rainfall in history have shaped the Loess Plateau into numerous ravines. Likewise, the arduous life and the heavy past have bestowed most of the inhabitants on the yellow earth with deep wrinkles and frowns. These faces reveal the men's personality, past and thoughts. Many say that the sight of this kind of faces reminds them of the Terracotta Warriors, whose makers were believed to be slaves. With a glance at the weathered faces of Zhang Yimou and Chen Zhongshi, you can tell that they share the same ancestor.

**习大大**
Uncle Xi

以草根追星方式直播习近平而走红的网络微博“学习粉丝团”带火了一个词——习大大。在关中地区，“大大”这词一般用于称呼父亲的骨肉兄弟、叔伯长辈，透着股自家人的亲切劲儿。

A band of ardent admires, the “Xi Fans Club” on Weibo went popular for its passionate live broadcasting on Xi Jinping. Meanwhile, it popularized the word “Xi dada” (Uncle Xi). In Guanzhong, “dada” is used to call father’s older brother, and suggests a kind of affection that only a family member has.

**凤翔泥塑**
Clay Sculptures of Fengxiang

1998 年，克林顿到西安的时候，凤翔胡家的传人把一个斗牛的泥塑挂在了他的脖子上。这种产自陕西凤翔六营村胡家的彩绘泥塑，声名远扬已有几百年了，被当地人称为“泥货”，多为造型夸张、色彩艳丽的动物形象。逢年过节或赶庙会，当地人都以泥塑为礼品。2002 年马年的生肖邮票选中的也是胡家泥塑。

When Bill Clinton visited Xi’an in 1998, a descendent of the Hu family in Fengxiang hung a clay sculpture of a fighting bull around Mr. Clinton’s neck. This kind of painted sculptures, made by the Hu family in Liuying Village has been widely known for several hundred years. These “clay wares”, as locals call them, are usually exaggerated animal models with bright colors. Locals send clay sculptures as presents during the Spring Festival and temple fairs. The zodiac stamp for 2002, the Year of the Horse, chose Hu family’s clay sculpture as its imagery.

摄影：尚洪涛

**典雅的陕西话**

The Elegant Dialect

陕西话曾被冠以“土”的标签，但在贾平凹看来，如果依音笔写出来，那便是文言文中的极典雅的词语。抱孩子不说“抱”，说“携”；口中没味不说“没味”，说“寡”；即使骂人滚开也不说“滚”，说“避”。

The Shaanxi dialect was once labeled “crude”, but Jia Pingwa, a famous writer, argues that if the spoken words were written down, they would actually turn out to be the elegant terms in classic Chinese. To say holding a baby, one would not use hold but “carry”. To describe something tasteless, one would use the word “insipid”. Even when telling another person to get lost, one would say “evade”.

**“吹”出来的产业**

An Industry “Played Out”

西安逛街，最常见的就是埙这种古老的乐器。贾平凹说，埙发出的是土声地气，在更多人听来，埙声带着苍凉、神秘、悠远的气息，更似化身穿越远古的音乐使者。最早的埙距今约有 6700 年。西安人喜欢把玩和吹奏这种掌间乐器，也许因为血脉感情。沾了祖先的光，做埙、卖埙，如今在西安已成为产业。

Strolling on the streets in Xi’an, the instrument you’ll see most frequently is the ancient one called *xun*. In the words of Jia Pingwa, the sound that the *xun* makes is that of the clay and earth, and for many people, the solemn, mysterious, and melodious sound is more like a messenger of music from the ancient times. The oldest *xun* was made about 6,700 years ago. Perhaps because of their traditional obsession with the instrument, the Xi’anese enjoy playing the *xun*. And thanks to this historical heritage, the production and sales of *xun* have evolved into an industry in Xi’an.

摄影：贾庆华

**千里送石榴**
Pomegranates from Afar

2013 年 3 月 22 日，云南 4 岁男童小博癌症晚期，特别想吃石榴，父母跑遍了云南的市场也没买到。发在云南贴吧的这条消息被西安网友发现，热心的西安人全城大接力，7 小时后，12 个临潼甜石榴“飞”到了孩子的病床边。小博的父母特别激动，他们说怎么也没想到，那么远的地方还有那么多人关心着他们的孩子。

On March 22, 2013, Xiao Bo, a four-year-old boy in Yunnan in the late stage of cancer, felt like some pomegranates, yet his parents tried in vain to get any in the markets across Yunnan Province. When this information got online, it was noticed by some Xi'an netizens. These warm-hearted Xi'anese teamed together, and within 7 hours, 12 sweet pomegranates from Lintong flew over to the boy's sickbed. Xia Bo's parents were deeply touched. By no means could they have expected so many people from a place so far away cared about their son.

**贵族作家叶广芩**
A Writer of Noble Birth

叶广芩是清皇室后裔，是一位生活在西安的贵族作家。废弃的深山旧城，因她的《老县城》引起广泛关注；傥骆道上默默无闻的魏家大院，也因她的《青木川》而成为旅游热点。叶广芩的妙笔，成就了被时光遗弃的两座古镇。

Ye Guangqin, a descendent of the royal family of the Qing Dynasty, is an aristocratic writer living in Xi'an. Because of her work *Old Town*, an abandoned city deep in the mountains received great attention. And thanks to her work *Greenwood Riverside*, the little known Wei Family Courtyard on Tangluo Road became a tourist hot spot. It is her wonderful writings that have brought new lives to two deserted towns.

**关中学派**
The Guanzhong School

从明张载起，吕大临、牛兆濂、李二曲、刘古愚等人树起了在亚洲思想领域极有影响的学派——关中学派。陈忠实在《白鹿原》中以这类隐居乡间的大儒为原型刻画了“朱先生”：隐居乡间教书育人，现世时敢于为民请命。他们千百年来影响关中知识分子和民风民俗，也让这里有了“一城文化，半城神仙”的注脚。

Zhang Zai (1020 -1078), a noted philosopher in the Ming Dynasty, along with scholars like Lü Dalin (1040 - 1092), Niu Zhaolian (1867 - 1937), Li Erqu (1627 - 1705), and Liu Guyu (1843 - 1903) established an academic school very influential in the realm of Asian thought, Guanzhong School. In *White Deer Plain*, Chen Zhongshi based the character Mr. Zhu on neo-Confucian hermits in the countryside. They educated younger generations as hermits, but fought for the benefits of the people if need be. For thousands of years, they have influenced the intellectuals in Guanzhong as well as local customs, distinguishing Guanzhong as a place full of intellectuals and hermits.

**早市**
**The Morning Market**

西安人的早晨从家门口的早市开始。因为城市发展的需要，西安市在人口密集的老城区设立 50 多个蔬菜早市，菜贩早晨四五点出门摆摊，九点前后撤摊。这些摆在社区街道的早市不仅有新鲜的蔬菜水果，还有胡辣汤、甑糕等早点，连日常杂货、服装鞋帽都有得卖。想要感受西安人的生活，不妨早起到早市上转转。

The morning of the Xi'anese starts with the morning market at the door. As a response to urbanization, the Xi'anese set up over 50 grocery markets in heavily populated old districts. Grocery vendors leave home at dawn to set up their stalls and finish around nine in the morning. Besides fresh vegetables, fruits, spicy soup, zenggao, sundries, clothing and shoes are all available. If you want to know what a Xi'anese life is like, you may well get up early and visit the morning markets.

**不吃面条，脸吊多长**
**A Lack of Noodles Is very Upsetting**

在关中有"不吃面条，脸吊多长"一说。对于关中人来说，你打他可以，骂他可以，但是不能不让他吃面条。那软软的、细细的、长长的面条，在关中人的肠胃中，起着非凡的作用。如果长时间吃不到这面条，他们可能坐卧不宁，烦躁不安……总之，看什么都不顺眼。美美吃上一顿面条，他们会立刻感到气顺心和。

As a saying in Guanzhong goes, "Nothing is more upsetting than the lack of noodles". The people of Guanzhong can stand being beaten or cursed, but they cannot live without noodles. Soft, thin and long, noodles work magic in the Guanzhong people's stomach. If deprived of noodles for a while, they become very irritated and unable to sit or sleep well. In short, everything seems to be wrong for them. A bowlful of delicious noodles, however, will pacify them immediately.

**属于西安人的本土 party**
**Xi'anese Local Party**

"过会"的传统在西安尤其是长安自古有之，指秋收结束以后，人们（通常以村为单位）在约定的日期全回村，和亲朋好友见个面，唱戏喝酒聊天，开个大 party。这一充满地域性的"节日"被本地人极为重视，因为它意味着情感回归。

The tradition of "*guo hui*" (gathering) in Xi'an has long existed since the time when the city had the name of Chang'an and was the capital of the nation. It refers to a large party that occurs after the autumn harvest, where everyone (usually each village as a unit) returns to the village on a set date, meets up with friends and relatives, enjoys operas, has a couple of drinks, and chats away. Locals place high significance on this regional "festival", because it means going home with affection.

## 唐槐
The Tang Pagoda Tree

西安人敬称槐树为“唐槐”。《说文解字》中说：“槐，木也，从木，鬼声。”故而汉代以来，槐树多被寄寓为“通灵之树”，常被栽于庭院门前，民间更有“门前一株槐，招宝又进财”的说法。又因为槐树根深，叶密浓荫，夏季时，人们多喜欢在槐树下“畅话古今，纳凉纳吉”。

The Tang pagoda tree is a respectful term for the pagoda tree in Xi'an. According to *Shuowen Jiezi* (*Explaining and Analyzing Characters*), "槐 is a kind of tree with a radical for trees, and a pronunciation after 鬼, the spirit". Thus, the pagoda tree has been called "the tree that convenes with spirits". Also, because it is often planted in courtyards, there is the saying "a pagoda tree in front of the door attracts fortune and brings in money". Since pagoda trees are deeply rooted and their thick leaves provide a large shade, in the summertime, people like to converse and relax under it.

## 老谚语
Old Proverbs

虽地处八百里秦川富饶之地，陕西人却勤劳肯干。流传最多的祖训是“勤俭持家”，民间谚语也多有如此教导：“指亲戚，靠邻里，不如自己学勤俭。”“毛毛雨，湿衣裳；分分钱，花家当。男人是个耙耙，女人是个匣匣。不怕耙耙没齿，就怕匣匣没底。”

Although Shaanxi is located in a land of prosperity, its people are diligent and hard-working. The most widespread ancestral commandment is "be hardworking and thrifty in managing the household". Proverbs with similar connotations: Industry and thrifty are preferable to dependence on either the relatives or the neighbors. A drizzle would wet the clothes; a penny would drain the fortune. The husband is a rake, and the wife a money box. More terrible is the bottomless box than the toothless rake.

## 盲人卖蛋
The Blind Egg Vendor

离西安城40公里外的长安郭杜镇，有个叫张喜平的盲人，每日天不亮，牵着自己做的四轮轴承车，载着满满一筐鸡蛋，搭长途倒公交，到达城里的农贸市场。虽然目盲，他的称秤功夫却是了得，以指揣摩，钱两不差。很多市民都爱买他的鸡蛋。司机、乘客、警察和路人的悉心关怀，点亮了这个盲人的路途。

There is a blind man named Zhang Xiping in Guodu Town, 40 kilometers out of the city of Xi'an. Zhang drags a self-made cart fully loaded with eggs to the bus station before dawn. He takes a coach bus, transfers, and finally makes his way to the farmer's market in the city. Blind as he is, he has an amazing skill in weighing. With his fingers, he could figure out the exact weight. A lot of people come all the way just to buy eggs from him. The care of the bus drivers, passengers, policemen, and pedestrians light up this blind man's journey.

## 陈忠实和秦文化

## Chen Zhongshi and the Culture of Qin

陈忠实是活着的秦文化的象征。很多外乡人第一次见到这位大名鼎鼎的陕西作家的反应是：像！腰杆子笔直，目光如炬，满脸褶皱，一支雪茄香烟，满口关中乡语。像黄土高坡的纵横沟壑，深刻而沧桑；像热气腾腾的羊肉泡馍，醇厚而地道。

Chen Zhongshi is a living symbol of Qin culture. When visitors meet this well-known writer for the first time, their first impression is "a descendant of Qin indeed". With a straight back, two piercing eyes, a wrinkled face and a glowing cigar, he speaks with a strong Guanzhong accent. Just like the timeworn ravines on the Loess Plateau, he is profound and weathered. Meanwhile, he is as pure and genuine as a bowl of steamy *yangrou paomo*.

摄影：尚洪涛

**醋溜普通话**
Quasi-Mandarin Chinese

就像四川人的“川普”，融入了陕西口音的普通话被本地人称为“醋溜普通话”，透着那么点别扭的洋腔洋调。其实，地处北方方言区的西安，普通话使用很普遍。一个满口“忒色”的西安人转头就能给你讲出一口字正腔圆的普通话。

Just like how it is with Sichuan people's “Chuan-style Mandarin”, Mandarin Chinese mixed with Shaanxi accents is called “Quasi-Mandarin”, which sounds exotic and awkward. The truth is, in Xi'an, a part of the northern dialect region, Mandarin Chinese is widely used. A Xi'anese with a strong local accent could shift to Mandarin at any time.

**关中女子**
Guanzhong Girls

西安人统称未婚女性为“女子”，已婚的叫“婆娘”。《秋菊打官司》是典型的关中女人戏，主人公秋菊处理家里事和家外事的方式与思维，诠释了“犟（硬气）女子”和“歪（厉害）婆娘”的内涵，像极了关中女人直爽实诚、勤谨顽韧。

An unmarried woman is called “女子” (girl) and a married one “婆娘” (wife) in Xi'an. *The Story of Qiu Ju* featured a typical Guanzhong woman. The way the protagonist Qiu Ju deals with domestic and social affairs demonstrates the characteristics of the “stubborn women” and “tough women” in Guanzhong, who are typically candid, earnest, diligent, prudent and resilient.

**一字品“性”**
Traits in a Character

西安话说“中午不回家，在单位搞（gào）着吃”，指将就吃一点。“搞磨”指不认真。“适搞干”指草草地干。“搞着说他两句”，指轻微批评。一个“搞”字，说尽西安人的随性、粗犷和豁达。

In the Xi'an dialect, a single character “搞 (gào)” embodies the major Xi'anese characteristics: easygoing, tough and optimistic. “Not going home during lunch break, they will 搞 (gào) 着吃, i.e. make do with a quick snack at the company. “搞磨” means facetious; “适搞干” means to do something half-heartedly; and “搞着说” means to criticize in a mild way.

**“愣娃”**
Rash Lads

有人也称陕西男子为“愣娃”。一个“愣”字，不失幽默地抓住了陕西男子的特点，比如为人老成正统、待人温厚诚恳、脾气倔强坚毅等，但如果您就此以为“愣娃”就是老实巴交的笨人，那就大错特错了，“愣娃”们精着哩，大智若愚，心头比谁都有数。

A rash lad is referred to as “愣娃” in the Shaanxi dialect. This phrase captures the characteristics of Shaanxi men humorously, including honesty, righteousness, kindness, earnest, stubbornness and resilience. However, if you take “a rash lad” as a gullible silly guy, then you couldn't be more wrong. The rash lads are quite smart. Slow-witted as they appear, they know better than anyone else.

摄影：翟小雪

舌尖 · 味道
A Bite of Xi'an

**西安的饮食哲学**

**The Philosophy of Xi'an Cuisine**

本土作家袁林说，西安的饮食受到两种因素的影响，第一是中国儒家天人合一的哲学思想，五味杂陈；第二源自本地历史地理环境的制约，深沉厚重。在西安的饮食中，酸咸麻辣均有，但是并不特别突出任何一种味道，西安的饮食风格，最接近中国的传统文化，中庸、融和，不偏不倚。

Local author Yuan Lin contends that the cuisine of Xi'an is underpinned by two factors. The first is the Confucian idea of "Harmony between Man and Nature", which stresses the integration of diverse flavors. The second is the historical and geographic context, characterized by profundity and solemnity. Hence, Xi'an cuisine offers all flavors like sour, salty, and spicy, yet none stands out. It is symbolic of traditional Chinese culture, valuing golden mean, inclusiveness and fairness.

**谁家的泡馍**

**Which Restaurant Did He Go to?**

2003 年，美食家蔡澜陪金庸参加"华山论剑"，之后他在一篇文章中平淡地描绘："在西安，吃来吃去，总离不开'馍'。所谓的羊肉泡馍，就是把烧饼撕开，放进碗中，再淋汤罢了。羊肉的分量真是少得可怜。"西安的吃货们倍感失落，直追问栏目组"究竟带他吃的哪一家"。

Food critic Chua Lam accompanied Louis Cha to Shaanxi to a forum in 2003. After the visit, Chua Lam described his experience in an article quite apathetically: "In Xi'an, whatever you eat, it always comes down to cake. The so-called '*yangrou paomo*' is a simple dish. you tear cakes into pieces, toss them into a bowl, and pour stew onto them. Pitifully there is little mutton in it." Foodies in Xi'an were disappointed by his comments and questioned the program's crew: "Which shabby restaurant on earth did you take him to?"

**烤红薯**

**Roasted Sweet Potato**

一辆平板车，上面放着用废弃油桶做成的烤炉，灰头土脸的，可这毫不影响烤红薯焦香的味道在街头蔓延。衣着时尚的情侣边走边分吃着热腾腾的烤红薯，显得那样甜蜜而和谐。几十年来街巷变迁，但西安人却依然执着地保留着那老烤炉和那老味道。最古老的和最现代的，都可以在这座城市水乳交融。

A stove transformed from an abandoned oil drum sits on a dray, covered in ashes. The tantalizing aromas of roasted sweet potatoes fill the air. While walking in love and harmony along the street, a trendy couple would share their hot roasted sweet potato. Over the last few decades, much change has taken place to the streets and lanes, but Xi'anese still hold onto this traditional stove and the traditional flavor. The most ancient is wedded to the most modern in this city.

### 羊肉泡馍的滋味
### A Bite of Mutton Stew

马未都说自己二十几岁时到陕西出差，第一次吃羊肉泡馍就留下了深刻的印象。他想象：一个人在陕北塬上长途跋涉，三九隆冬，大雪纷飞，饥寒交迫，吃这样一碗羊肉泡馍，那该是什么滋味！也许山珍海味都没能有这个效果。

Antique collector Ma Weidu recalls that on a business trip to Shaanxi in his twenties, he was much impressed by *yangrou paomo* when he had it for the very first time. He was confident that it would be sheer ecstasy if a guy, cold and hungry, could have a bowl of *paomo* after treading amongst the ravines of the Loess Plateau in the depth of a snowy winter. No delicacy on earth compares.

摄影：翟小雪

摄影：翟小雪

**腊牛肉**
**Preserved Beef**

逢年过节，腊牛肉是老西安人饭桌上必不可少的一道菜。坊上最有名的刘纪孝腊牛肉店，门口队伍堪比春运购票大军，常年如此，年前尤甚，已成为西安的一道风景线。“左手火车票，右手刘纪孝”——在春节前做到这一点，就是当之无愧的最牛西安人。”网友的趣话，足以看出西安人对腊牛肉的感情。

Preserved beef is indispensable to the table at every major festival in Xi'an. In front of Liujixiao Preserved Beef Store, the most famous one on the Muslim Street, there is always a queue comparable to those purchasing train tickets before the Spring Festival. As a netizen put it, "You are the greatest Xi'anese if you could hold a train ticket in the left hand and a bag of Liujixiao in the right." The bantering tone gives expression to the Xi'anese passion for preserved beef.

**油馍**
**Oil Cake**

油馍，是在烧饼两面抹上油撒上辣椒面、孜然等调味品烤制而成的一种小吃。是大多数西安人吃烧烤时必点的一道主食，在夜市的烤肉摊上随处可听到：“老板！烤个油馍，油渗到，辣子、孜然多。”

Oil cake is a baked cake with both sides brushed with oil, chili powder and cumin. It is an essential staple most Xi'anese order when they have barbeque. At the barbeque stands at night markets, you often hear: "Bake an oil cake, drenched with oil, with extra chili and cumin."

**油泼面**
Oil Sprinkled Noodles

正宗的油泼面，面条筋道，辣子味道冲，吃起来十分痛快。电影《白鹿原》里扮演黑娃的段奕宏谈起吃面的戏份，说："其实也观察到陕西当地农民吃面，他们蹲着，吃得很快，那不是'吃'而是'大口吞咽'。就感觉他们眼里只有那碗面而没有其他，'好吃，好吃'，那都不是演出来的，都是下意识的。"

The authentic *youpomian* (oil sprinkled noodles) features chewy noodles and strong spice, which make quite a hearty eating experience. Actor Duan Yihong, who played the role Heiwa in the film *White Deer Plain*, had thus spoken of the filming of a noodle-eating scene: "I noticed that when Shaanxi farmers eat noodles, they squat and eat quickly. They are not eating, but devouring. It seems to them the whole world was nothing but a bowl of noodles. When they exclaimed 'yum, yum', it was not an act, it was involuntary."

**小吃的洋名字**
Local Snacks with Foreign Names

怎样向老外解释西安小吃的风味与内涵？网络吃货们试着给西安小吃起了西餐洋名。慢炖五花肉浇汁配香烤面饼——肉夹馍；香煎临潼火晶红柿软面饼配果仁黄桂酱汁——黄桂柿子饼；精炖顶级小羊肉烩陕西硬面饼配腌渍香蒜、红椒汁——羊肉泡馍。那么，醇香肉圆汤精炖杂菜，猜猜看是什么？肉丸胡辣汤！

How could one explain the unique taste and contents of Xi'an snacks to foreigners? Foodies online tried to give Xi'an snacks Western names: slow-stewed pork belly with sauce and baked buns—*roujiamo*; fried crystal red persimmon bread with nuts and cinnamon sauce—deep fried persimmon pastry; stewed top-quality mutton with Shaanxi peta bread finished with garlic and red pepper sauce—*yangrou paomo*. Guess what dish fragrant meatball soup with vegetables is? Pepper soup with meatballs.

**温情爱意打搅团**
The Love and Care in Cooking *Jiaotuan*

做关中搅团，需要边向锅里均匀撒苞谷面，边用木勺搅动，因此往往两人配合才能做好。陈忠实说：搅团这种关中饭食的操作过程，常可看出农家夫妻的温情爱意。夫妻间闹了气儿，男方或女方企图结束冷战，便会提议打搅团。在灶下和锅台上近在咫尺的夫妻配合中，搅团打成了，夫妻关系也重修旧好了。

To cook *Jiaotuan*, a paste-like local food made from cornmeal, involves good teamwork, with one sprinkling cornstarch into the wok evenly and the other stirring with a wooden spoon. Chen Zhongshi, a famous writer in Shaanxi, says the cooking process often reveals the loving care between husband and wife. When a couple gets in a fight, the husband or wife will suggest cooking *jiaotuan* to make up, with both aware that the teamwork provides the best chance for reconciliation.

**三秦套餐**

**A Combo Meal**

无论中午或者晚上，走在西安的大街小巷，随处可见吃着凉皮、就着肉夹馍、喝着冰峰汽水的景象。这就是西安人民经典的午饭，老西安亲切地称之为“三秦套餐”。

Whether at noon or in the evening, it is easy to spot people eating *liangpi* (cold noodles) and *roujiamo* (Chinse hamburger) while drinking Ice Peak soda. When combined, this meal is called "Qin's combo meal", a classic one in Shaanxi.

摄影：李念

**水果之乡**
**Land of Fruits**

全球每六个苹果当中就有一个是陕西生产的。作为中国水果生产第一大省，陕西水果的丰富程度绝不逊于小吃。苹果、红枣、石榴、柿子、猕猴桃、樱桃、葡萄等都享誉全国，其中像洛川苹果、佳县红枣、周至猕猴桃、临潼石榴、户县葡萄、灞桥樱桃等一大批农产品，还是国家地理标志产品。

One out of six apples in the world comes from Shaanxi. As the number one fruit producer in China, Shaanxi abounds in both fruits and snacks. Shaanxi apples, dates, pomegranates, persimmons, kiwis, cherries, and grapes are famed nationwide. Moreover, farm produce like Luochuan Apple, Jianxian Date, Zhouzhi Kiwi, Lintong Pomegranate, Huxian Grape, and Baqiao Cherry have been designated as National Geographical Indication Products.

**神仙粉**
**The Fairy Jelly**

蓝田县古为华胥国，又称“神仙国”，神仙粉就是这个神仙国度的标志性美食。春夏时节秦岭中有一种特有的野生乔木，椭圆型叶子，当地人称糜子梢。采摘这种树叶煮熟，双手揉搓成泥糊状，放冷后变成了一种深色的凉粉，口感清凉爽口，是百分百纯天然的消暑小吃。

In ancient times, Lantian County was called Huaxu Kingdom or Fairyland. Fairy jelly is an iconic snack here. In spring and summer, a unique species of wild arbor in the Qinling Mountains produce oval leaves, called “millet’s tip” by the locals. If you pick the leaves, boil them, knead them into paste, and cool for some time, you’ll have a dark-colored jelly. With a refreshing and smooth taste, it is a 100 percent gift of nature for summer.

**钟楼小奶糕**
**Bell Tower Popsicle**

小时候每次去钟楼，最开心的事莫过于“五毛钱买一根小奶糕”。奶糕口味众多，但最经典的还是奶油的，奶味儿很浓。小奶糕由钟楼食品店推出，并在钟楼地段销售，因此昵称“钟楼小奶糕”，是几十年来最受西安人民欢迎的冷饮。如今，钟楼小奶糕已经脱离了商品最基本的层面，转变成了城市的一种文化符号。

When I was little, the happiest thing about going to the Bell Tower was getting a 50 cent milk popsicle. Popsicles came in many flavors, but the most classic was cream, which had a heavy milk taste. The milk popsicles were promoted by the Bell Tower convenience store and sold nearby. Thus, it was nicknamed the Bell Tower Popsicle, and has been the Xi’anese favorite cold snack for decades. Now, the Bell Tower Popsicle is more than a commodity; it has become a cultural symbol of the city.

**肉夹馍**
"Meat Wrap Cake"?

外地人首次听说肉夹馍，都认为是病句，肉怎么能夹馍？一种说法认为，肉夹馍的叫法源自古汉语，其实是"肉夹于馍"。老百姓无须文绉绉地讲之乎者也，加上西安人性急、直爽，省去"于"字，喊起来便当。

When nonlocals first hear *roujiamo* (literally, "meat wrap cake"), they think it is grammatically incorrect: how can a cake be wrapped in meat? The term actually stems from ancient Chinese. It is supposed to be "rou jia yu mo" (meat be wrapped in a cake). Common people pay no heed to grammar and the Xi'anese are quick and straightforward, so they change the passive voice simply into an active one for the sake of convenience.

**"河漏"**
"*Helou*"

饸饹，陕西方言中念为"河漏"。元代王祯在《农书·荞麦》中记载："北方山后，诸郡多种，……磨而为面或作汤饼，谓之河漏。"用荞麦面制成的面团搁在饸饹床子里，从漏孔中轧出面条，煮熟即可，夏天凉拌，冬天浇汤。在西安，几乎每家饸饹店都会把饸饹床子摆在大门口现场轧，也算是最显著的招牌。

In Shaanxi dialect, buckwheat noodles is pronounced "*helou*" . Wang Zhen (1271 - 1368) documented in the chapter on buckwheat from the Yuan Dynasty book *Book of Agriculture*: "behind the mountains in the north, counties mostly plant (buckwheat)... grounded and made it into noodles or soup cakes, which are called *helou*." Put the buckwheat dough on the noodle maker, and squeeze it into noodles through the holes. Boil the noodles, and you can serve it cold in the summer or pour hot soup on it in the winter. In Xi'an, almost every buckwheat noodle restaurant places the noodle maker at the door, and noodle-grind in public, which could count as a distinct telltale sign.

**口水一条街**
A Street for Foodies

车家巷在南院门附近，究竟因何得名，是因为曾经水车云集，还是因为居住过"车"姓人家，如今已无从考证。对于吃货们来说，他们更喜欢谈论这里的美食。一条街走过去，摆汤面、裤带面、米线麻辣粉、泡馍、腊汁肉揪面片、三鲜煮馍、丸子汤以及冷热拉面，光听这些名字，流的口水都能装一车了。

The origin of the name Che Jia Lane near Nanyuanmen, whether from the fact that once carriages congregated here, or that a family surnamed "Che" once lived here, is lost in time. Foodies, however, love talking about the food here. Walk down the street, and you'll come across noodles in hot and sour soup, girdle-shaped noodles, spicy noodles, *paomo*, noodles with braised meat in preserved sauce, pancakes with three delicacies, meatball soup, and warm and cold ramen... Just hearing these makes one salivate.

**麻食**
Cat-eared Noodles

左手持面团，右手的拇指、食指轻轻一捏，捏出个蚕豆大小的面疙瘩，滚过干净的草帽，搓成一粒粒空心的小面卷，将豆腐干、萝卜、香菇和肉丁炒成香喷喷的臊子一起下锅，这就是西安的“草帽美食”——麻食。冬天来了，来一份热腾腾的砂锅麻食，怎样？

Hold the dough in the left hand, and pinch it with the thumb and index finger of the right hand to make small chunks the size of a broad bean. Roll them across a clean straw hat, and then into smaller rolls hollow at the center. Toss them into the pot along with fried tofu, radish, mushrooms and minced meat. Then you get Xi'an's "Straw Hat Cuisine"—*mashi* (cat-eared noodles). Now that winter is here, how about a hot pot of *Mashi*?

**甑糕**
*Zenggao*

尽管陕西人喜食面食，但以大米为原料的小吃也别具风味，甑糕便是其中之一。甑是一种特制的大蒸锅，制作甑糕要先将糯米淘洗加工，在锅中铺上一层米、铺上一层蜜枣；再铺一层米，再撒一层红大豆，逐次盛满。然后将甑锅加盖密封，大火蒸制。蒸好的甑糕糯米黏软，枣香甜郁，这是陕西人最钟爱的早点之一。

Although Shaanxi people dote on flour food, the province's snacks made from rice are also delicious. *Zenggao* (jujube glutinous rice cake) is one such specialty. *Zeng* is a type of specially made steamer. Before making *zenggao*, first wash the glutinous rice. Then spread a layer of rice on the bottom of the steamer, on top of which lie another layer of candied jujube, then another layer of rice, and another layer of red beans until the steamer is all filled. After that, seal the steamer with a lid, and steam at high heat. When done, the glutinous rice tastes sticky and soft, while the jujubes smell sweet and strong. This is one of the most loved breakfast food in Shaanxi.

摄影：贾庆华 魏影

**九大碗**

Nine Big Bowls

关中人过年过节、婚丧嫁娶时，有种特别“隆重”的宴席格局，叫作九大碗，烹饪方法一般是蒸或烩，包括条子肉、米粉肉、小酥肉、大丸子、豆腐、粉条、白菜、萝卜、全家福（大烩菜），大户人家还有海参、鱼翅等。

At festivals, wedding or funeral feasts, Guanzhong people serve a special banquet called "nine big bowls". The dishes are usually steamed or braised, including braised pork, steamed pork with ground glutinous rice, crisp meat, large meatballs, tofu, vermicelli, Chinese cabbage, radish, and mishmash. Affluent families also serve sea cucumber, shark fin and other fancy dishes.

**西安街头的“爆米花神器”**

The "Popcorn Cannon" on Xi'an Streets

美国著名探索节目《流言终结者》让中国“神器”爆米花机火了一把。其实，在西安的背街小巷、城门下还不时能循声找到这种手摇式的黑葫芦爆米花机。“嘭——”，只要听到这熟悉的声音，闻到爆米花焦香四溢的味道，不少怀旧的西安人就会赶来光顾，拎着大米、玉米等各种原料前来加工，生意出奇的红火。

Famous American show "Mythbusters" made China's "popcorn cannon" very popular. Even in Xi'an today, in the back alleys, narrow streets, and by the city gate, one can still trace this type of hand-cranked gourd-shaped black popcorn machine by its sound. "Boom!" As soon as the locals hear the familiar sound and smell the outpouring attractive fragrance of popcorn, they rush over with such ingredients as rice and corn to be popped. The business is always flourishing.

摄影：张宇明

**西安人最靠谱儿的一周食谱**
Weekly Diet

网友@西安调调在微博上列出了西安人最靠谱儿的一周食谱。周一：肉夹馍、羊肉泡馍、烩麻食；周二：擀面皮、酸汤饺子、醪糟+甑糕；周三：胡辣汤、臊子面、荞面饸饹。周四：鸡蛋饼+葱花饼、扯面、洋芋擦擦……看罢，有网友戏言，在西安莫谈减肥，因为减肥的敌人太强大。

Weibo user "Xi'an Style" made a list of the most authentic Xi'an diet for a whole week. Monday: *roujiamo*, *yangrou paomo*, and braised *mashi*. Tuesday: dough wrappings, dumplings in sour broth, and fermented glutinous rice cake. Wednesday: spicy soup, noodles with minced meat, and cold buckwheat noodles. Thursday: egg pancakes and green onions pancakes, *chemian* (hand-ripped noodles), and potato shreds steamed with flour... After reading the list, other netizens joked that there'd be no point trying to lose weight in Xi'an, because the enemies to weight losing are too powerful.

**从主菜到调料**
From a Main Dish to Seasoning

陕西八大怪里有"油泼辣子一道菜"之说。过去，它不只是道菜，还是老陕人餐桌上的一道主菜。而今，随着经济发展，新鲜蔬菜、生猛海鲜一年四季都有，油泼辣子虽然仍出现在秦人饭桌上，但它已不是主菜，而是降格为调料。只是这味料真少不了，不然陕西的凉皮、羊肉泡馍等不知要少了多少风味呢！

Among the "eight weird things of Shaanxi", one is "oil-sprinkled hot pepper". In the old days, it was more than a dish—the main dish on the Shaanxi people's dining table. Economic development has made fresh vegetables and seafood available all year round. Hot pepper is still a dish, but it has downgraded from a main dish to a seasoning. To tell the truth, this spice is indispensible, otherwise Shaanxi's cold noodles and *yangrou paomo* will be so bland!

**两根面就吃饱**
Two Strands of Noodles Make One Full

你一般吃几根面？什么？卖面都是按碗或两算，谁能数得清有多少根？关中地区有一种蘸水面，一米长一根，每根二两。每次吃蘸水面，你都会被它强大的气场震撼。一般的人两根吃饱，能吃三根以上的就算大胃王了。

How many strands of noodles do you usually eat? Come again? Noodles are sold by bowls or weight. Who would be able to count the strands of noodles? Well, in Guanzhong area there is a kind of *zhanshui* (dipped) noodle, each strand of which is one meter long and weighs two *liang* (equals 100 grams). You'll be overwhelmed by it every time you eat *zhanshui* noodles. An average person becomes full with two strands, and a guy who takes three must be a great eater.

**肉夹馍的误读**
Misreading Roujiamo

正宗的西安肉夹馍是白吉馍夹上腊汁肉。腊汁是指老汤，腊汁肉即老汤煨出的五花肉。没有香菜，没有葱花，没有生菜，没有青椒，不是红烧肉，不是里脊肉！在外地见识到各式山寨肉夹馍后，西安人难免捶胸顿足。转回头一想，西安的“兰州拉面”“北京烤鸭”“广东早茶”，又何尝不是融合了本地口味的创新美食呢？

An authentic *roujiamo* in Shannxi has only two parts: a cake and some preserved meat in between. There is usually no coriander, green onions, lettuce, green pepper, red-braised pork or tenderloin. And *lazhi* meat is streaky pork stewed in the broth that has been cooked for a long time. The Xi'anese get really frustrated with any copycats of *roujiamo* in a place other than Xi'an. But on the other hand, the Lanzhou hand-pulled noodles, Peking duck, and Cantonese dim sum in Xi'an are also adapted to the locals' preferences.

**油泼辣子**
Oil-sprinkled Pepper

遍览各地对辣椒的食用方法，学者商子雍说，秦人的油泼辣子堪称独出心裁——第一步，令辣椒变干，去掉水分，辣味更烈；第二步，粉碎辣椒使其成为辣椒面，为烹制时达到充分境界做好准备；第三步，用滚烫的油泼向掺和有少量精盐的辣椒面，将辣椒的本味、真味充分激出。如此炮制，简单明了，淋漓尽致！

Having seen how pepper is consumed in different regions, scholar Shang Ziyong concludes that the way the Xi'anese use pepper is really ingenious. The first step: dry the peppers to remove the water and increase the spiciness. The second step: crush the peppers into powder so that the taste will be fully unleashed when cooking. The third step, blend a little salt into the powder, and sprinkle boiling oil onto it so that the original flavor and taste of pepper can be maximized. Simple, easy-to-follow, and superb!

**来得晚就吃不上了**
Sold Out Early

“对不起，来得晚了，馍卖完了。”和任何一家超牛的人气小吃店一样，东木头市的秦豫肉夹馍只卖到中午 1 点就打烊。 美食纪录片《舌尖上的中国》介绍西安肉夹馍就是在他们家取的景。尽管没有拍摄门口的招牌，但细心的本土吃货们还是一眼就认出那个慈眉善目的老板和厨房里高效运转的打馍炉子。

"Sorry, you got here too late. Our cakes are already sold out." Like any other popular snack eateries, the Qinyu Roujiamo store on East Mutoushi closes early at 1PM. The episode in *A Bite of China*, a documentary series about Chinese cuisine, that introduces *roujiamo* in Xi'an, was filmed in this store. Although the crew didn't shoot the signboard of this store, local foodies recognized the kind-looking owner and the fast-spinning cake maker in the kitchen right away.

**长安第一味**
**The Number One Cuisine in Chang'an**

有"长安第一味"之称的葫芦鸡，历来是西安人待客的必点菜。据传，葫芦鸡的创始人是唐玄宗礼部尚书韦陟的家厨。一次，韦陟命家厨烹制酥嫩鸡肉，前两个厨师都没成功，第三个厨师吸取前者的经验，把鸡捆起来，先煮，后蒸，再油炸，做出来的鸡不仅香醇酥嫩，而且整形似金灿灿的葫芦，葫芦鸡由此得名。

Gourd chicken, crowned "number one cuisine in Chang'an", has always been the dish that Xi'an locals order when treating their guests. According to legend, Gourd Chicken was invented by a family cook of Wei Zhi, the chancellor of the Tang Dynasty. Wei Zhi (697 - 761) ordered his cooks to make tender and crispy chicken. The first two failed, and the third learned from his predecessors. He tied the chicken, boiled it, steamed it, and then fried it. The chicken he cooked did not only taste crispy and tender, but also took the shape of a golden gourd. Thus the dish was named "gourd chicken".

摄影：王旭东

摄影：翟小雪

**麦饭**
**Alfalfa Dish**

西安人爱吃馍，也爱吃除了馍以外的许多面食，比如春季的麦饭。陈忠实就对麦饭情有独钟。苜蓿芽儿用水淘了，拌上面粉，揉、搅、搓、抖均匀，摊在木屉上，放在锅里蒸熟。出锅后，用熟油拌了，便用碗盛着，整碗整碗地吃，伴着一碗玉米糁子熬煮的稀饭，可以省下一两个馍来。

The Xi'anese love not only *mo*, but also other flour food, especially alfalfa dish in spring. Chen Zhongshi, a famous writer, is crazy about it, "Take alfalfa sprouts, wash them in water, and mix them in flour. Knead, stir, rub, and shake them even, then put in the pot to steam. Once it's done, sprinkle it with boiled oil and stir, put it in bowls, and eat with a bowl. To go with a bowl of porridge made of corn and you can save a piece or two steamed bread".

**最百搭的美食**

Cake Goes Well with Everything

在西安，馍可说是最百搭的美食。肉嫩汤鲜、肥而不腻，由猪大肠与馍组成的“葫芦头”；肉烂汤清、号称“六月鲜”的水盆羊肉；还有将肉丸子、橡皮、老豆腐一起煮的“煮三鲜”，都少不了馍这个配搭。这里所说的“馍”并非馒头，而是烙得半熟或全熟的白面烤饼，秦人一番烹煮，热锅浓汤里盛出的馍就成了绝佳美味。

In Xi'an, a cake goes well with almost everything. Pig intestines and a cake make “intestine stew”, which is a dish with tender meat and savory soup. The meat is fat but isn't greasy. When stewed with lamb, it is called “June Delicacy”, which is accompanied by chewy meat and light soup. “Three Stewed Delicacies” consisting of meat balls, fried pig skin, and tofu, must not be eaten without cakes. The cake concerned here is a kind of half-baked white pancake. Cooked by the Qin people, cakes in the broth becomes a wonderful delicacy.

**头汤泡馍**

*Paomo* in the First Batch of Broth

许多老西安一大早吃泡馍，目的是吃“头汤”，据说刚煮好的汤味道最正最香。其实汤味的好坏一是取决于自身品质；二是师傅的“破汤”，就是原汤中加水，是三七破，还是四六破。一早上肯定都是四六破汤，汤味自然就浓香；午上人多就变成三七了。老吃家会喊一声“肉瘦汤肥”，老板自会了然。

Many Xi'an natives eat *paomo* early in the morning to enjoy the first batch of broth. It is said that this fresh cooked broth tastes the most authentic and especially delicious. Actually the taste of broth depends on its ingredients and the proportion of water to the broth. Early in the morning, the broth is definitely 40 percent, meaning 40 percent of it is the original broth, so the flavor is the fullest. Later as more customers come, the broth decreases to 30 percent. When the regulars shout “lean meat, rich soup”, the owner will instantly understand.

摄影：翟小雪

摄影：贾庆华

## “化石”石子馍
## Cobble Cakes

西安农村有一种制作奇特、风味别致的食品，叫石子馍。它是用烧热的石子作为炊具烙烫而制，表面坑坑洼洼，因而得名。石子馍因具有我国烹饪史上石烹时代的明显特征，被称为“食品中的活化石”。据传，周代“燔黍，以黍米加于烧石之上，燔之使熟也”，石子馍就是由这“燔黍”演变而来。

In rural Xi'an, there is a kind of specially made food called "cobble cakes" with a unique flavor. Baked on hot cobbles, the cake has a surface full of bumps and hollows. Because the "cobble cake" inherits the obvious characteristics of China's stone-cooking era in history and is thus called "the living fossil of food". It is said that in the Zhou Dynasty, "people put millet on burning hot pebbles as a way of cooking", hence the name of "pebble cake" in early times.

## 小吃之城
## City of Snacks

虽然陕菜在国内不及川菜、鲁菜等闻名，但西安的小吃却在国内首屈一指。2011 年西安入选亚洲十大最佳小吃城市，也是中国内地唯一入选榜单的城市。据统计，西安小吃多达 200 多种，是小吃品种最多的城市之一。如果你觉得自己还算得上是一个“吃货”，可千万不要让味蕾错过西安的美食。

Although Shaanxi cuisine is not as famous as Sichuan cuisine or Shandong cuisine, Xi'an snacks rank the top quantitively and qualitively in China. In 2011, Xi'an is on the list of Top 10 Cities for Best Snack in Asia, the only city in Chinese Mainland that made it onto the list. Statistics shows that Xi'an boasts as many as 200 types of snacks. If you still consider yourself a foodie, don't you ever miss Xi'an snacks.

摄影：翟小雪

摄影：翟小雪　魏影

**火晶柿子**

**Fire Crystal Persimmon**

临潼区不仅有赫赫有名的秦兵马俑、华清池、骊山等黄金级景点，还有一个黄金级的果品——火晶柿子。它表皮光滑，色泽红润，浆汁丰满。相传是一位美丽的“火晶”姑娘与善良的“四子”小伙相爱种下的爱情果实，怪不得味美甘甜。秋季，红彤彤的火晶柿子挂满枝头，远远望去像挂满了小红灯笼，甚是喜人。

Lintong District of Xi'an boasts not only top sights such as the famous Terracotta Army, Huaqing Pond and Mt. Li but also a kind of top fruit, Huojing persimmon,which has smooth crimson peel and juicy flesh. Legend has it that this is the fruit of love planted by a beautiful girl named Huojing (meaning "fire crystal"), and a kind boy, Sizi (meaning "the fourth son"). No wonder it tastes so sweet. When autumn comes numerous red Huojing persimmons hang on trees like tiny red lanterns, posing as a delightful sight.

**泡馍的五种吃法**

**Five Ways to Eat *Paomo***

泡馍绝对是西安小吃的代表，但泡馍吃起来却很有讲究。除了掰馍的方法有要求外，光泡馍的制作方法就达五种之多，是做法最多的地方小吃之一。根据汤量的由少到多，泡馍分为“干泡”“口汤”和“水围城”。此外还有将肉夹在馍里吃的“单走”以及加入众多菜品制造的“小炒”。

*Paomo* is definitely the representative of Xi'an snacks, but there are many ways to enjoy it. Aside from the specific requirements to tearing the cake, there are more than five ways to soak the cake. According to the amount of broth used, *paomo* can be divided into "*ganpao*" (dry soaking), "*koutang*" (with just enough broth), and "*shuiweicheng*" (city surrounded by water). There is also "*danzou*" (go alone), meaning eating the cake sandwiched with meat, and "*xiaochao*" (stir fry) when mixed with other ingredients.

**蓼花糖**

**Knotweed Candy**

蓼花糖起源于陕西三原县，因食者交口称赞“嫽，嫽得太！”故称为“嫽花糖”。相传慈禧和光绪逃到西安时，慈禧对陕西小吃“嫽花糖”赞不绝口，慈禧见“嫽花糖”的形状酷似她在草原上见过的一种蓼花果实，遂改“嫽”为“蓼”，之后人们便改称为“蓼花糖”，列为贡品。

The snack knotweed candy originated in Shaanxi's Sanyuan County. When Empress Cixi (1835 - 1908) and Emperor Guangxu (1871 - 1908) fled to Xi'an, Cixi was won over by the snack *liaohuatang*. The shape of the candy reminded her of a type of knotweed she had seen on the prairie, and changed its name. Later it entered the list of tribute to the court.

**稠酒**
**Thick Liquor**

稠酒又名“黄桂稠酒”，因其配有芳香的黄桂而得名，用糯米和小曲酿成，状如玉液，绵甜醇香，回味悠长。稠酒年代久远，据说盛唐时期朝野上下无不饮之。郭沫若曾赞誉它：“不像酒，胜似酒。”现代人则说：“称其为饮料更恰当些”。

Osmanthus wine received its name for the fragrant osmanthus ingredient. Fermented with glutinous rice and distilled liquor, Osmanthus wine looks clear as crystal, tastes sweet and mellow, with a lingering delicious flavor. Its history is so long that it is said that during the heyday of the Tang Dynasty, everyone drank it. Guo Moruo (1892 - 1978) complimented that it is “more than wine”. Nowadays people regard it as a kind of beverage.

**一瓶汽水的情怀**
**What a Bottle of Soda Stands for**

如今各种口味的饮料多如牛毛，但西安销量最好的还是西安自产的橘子水“冰峰”，这个诞生于1953年的饮料始终保持着最初的味道。除了是“三秦套餐”中不可缺少的饮料，还是家的代名词，从外地回家的西安人总要喝上一瓶“冰峰”，体现着故乡情结和陕味文化。

Although there are numerous soft drinks with varying flavors, the bestselling one in Xi’an is still the local orange soda “Ice Peak”. Since its creation in 1953, this soda has retained its original flavor all along. It is not only an essential part of the “Qin’s combo meal” but also the symbol of home. When a Xi’anese returns to his hometown from other places, he or she will drink a bottle of “Ice Peak”, which has become a hometown complex and a part of Shaanxi culture.

**关中“过桥米线”**
**Soup Noodles**

获誉“中华名小吃”的户县摆汤面，颇似过桥米线。摆汤面的那碗汤尤为重要，配上臊子和陈醋，放入炒好的豆腐、鸡蛋饼丝，上面漂满切碎的韭菜叶、葱花。吃的时候，夹一筷子面放入汤里摆一摆，然后再吃。面薄筋光、酸香适口。民间有言：下到锅里碗里转，捞到碗里叠丝线，吃到口里嚼不断，咽到肚中香半年。

Hu County’s *baitang* noodles (noodles with broth that tastes spicy and sour), a famous Chinese snack, is quite similar to the famous “crossing-the-bridge rice-flour noodles” in Yunnan Province in southern China. The broth of *baitang* noodle is very important, seasoned with meat sauce and vinegar, decorated with fried tofu and slices of egg pancakes, and flavored with chive and green onion. To eat the noodle, you take a chopstick-full of noodles, dip them in the broth, and then eat it. The noodles are thin and chewy, with a sour and delicious taste. There is the saying, “Noodles into the pot and sauces into the bowl, / Noodles into the bowl and add the ingredients, / Noodles into the mouth and are elastic and chewy, / And noodles into the stomach would savor for half a year.”

**吃掉"乌鸦头"**

Eating the "Crow's Head"

西安有种命名奇特的传统小吃——"老鸹萨"，老鸹是乌鸦的意思，"萨"在陕西方言里指的就是头。这么叫是因为老鸹萨做好之后的样子，和缩小版乌鸦的头差不多。这种面食，也因此被关中农家给予了对收成的渴望——吃掉老鸹萨，就等于吃掉了偷吃粮食的乌鸦们。

There is a traditional snack in Xi'an with an odd name, *laoguasa*. *Laogua* means "crow" while sa means "head" in Shaanxi dialect. The snack got its name because it looks like a miniature of a crow's head. As crows feed on grains in the field, eating this crow head shaped snack states Guanzhong farmers' hope for a good harvest.

**像蝌蚪的"鱼"**

Tadpole-like "Fish"

夏天来到西安，一定会见到一种叫"浆水鱼鱼"的小吃。虽然曰"鱼"，其实这小吃的形状更像蝌蚪。陕西人叫它"蛤蟆骨朵"，意即小蝌蚪。"鱼鱼"一般有两种，分别用玉米面和白面制成。漏鱼浇上炝好的浆水、红辣子，浆水菜咯咯脆，鱼鱼溜溜滑，轻轻一吸，似乎要溜进喉咙里去，舌尖轻轻一顶，又似乎雾散云消。

If you come to Xi'an in summer, you will surely encounter a snack called *jiangshuiyuyu* (浆水鱼鱼, literally, "starch goo fish"). Although it is called fish, the snack actually looks more like tadpoles, and that is why people in Shaanxi call it "tadpoles". There are two kinds, one made with corn flour and the other with wheat flour. With the pre-cooked starch solution and red pepper sprinkled on the "fish" and crunchy vegetables in the dish, the "fish" will taste smooth. It is not you who are eating it, rather it is the "fish" that are swimming down your throat. Slightly pushed by the tip of your tongue, they go straight down.

**秦碗**

Bowls of Qin

民间谚语"鲁盘秦碗，撑死壮汉"恰好体现了鲁秦两地的文化，山东人好义，席宴场面雍容；陕西人性直，热衷各式肉类佐以烈酒。无论是肉或酒，最后收场的定然是面。去耀州古窑址去看，最深的是酒碗，最宽的是面碗。陕西的大碗里什么配菜都有，一碗油泼面便足以吃饱肚腹。

As the saying goes, "The food in Shandong's plates and Shaanxi bowls make strong men stuffed to death". It demonstrates the two local cultures perfectly: while people in Shandong value human relations, so banquets are always extravagant; people in Shaanxi are forthright and love to drink strong liquor while eating meat. After the meat and wine, the meal always ends with noodles. If you visit the ancient kiln site of Yaozhou, you will see that the deepest bowl is for wine, and the widest bowl for noodles. In Shaanxi you can find all kinds of ingredients in a big bowl, and a bowl of *youpomian* (oil sprinkled noodles) is more than enough.

### 闻香下马 丢乌纱

### Fired for a Delicious Smell

“提起似金线，放下像松塔”，西安的金线油塔好看又好吃。金线油塔早在唐代就有，当时名为“油塌”。唐《朝野佥载》记述，当时官员张衡退朝归来，路过街市，被刚出笼的热油塌引得垂涎欲滴，悄悄买了一个在马背上就食，却因此被御史弹劾，丢了乌纱。但这倒霉事却让令人“闻香下马”的油塌名声大噪。

“Looks like a ball of golden thread when picked up, and pine cones when laid down,” the *jinxianyouta* (金线油塔, Golden Thread Oil Cones) in Xi'an looks appealing and tasty indeed. The snack had already existed in the Tang Dynasty, and was called *youta* at that time. As recorded in *The Sui Dynasty and Tang Dynasty Government Rumors*, when official Zhang Heng (? - 612) returned from the imperial court, he passed by the street market and was caught by the smell of freshly-made hot *youta*. He bought one stealthily and climbed back onto the horse to eat it. However, because of this incident, he was reported by the imperial inspector and lost his job. However, this misfortune brought great fame to the deliciously smelled *youta* that got Zhang off the horse and removed from his post.

摄影：李念　翟小雪

摄影：贾庆华

## 水晶饼
## Crystal Cake

传说大清官寇准回老家渭南探亲，有人送来一盒如水晶石一般的点心。还放着一张红纸，写着首诗：“公有水晶目，又有水晶心，能辨忠与奸，清白不染尘。”落款是渭北老叟。后来，寇准的家厨也仿照做出了这种点心，寇准便给它取了一个好听的名字“水晶饼”，如今这种饼已经是西安名产了。

Legend has it that when Kou Zhun, an honest and upright official in the Song Dynasty, went back to his hometown on the south of the Wei River, he received a box of crystal-like desserts. In the box lay a piece of red paper, on which was a poem: “You have two eyes and a heart clear as crystal. So you can distinguish the loyal from the conniving because you have a clean record.” There was a signature: “An Old Man from Weibei”. Kou Zhun took fancy in it and asked his cook to imitate this kind of dessert. Kou Zhun gave it a beautiful name crystal cake’. Now, crystal cake has become a famous snack in Xi’an.

## 天然维生素
## Natural Vitamins

在陕西，能吃到别处少有的卤肉菠菜面。菠菜面的绿，好似晶莹的翡翠，卤肉的红，吸满卤汁透亮。糅合了肉的“香”和菜的“爽”，夹一缕菠菜面放在嘴里，仿佛大口大口嚼着天然维生素。

In Shaanxi, one can eat a kind of gravy spinach noodles rarely found elsewhere. The noodles look as green as shimmering translucent emeralds, and the accompanying braised meat is transparently red in the broth. Fragrant and delicious is the meat and fresh and crisp are the vegetables, and they provide plenty natural vitamins.

**卤汁凉粉泡馍**

**Cold Noodles and *Paomo* with Gravy**

西安有一样卤汁凉粉泡馍，想必是外地少有的。滑溜溜的凉粉与馍块一齐放进大碗里，浇上浓稠的秘制卤汁，淋上香滑的芝麻酱，配上咸鸭蛋，加香醋、蒜泥等佐料，点睛之笔当然少不了地道的油泼辣子。关中口味的酸辣遇上芝麻的浓香，咬一口凉粉滑入口中，自然妙不可言。

There is one dish in Xi'an that you probably won't find elsewhere: cold noodles and *paomo* with gravy. The smooth cold noodles are put into a big bowl with pieces of *mo*, sprinkled with specially prepared thick gravy in addition to a salted duck egg and ingredients like vinegar and smashed onions. To top it off, this dish is incomplete without authentic oil-sprinkled spices. With typical sour and spicy flavor of Guanzhong along with the fragrance of sesame, the cold noodles slip into the mouth in just a single inhaling. It is really wonderful beyond words.

**枣肉沫糊 "不见"枣**

**Invisible Dates in Date Gruel**

国菜中红枣大都作为辅料，但西安的枣肉沫糊，却是以它为主料制作饭食的佼佼者，其中又属大荔县的最有名。用"马牙枣"细细熬制，直到把枣熬得"不见了"，喝一口，枣香溢满全身。在学者商子雍眼中，枣肉沫糊是对红枣的去粗取精，从牙牙学语的小儿到古稀老翁，皆可百喝不厌。

In Chinese cuisine, red dates are usually used as an auxiliary ingredient, yet date gruel is an amazing snack which uses red dates as the main ingredient. Date gruel in Dali County is the best known. Maya dates are cooked on soft fire for a long time until they melt into the gruel. One sip fills your whole body with the fragrant smell of dates, yet if you inspect closely, no traces of the dates could be seen. The scholar Shang Ziyong regards the snack as the essence of the red dates, which everyone, from infants to the aged, enjoys.

**梆梆肉**

**Bangbang Meat**

什么时候去买梆梆肉，那里总围着许多饕餮之徒不停叮咛老板：要肥的要肥的！普通的猪大肠，被特殊的卤汁熏制程序逐一料理，却成了许多离开西安的人总思念的一款美味。这种熏制出来的吃食有种强烈风味，有老饕戏称它是吃起来最配得上"大快朵颐""饕餮之徒"两成语的——因为吃得给劲！

Whenever you go and buy bangbang meat, you'll always hear some gourmets telling the seller repeatedly, "I want the fat parts!" Ordinary pork chitterlings, after stewed in special gravy sauce and smoked, turns into a delicious dish that people always miss after leaving Xi'an. This smoked meat has a distinctive flavor. And foodies say that enjoying it can be described properly by the two idioms *dakuaiduoyi* ( 大快朵颐 , meaning "eat to one's heart's content") and *taotiezhitu* ( 饕餮之徒 , meaning "gluttons").

## 千姿百态的馍
## Bread in Various Shapes

馍只能是个圆面团？西安人说，大错特错！这里代代因袭流传寄托希望的“馍”文化——清明祭奠的馍顶有面龙，叫“蟠龙馍”；嫁娶喜事要送对蒸得大大的“老虎馍”；农历年农家蒸出“麦积子馍”祈望丰收；过年时做“银子盎盎馍”；七月七要给女孩蒸“蒲篮馍”，给男孩蒸长形或圆形的“砚台馍”“笔架馍”。

Is *mo* just dough in a round shape? According to Xi'anese, you are all wet to think so. Here, the "*mo* culture" that carries people's hope has been passed down by generations. On the top of the *mo* that is sacrificed to the dead during the Tomb Sweeping Festival lies a dragon, and is called a "coiled dragon *mo*"; for weddings, one needs to prepare large "tiger *mo*"; to celebrate the Lunar New Year, farmers steam "haystack mo" in hope of a good harvest; during the Spring Festival, families make "silver filled *mo*"; during the seventh evening of the seventh moon of the lunar calendar, "bamboo basket *mo*" is prepared for girls, and "ink stone *mo*" and "pen rack *mo*" for boys.

摄影：王幼健

摄影：王幼健

**每样都尝尝**
A Taste of Every Delicacy

台湾历史学教授逯耀东先生以讲授中国饮食文化史而广受欢迎。有一年，他陪同曾在西安度过童年的妻子回乡，一连多日流连在回民街"搜食"。他一面咬着饦饦馍夹腊牛肉，一面对妻子说："这条巷子真可爱，这么多的吃食。"妻子提醒他："注意肚子啊。"他只顾答："尝尝，只是尝尝，每样都尝尝。"

Mr. Lu Yaodong, a professor of history in Taiwan, enjoys widespread popularity for his lectures on the history of Chinese culinary culture. One year, when accompanying his wife, who grew up in Xi'an, to her hometown, he lingered for several days on the Muslim Street to search and enjoy local special food. Chewing the *mo* sandwiched with curbed beef, he remarked to his wife, "This alley is so lovely as there are so many nice snacks." His wife reminded him, "Mind you don't get a beer belly". He replied, "Just a taste, just a taste of everything".

**"爱饺及盘"**
Love the Dumpling, Love the Plate

曾五出国门的德发长饺子宴是西安小吃对外交流的"使者"。80多个国家的政要和名流都曾品尝过德发长饺子宴，与饺子发生的趣事也不少。有一次，德国奔驰公司总裁赫尔米特·沃纳品尝完饺子宴说："我特别喜欢这些饺子，要把餐具带回去做个纪念。中国有句成语叫'爱屋及乌'，我这是'爱饺及盘'呀！"

Defachang Dumpling Banquet "went abroad" five times, and has acted as an "ambassador" of Xi'an cuisine. Politicians and celebrities from over 80 countries have enjoyed the Defachang Dumpling Banquet, which in turn gave births to many "dumpling" anecdotes. Helmut Werner, former chairman of Mercedes-Benz, once said after a dumpling banquet, "I like these dumplings so much that I really want to bring back the tableware as a souvenir. There is a Chinese idiom, *aiwujiwu* ( 爱屋及乌 , meaning "love me, love my dog"). In my case, it's 'love the dumpling, love the plate'!"

**咥面**
Noodle Eating

"红日当午，几个汉子各端上一大碗捞面，盐搁得重重的，醋放得酸酸的，辣子撒得红红的，浇一勺滚油，再捏上一头大蒜，往门槛前一蹲，长长挑起一筷头裤带般的长面，筋亮油光，酸辣喷香……连吞带咽，一老碗黏面三五下就咥完了。"《大秦美食》中这段描述活灵活现地再现了陕西人咥面的生动场景。

"The sun hangs high in the sky. A couple of men each brings over a huge bowl of *laomian* (boiled and strained noodles), really salty, sour, and spicy, with one spoon of boiling oil on top of the noodles, and garlic in their hands. They squat in front of the door and pick up a load of long girdle-shaped noodles shiny with oil, fragrant, sour and spicy..." The description in *Delicious Food of Qin* vividly portrays the way Shaanxi people eat noodles.

**百变的面条**
**Varieties of Noodles**

在作家朱鸿看来，西安人变魔术般把面条做得多姿多彩，出神入化：扯面扁而韧，拉面圆而筋，揪面有起有伏，像散文小品，削面有棱有角，像唐诗宋词……擀面则以一根杖和一块案做成，有旗花面、韭叶面、裤带面、片片面、线线面，还有臊子面、蘸水面等等，真是各有形状，更各有口感！

In writer Zhu Hong's eyes, Xi'anese are like magicians who can turn noodle making into something fascinating, vibrant, and marvelous. Hand-ripped noodles are flat yet tough; hand-pulled noodles are round and chewy; flaked noodles rise and fall like a piece of prose; pared noodles are angular like ancient poetry... Roll-and-cut noodles are made with only a rolling pin and a cutting board, and there are also other varieties like *qihua* (flag-shaped) chives noodles, girdle-shaped noodles, peeled noodles, string noodles, noodles with minced meat, and noodles with sauce in another bowl. Each has its unique shape and taste!

**腊汁肉揪面片**
**Flaked Noodles with Braised Meat in Preserved Sauce**

如果食物也按口味分男女的话，腊汁肉揪面片就是食物里的“纯爷们儿”。大老碗，很实在的腊汁肉块，软烂醇香；厚厚的面片，筋道爽滑，放进嘴里好像自动就会往嗓子眼里滑；再加上各种调料，有点酸，有点辣，吃起来很是过瘾。如此美味的面食，您只有到西安才吃得到。

If food has gender according to their flavors, flaked noodles with braised meat in preserved sauce would be the “macho man”. Big chunks of braised meat in preserved sauce in an old big bowl are tender and delicious. Those flakes of noodle are thick and chewy, yet so smooth that they would slip down the throat by themselves. A little sour and spicy, it is really an enjoyable cuisine. But you can get it only here in Xi'an.

**花奶奶的酸梅汤**
**Granny Hua's Plum Juice**

花奶奶，姓花，一位和蔼的回族老人。酸梅汤在回坊小吃街上几乎家家都有，她的摊点只有资深吃货才知晓。老人几十年如一日守在大皮院，天天熬一锅酸梅汤，在人来人往的小街上颇为低调。现在，奶奶年事已高，售卖的活儿交给儿女来干，慕名而来的人偶尔还会遇见坐在路南藤椅上晒太阳的这位老奶奶。

Granny Hua is an affable elderly lady of the Hui ethnic group. Although plum juice is sold in almost every store on Huifang Snack Street, experienced foodies choose Granny Hua's stand. For decades, this old lady has been staying in Dapiyuan, cooking a pot of plum juice day after day, and living a peaceful life on this bustling street. Now, Granny Hua has passed the selling work to her children because of her old age. Occasionally, visitors who are attracted by the stand's reputation still run into this old granny, who is sitting in the sun in a bamboo chair.

摄影：王健

摄影：王幼健

### 像筷子一样粗的面
### Noodles as Thick as Chopsticks

西安有一家极费腮帮子的柳巷面，藏在小巷口，门口天天排队，面条粗细与筷子相当。喜欢它的人，爱它豪爽的牛肉块和十足的嚼劲，更爱厚厚一层的油泼辣子；不喜欢它的人嫌面条太粗、硬度太高，嚼起来费劲，还不易消化，属于重油、重口味。面对如此结实的面食，想不想挑战一下自己的牙齿？

Liuxiang ( 柳巷 , Willow Alley) noodles served in a restaurant in Xi'an is a challenge for the jaw. Hidden in the valley, this restaurant always attracts a long queue of customers. Its noodles are as thick as chopsticks. Those who favor it love its large chunks of beef, the chewiness, and especially the thick layer of oil-sprinkled spices. Those who aren't fond of it dislike the thick noodles, the hard texture, and the difficulty in chewing, not to mention that it is very hard to digest and is heavy on oil and taste. Would you dare challenge your teeth to chew the solid noodles here?

### 蒸馍和烙馍
### Steamed Bread and Baked Cake

在关中，馍有两大类做法：蒸和烙。仅仅是蒸出来的便有花卷、油塔、糕和包子等。而烙出来的馍则有锅盔、太后饼、胡麻饼、油旋、饦饦、菜盒等。老幼妇孺宜于蒸馍，因为它柔、软、容易消化，而壮者则嗜烙馍，它瓷、实、耐饿久饱，当然也考验牙和胃。

There are two major ways to make *mo* in Guanzhong. One is steaming and the other is baking. Steamed ones include steamed rolls, crispy fried noodles, glutinous rice cake, and buns. Baked ones include *guokui* (baked wheaten cake), empress dowager cake, oil cake of flax seed, *youxuan* (coiled pancake), Arabic turml, and dumplings with leek. Steamed ones are for the elderly, women, and children, as they are soft and easy to digest. Strong men prefer baked ones, as they are solid, firm. But they are a challenge for one's teeth and stomach.

### 玫瑰镜糕
### Rose Mirror Cakes

西安土话将甑糕也念成“镜糕”，不过这“玫瑰镜糕”和“甑糕”可完全不是一回事。玫瑰镜糕很小，只有掌心大，是将糯米粉放入小笼里蒸制而成，白白嫩嫩，状如小圆镜，故而得名“镜糕”。吃的时候，用竹签扎一块，蘸上白糖、玫瑰酱、黑芝麻、花生碎之类，绵软香甜，好看又好吃。

In Xi'an dialect, *zenggao* ( 甑糕 , jujube glutinous rice cake) is also pronounced "*jinggao*" ( 镜糕 , mirror cake), but *meiguijinggao* ( 玫瑰镜糕 , rose mirror cake) is completely different from *zenggao*. It is small as a palm, made with steaming glutinous rice flour in steamer. White and fluffy in the shape of an oval mirror, it is named "mirror cake". To enjoy it, you need to pick one up with a bamboo slip, dip it in sugar, rose petal jam, black sesame, and peanut crumbs. Soft and sweet, it is really a delight to the eye and a treat to one's craving .

HOTEL XIAN
摄影：刘问

# 都市·风尚

Metropolitan Trends

**不拘一格的小资**
The Carefree Petty Bourgeoisie

有人感叹：其他城市的金领小资们刻意标签化模式化，穿什么用什么在哪里消费都很固定，而西安的金领小资们却完全不同，他们可能刚刚从德福巷的某个咖啡馆、茶秀走出来，然后又直奔羊肉泡馍馆或凉皮摊，坐在油迹斑斑的长条凳上海吃一碗。这种随意而为，大概缘于他们身上秦皇汉武的皇族血脉吧。

It is said that unlike the petty bourgeoisie in other cities who have deliberately identified themselves with certain labels and stylized their life, those in Xi'an are completely different. As soon as they leave a coffee bar in Defu Lane, they may straightly head for a restaurant for a big bowl of *yangrou paomo* or to a street stand for a big plate of cold noodles known as *liangpi*, not in the least minding the oily stained benches. Their carefree behavior probably originated from the royal style of the Qin and Han dynasties.

**最青春活力的商圈**
The Most Dynamic Commercial Hub

小寨是西安的美女聚集地，是一个无处不时尚的地方，它得名于明代村落，城市化后便与农业文明无干。现在其周边名胜和高校众多，被誉为西安最具青春活力的商圈。每逢休息日，大学生情侣手牵着手穿行于此，他们没有太多钱，不会去消费高的地方，来小寨轧马路、吃小吃、品甜品和偶尔“血拼”最令他们开心。

A completely trendy place, Xiaozhai is a favorite place for beauties of Xi'an to gather. Although the name of the place was derived from a Ming Dynasty village, it has lost all associations with agriculture after the place was urbanized. Surrounded by famous scenic spots and universities, Xiaozhai has been crowned the most dynamic commercial hub in Xi'an. Every weekend, courting couples from colleges around stroll here hand in hand. With thin wallets, they can't afford to visit expensive places. So they come here to take a walk, taste snacks, savor desserts, and occasionally, "shop till they drop", all guaranteeing the best of times.

**夜西安**
Xi'an at Night

旅游达人建议：坐飞机到西安尽量选择晚上的航班，因为只有这样才能看到辉煌的夜景。桂林一位网友曾在微博上传一张从飞机上俯瞰西安夜景的照片，吸引了无数网友欣赏、赞叹。照片中的夜西安绚烂夺目，璀璨的灯光点亮了横平竖直的主干道路，棋盘式布局一目了然。

Experienced travelers suggest evening flights to Xi'an for the spectacular night skyline. A netizen from Guilin once posted a photo he took on the plane of the city's skyline at night, and it received abundant appreciation and praises. The photo shows a dazzling Xi'an as the resplendent lights light up all the major roads of the city's grid layout.

摄影：翟小雪　贾庆华

### 西安细腻的一面
### The Exquisite Side of Xi'an

如上海衡山路、北京三里屯，西安也有个街巷定义城市的浪漫——德福巷。这个中间拐弯的巷子，在西安横平竖直的街道中是个特例，它也阐释了西安人的“小资”。豆瓣网“德福巷小组”说：德福巷的个性、浪漫与柔情，令西安人在吼秦腔、看秦俑外，有了可以品味自己细腻生活的一面。

Just like Hengshan Road in Shanghai and Sanlitun in Beijing, Defu Alley in Xi'an defines the city's romance. Zigzagging in its middle section, the alley is an exception to Xi'an's grid patterned streets. This alley in a way also illuminates the "petty-bourgeoisie" in Xi'an. The Defu Alley Team on Douban.com describes: Defu Alley's individuality, romance and tenderness give Xi'anese a chance to savor the exquisiteness of life, aside from the bellowing of the Qinqiang opera and the displaying of terracotta warriors.

**我国唯一的卫星测控中心**

China's Only Satellite Control Center

每次发射神舟飞船或者其他卫星的时候，总会听到西安的名字，因为不管是运载火箭还是卫星、飞船的飞行和控制都离不开西安卫星测控中心。卫星测控中心就像是个遥控器，主要任务就是对航天器进行跟踪测量、控制及回收等；还要对在轨的航天器进行长期的运行管理等。这可是我国唯一的卫星测控中心。

Every time satellites or spaceships are launched, Xi'an would be mentioned. Whether a carrier rocket, a satellite, or a spaceship, the Xi'an Satellite Control Center is indispensible for their launch, the only one of its kind in China. Like a remote control, this center assumes the duty of tracking, controlling, and the retrieval of spacecrafts as well as long-term management of spacecrafts in orbit.

**纺织城艺术区**

A City of Textile Art

东郊纺织城的"唐华一印"是苏联援建的项目。90 年代起，纺织行业繁华不再，纺织厂几近倒闭。2007 年，西安艺术家自发聚集在一印开设画廊、工作室，让原本充满工业痕迹与时代感的厂区在艺术家的"文艺复兴"下，焕发出全新的气质，使这里成为西安本土的当代艺术区。

Tanghua No. One Printing and Dyeing Mill (known as Yiyin) in the Textile City in the eastern suburbs of Xi'an, was built with the aid of the former Soviet Union. In the 1990s, the heyday of the textile industry was over and textile mills were on the verge of bankruptcy. In 2007, artists in Xi'an teamed up to open galleries and studios in Yiyin. Thanks to the artists' "Renaissance" effort, the original area of the mill once marked by industrialism and the feel of a bygone era has turned into Xi'an's contemporary art district with an entirely new look.

摄影：翟小雪

**巷口**
At the Entrance to an Alley

巷口两间店，西家“老刘家烤肉”，东家“松鼠家咖啡”。寒冬夜幕降临，老刘家肉串的香味在炭火中滋长，人们坐在街边的小凳上甩开膀子，喝喝啤酒聊聊家常；在松鼠家木桌上找一本有趣的旧书，窝在沙发里捧着大杯的研磨咖啡暖暖手。西安的两种味道，一样的闲适调调。

There are two stores at either end of the alley, namely Old Liu's Barbeque in the west, and the Squirrel Café in the east. When cold winter night falls, the delicious smell of Old Liu's Grill grows stronger above the burning coal. People sit on stools by the road, drinking beer and chatting idly. At the Squirrel Café, one can sit at a wooden table, pick an interesting secondhand book, curl up on the couch, and warm his hands with a large cup of ground coffee. Although their flavors are different, the easiness of Xi'an never gets lost.

**最有味道的地下通道**
The Most Romantic Underpass

就像很多城市一样，西安也有不少地下通道，其中最具味道的当数南门里的那一条。这里从早到晚都有流浪歌手弹唱着许巍们的歌，虽然许多年来这里的歌手换了一个又一个，但专属西安的那种沧桑嗓音却从未更换。伴着他们的木吉他，慢步走出通道，抬眼便见南门，那一瞬间你就能体会到这座城市独有的温度。

Like in many other cities, there are a lot of underpasses in Xi'an. Among them, the most romantic one is at Nanmenli. From morning till evening, vagabond singers play and sing songs composed by famous popular song writer Xu Wei. Although singers come and go, the aged voice of Xi'an never changes. Enjoying the melodies of their wooden guitar, sauntering in the underpass, and taking a glimpse of the South Gate when looking up at the end of the underpass, you can always feel the unique warmth of this city.

**外国人的新故乡**
A New Home for Foreigners

西安是一座包容的城市，不仅包容外乡人，也包容外国人。很多来西安旅行或学习的老外都留在了西安。克里斯在西安经营一家小公司，领略过世界各地美景的他说：“西安就是我想象中的古城，城墙太美了，在日出日落中显得那样迷人。”而闲暇时，克里斯会和朋友们骑上摩托车，去秦岭山中感受大自然的美妙。

Xi'an is an inclusive city for non-locals and foreigners. A lot of foreigners who come here as tourists or to study would decide to stay or even settle down. Chris, for example, now runs a small business in Xi'an. Having seen numerous beautiful sceneries around the world, he said, "Xi'an has been an ideal ancient city in my imagination. The city walls are marvelous. They are so fascinating at sunset and sunrise". Whenever at leisure, Chris goes on motorcycle rides with friends to get immersed in the beauty of nature in the Qinling Mountains.

**两个半坡**
Two Banpo Sites

西安东郊有两个半坡。一个是众所周知的新石器时代村落遗址，另一个则是与此一墙之隔的半坡国际艺术区，这是西安正在精心打造的具有国际色彩的文化艺术产业创作与输出基地。学者商子雍感叹，一个半坡展示着沉积了几千年的厚重历史，而另一个则洋溢着先锋文化的蓬勃活力，左顾右盼，令人浮想联翩！

There are two Banpo sites in the eastern suburbs of Xi'an, the Neolithic Village, a well-known archeological site, and next to it the Banpo International Arts District, an international production and export base of culture and art industries elaborately built up by the city. Shang Ziyong, a famous scholar, was impressed and remarked: "One displays the history of thousands of years, while the other beams with the lively energy of culture of the art *d' avant garde*. The contrast fills one with wonder!"

**女子公交**
The Women's Bus Route

"全国三八红旗集体"19路公交车，从南郊航天大道西口到东郊纬什街，因劳模多、美女驾驶员多，民间誉其为"最美线路"。近60名女驾驶员占到了司机总数的80%，是陕西唯一一条女子公交线路。从梳着大辫子的姑娘，开到渐露白发的"资深美女"，方向盘上留下了她们的心路与青春。

The crew of No. 19 Bus has won the honored title of "National 'March Eighth' Red Banner Holding Collective". This bus runs from the west intersection of Hangtian Avenue in the southern suberbs to Weishi Street in the eastern suburbs. It is known as the most beautiful bus route for its large number of model workers and beautiful drivers. 80 percent of the drivers of this route, that is, nearly 60 of them, are female, which makes it the only bus route in Shaanxi, most drivers of which are women. From girls with braids to "senior beauties" with gray hair, they leave their passion and youth on the driving wheel.

**外籍西安人**
Xi'anese of Foreign Citizenship

五年前，Stephen从美国来中国时，爸爸送了他一台单反相机。如今，他作为杂志编辑游走在西安的大街小巷，带着这台相机到处采集有趣的餐厅或酒吧信息。像Stephen一样常驻西安的外籍人士数以万计，有教师、演艺者，也有创业青年，他们完全融入这里的生活，成为西安的一分子。

Five years ago, when Stephen came to China from America, his father gave him a single lens reflex camera. Now as an editor of a magazine, he roams the streets of Xi'an with this camera to explore interesting restaurants and bars. There are tens of thousands of expatriates in Xi'an like Stephen. Some are teachers, some are performers, and some are young entrepreneurs. They have already adapted themselves to the life here and have now become a part of this city.

## 八水润西安

## Eight Rivers Nurituring Xi'an

两千多年前，东浐灞、北泾渭、西沣涝、南潏滈就为西安赢得了“八水绕长安”的美誉。今日的西安通过引水、治水工程的建设，正在形成“东有浐灞广运潭，西有沣河昆明池，南有唐城曲江湖，北有未央汉城湖，中有明清护城河”的“新八水”格局。市委书记魏民洲将此称为“八水润西安”。

When young people have their wedding photos taken in Xi'an, they always go to the banks of the Chan River, the Ba River or the Qujiang Lake for the beautiful scenery. Two thousand years ago, the rivers of Chan and Ba to the east, Jing and Wei to the north, Feng and Lao to the west, and Ju and Hao to the south won Xi'an the reputation of "eight rivers around Chang'an". Now, through irrigation and water control projects, Xi'an has made a new eight-river landscape that features the Chan River, the Ba River and the Guangyun Lake to the east, the Feng River and the Kunming Pool to the west, the Qujiang Lake to the south, Hancheng Lake to the north, with moat of the Ming and Qing dynasties in the center. Wei Minzhou, the Secretary of Xi'an Municipal Party Committee, calls it "eight rivers nurituring Xi'an".

摄影：王幼健

**垃圾桶也文艺**

Artistic Garbage Bins

“文艺的西安，连垃圾桶都文艺。应女友的要求，每逢垃圾桶必收藏。半年来跟女友走遍西安各大公园，收集了这66种垃圾桶。”@断尾壁虎H发的这条微博还附上了各式垃圾桶的照片，有古井形的、仿古木桶形的、树桩形的……而眼下，西安街头最新版的垃圾桶是有青龙白虎图案的“古典风”垃圾桶。

“Xi'an is so artistic that even its garbage bins form a kind of art. Upon my girlfriend's request, I took photos of every garbage bin I saw. In half a year, we have strolled across all of Xi'an's parks, and found 66 kinds of garbage bins.” Netizen “*duanweibihu* H” posted these words on Weibo with pictures of garbage bins in various forms and shapes: an ancient well, an old-fashioned barrel and a tree trunk... The most trendy garbage bins in the streets in Xi'an have a classical style: a pattern of the azure dragon and the white tiger.

**送你一个长安**

A Chang'an to You

西安2011世界园艺博览会成功举办，主题曲《送你一个长安》成为西安家喻户晓的歌曲：“送你一个长安，蓝田先祖，半坡炊烟……送你一个长安，李白杜甫，司马长卷……送你一个长安，一城文化，半城神仙……”好好听听这首歌，您会从自然、历史、文化等不同角度了解到西安令人心醉神往的原因。

The 2011 Xi'an China International Horticultural Exposition was a big success. The theme song “Give You a Chang'an” also became a hit in Xi'an, “Give you a Chang'an, where our Lantian forefathers once lived and smoke once rose from Banpo's chimneys... Give you a Chang'an, where great poets Li Bai, Du Fu once lived, and great historian Sima Guang who recorded history on long scrolls... Give you a Chang'an, a city full of culture, half filled with divinities.” Listen to the song carefully, and you will realize why Xi'an is so enchanting from every angle: its natural attraction, history, or culture.

**古城钟楼网上报时**

The Bell Tower Announces the Time Online

西安钟楼的钟声能传多远？“铛……”刷新最近的微博界面，你会发现满耳都能“听”到这种声音。一个名为“古城钟楼”的微博爆红网络，从2011年10月26日起，每天都进行“报时”。甚至连明星蔡康永都转发了@古城钟楼的微博并评论说：“我似乎有点理解钟楼的人生了。”

How far can the sound of the bell in Xi'an's Bell Tower travel? Refresh your recent Weibo, and you'll “hear” the clang from the bell. A weibo account named “Ancient City Bell Tower” is hot on social internet. It has been announcing time every day since October 26th, 2011. Even the celebrity Kevin Tsai reposted this weibo, and commented, “It seems that now I have got some idea about life in the Bell Tower”.

**天幕穹顶**

**An LED Sky Dome**

四季、星空、游鱼、飞鸟等各种三维影像在头顶变幻，将人们带入一个梦幻的视听空间。曲江“秦汉唐国际文化商业广场”顶部的这个总面积约3000平方米的巨型LED天幕穹顶，让来此休闲逛街的游客随时仰望“天际”，恍若置身于繁星似锦的童话世界。

Three-dimensional images depicting the alternate of seasons, the star-dotted sky, swimming fish and flying birds change magically overhead, all bring people into an audio-visual fantasy world. The 3,000-square-meter LED dome at Qin Han Tang International Culture and Commercial Plaza in Qujiang New District enables shoppers to gaze at the “sky” whenever they look up, and put them into a wonderland filled with twinkling stars above their heads.

摄影：贾庆华

### 汤峪温泉
### The Tangyu Hot Spring

桃花三月汤泉水，春风醉人不知归。每年三月，位于西安东南方的汤峪镇各家温泉馆都挤满了专程来泡汤的城里人。汤峪的温泉水温 61 度，属中高温热泉水，含硫酸盐，及铁、钼、碘等对人体有益的成分。西安人讲究在农历三月初三去泡一泡温泉，脱掉臃肿的冬装，在露天的温暖汤池中舒展四肢，放松身心，迎接春天。

It is said that in March, soaking in hot spring, intoxicated by peach blossoms and spring breeze, people are reluctant to go home. Every March, city dwellers swarm to Tangyu Town to the southeast of the Xi'an city, to enjoy hot springs there. The temperature of Tangyu's hot spring is kept at the medium high level of 61 degrees Celsius. The spring water here contains sulphate, iron, and trace elements such as molybdenum and iodine that are beneficial to people's health. Xi'anese are very particular about soaking in hot springs on the third day of the third lunar month. They take off their heavy winter clothes, stretch their arms and legs in the warm pool in the open, relax their soul, and welcome the arrival of spring.

### 西安的机场在咸阳
### Xi'an's Airport Is in Xianyang

西安咸阳国际机场是中国西北地区最大的空中枢纽，不仅有国内航班通达所有省会城市、重要工业城市、旅游城市，还有国际航班通达东京、首尔等城市。西安的机场并没有建在西安市，而是建在咸阳市境内，“机场建在邻居家”也算是一大特色了。

As the largest aviation transport hub in China's Northwest, Xi'an Xianyang International Airport has not only domestic flights to all provincial capitals, important industrial centers, and tourist cities in China, but also international flights to cities like Tokyo, Seoul, and etc. However, the airport of Xi'an is not located in Xi'an but its neighboring city Xianyang. A city airport built in the neighbor's place, this is something extraordinary.

摄影：王健

摄影：翟小雪

**快递广告牌**
Advertizing Boards for Express Delivery

“快递打包发往全国”。鼓楼北边的回坊风情步行街不仅云集了老字号的风味小吃，出售柿子饼、红枣等陕西特产的小店更是一家挨一家，方便游客选购礼物赠送亲朋。如果你不想背着大包小包赶飞机、挤火车，请留意每家特产店门前的快递广告牌。只需一个电话，快递员立刻来现场打包发货，想寄哪里寄哪里。

"Your parcels can be sent express to any place within China through express delivery." Gathered in the Huifang Pedestrian Street to the north of the Drum Tower are not only time-honored specialty stores selling local delicacies like persimmon cakes and red dates. The stores line up one by one so that tourists have many choices in buying gifts for their relatives and friends. If you don't want to catch your flight or train with loads of bags, please look at the advertising board in front of every store. Dial the telephone number on the board and a courier will rush over and pack the gift and send it to anywhere you intend.

**南非妈妈**
South Africa Mum

阿曼达是一个南非女人，2004 年漂洋过海来到西安，创办中国第一家由在华外国人设立的家庭寄养点——海星之家，168 名孤残儿童的命运因她改变。她是孩子们最喜爱的南非妈妈，无数的西安市民则是她最有力的亲友团。2012 年夏，阿曼达因突发重病不幸离世。临走前，她说“我把心留在西安了”。

Amanda, a woman from South Africa, traveled across the seas in 2004, arrived in Xi'an, and founded the first orphanage run by a foreigner in China, "Home of Starfish". She changed the fate of 168 orphans and disabled children. She was their most-loved "South African Mom", and millions of Xi'anese were her strongest backup. Unfortunately, in the summer of 2012, Amanda was hit by a severe illness and passed away. Before she left this world, she said, "I've left my love in Xi'an".

摄影：王旭东

**亚洲之最**

The Largest Train Station in Asia

亚洲最大的火车站在哪儿？很多人会猜东京、首尔以及我国的北上广。其实，她就位于西安城北。2011 年初投入使用的西安北客站，年发送旅客 6870 万人，远期将达到 8260 万人，是目前亚洲最大的铁路枢纽中转站。旅客通过站台下层出站通道进入集散大厅或广场，可与地铁、城市公交实现“零换乘”。

Where is the largest train station in Asia located? Many would guess Tokyo, Seoul, Beijing, Shanghai, or Guangzhou, yet in fact it is located in Xi'an. The Xi'an North Railway Station, which went into operation in early 2011, dispatches 68.7 million passengers annually, and the number is expected to increase to 82.6 million soon. It is the largest railway transport hub in Asia. Passengers exit through tunnels beneath the platforms and enter the terminal hall or square, where they can easily transfer to the subway or bus.

**西安人的菜园子**

A Xi'anese Vegetable Garden

杨凌是中华农耕文明的发祥地。1997 年杨凌成立示范区，是我国唯一的国家级农业高新区。这里聚集了多家农业科教单位，包括大学以及研究院所，因此，也被誉为“中国农科城”，还被亲切地称为“西安人的菜园子”。

China's agriculture stemmed from Yangling. In 1997, Yangling Agriculture Hi-Tech Industrial Zone, the only one of the state-level in China, was established. Many agro-scientific research institutions are based here, including universities and institutions. Thus, Yangling is also crowned "the town of China's agricultural technology", and affectionately called "Xi'anese' vegetable garden".

### 洋人活雷锋
### A Foreign Lei Feng

英国人托尼，卖掉三家公司、一处庄园及两辆跑车，原本想去印度修行，一次偶然机会来到西安后，他感到和这座城市有缘，于是便留在古城做起了善事——给流浪者发放包子和稀饭。托尼的“慈善厨房”七年多时间吸引了上千名志愿者加入。志愿者都叫他“活雷锋”，尽管他并不知道雷锋是谁。

Tony, an Englishman, sold his three companies, one villa, and two sports cars intending to practise Hinduism in India. Yet when he accidently came to visit Xi'an, he felt he was predestined to this city, so he settled down in this ancient city and started practicing charity by handing out buns and porridge to vagrants. Tony's "charity kitchen" attracted over a thousand volunteers to join him in seven years, who call him "the living Lei Feng", even though Tony himself didn't know who Lei Feng (1940 - 1962) was.

### 四点左右别打车
### Don't Hail a Taxi Around Four

西安出租车价格便宜，起步六块加一块燃油附加费，每公里一块五。可是看着满街跑的绿色出租车，空车可不多。好不容易停下一辆，要是司机先问你“去哪儿”，你八成又没希望了。而且，西安出租车交车时间统一在下午四点半，在四点前后千万别指望能打上出租车，还是坐公交或者想想其他办法吧。

Taxi fare in Xi'an is relatively cheap. The starting price is six *yuan*, plus one *yuan* for fuel surcharge. That makes one and half *yuan* per kilometer. You might see taxis painted in green running all over the place, but there aren't many vacant ones available. When you finally succeeded in signaling one down, if you let the driver ask you "where to" before you get in, then your chance of riding it is pretty slim. Also, taxi drivers in Xi'an change shifts around 4:30 pm, so don't even think about getting a taxi around 4 pm. You'd better take a bus or think of some other way.

### 西安最浪漫餐厅
### The Most Romantic Restaurant in Xi'an

在西安高新区鳞次栉比的高楼背后一条没有名字的小巷里，绿茉莉西餐厅门前的小花园很是养眼。地中海式的装修装饰，唯美温馨。服务员说，餐厅开业三年来，几乎每周都能看到手捧鲜花的年轻人在这里求婚，求婚成功率 99%，绿茉莉也被网友誉为西安“第一求婚餐厅”和“最浪漫的餐厅”。

In a nameless alley hidden behind the numerous skyscrapers in Xi'an Hi-tech Industries Development Zone, the little garden in front of the Green Molly Restaurant is a feast for the eyes. Furnished and decorated in Mediterranean style, the place is beautiful and cozy. Waiters say that in three years since its opening, the restaurant has witnessed young suitors proposing with flowers in their hands almost every week. The success rate is 99 percent, which is why netizens call Green Molly the best restaurant to propose and the most romantic restaurant in Xi'an.

摄影：翟小雪

**夜市**
The Night Market

炎炎夏日酷暑难耐，晚上邀三五好友去吃夜市已经成为很多西安市民喜欢的生活方式。西安摆夜市的摊点随处可见，大多以烧烤为主，也包括各种面食小吃等，比较集中的有回民街、东新街。要上一打啤酒，一把烤筋，几个烤油饼，两盘花生毛豆，边吃边聊，经常到半夜两三点还不散摊。

In swelteringly hot summer days, Xi'anese are used to inviting friends to eat out-doors at the night markets. This has become the favorite lifestyle of many Xi'anese. Food stands can be seen everywhere in Xi'an, mostly barbecue stands with some selling noodles and others selling cooked wheaten snacks. They are clustering around the Muslim Street and Dongxin Street. Xi'anese usually order a dozen beers, a batch of barbecued tendons, some deep-fried dough, and a couple of plates of peanuts or fresh soya beans, chatting while enjoying their food. The stands will not be packed up till two or three o'clock in the early morning.

**西安北京公交化**
The High Speed Railway Linking Xi'an and Beijing

2012 年 12 月 26 日，西安至北京高铁启动，全程 5 小时，平均一小时一趟，像坐公交一样方便。有吃货就发出这样的感叹："早上在西安咥羊肉泡，中午到北京吃烤鸭。"

On December 26, 2012, the high speed railway from Xi'an to Beijing was open to traffic. The whole journey takes five hours, averaging one train service per hour. It is almost as convenient as taking buses. Some foodies rejoiced that they could now "have *yangrou paomo* in Xi'an in the morning, and eat roasted duck in Beijing at noon".

## 外国人的聚集地
## A Gathering Place for Foreigners

Park Qin 酒吧是西安唯一的秦主题酒吧，里面有大大小小 1000 多个兵马俑，以兵马俑命名的鸡尾酒“秦俑士”口味独特。酒吧位于书院青年旅社的地下室，只接待会员和住宿的客人。这里还是外国人的聚集地，生活工作在西安的外国人经常相约在这里举办各种主题活动。

Park Qin is the only bar in Xi'an with the theme of the Qin Dynasty, where over 1,000 terracotta warriors of different sizes are on display. Here you can enjoy a cocktail with a unique flavor named "Qin Warriors". Located in the basement of the Shuyuan International Youth Hostel, this bar only serves its members and guests of this hostel. It is also the gathering place for foreigners in Xi'an. Living and working in Xi'an, they often gather here and host theme activities.

## 去 3D 照相馆打印自己
## Print Yourself in a 3D Photo Studio

看过 3D 电影买过 3D 电视，可你听说过 3D 打印吗？ 2012 年 12 月 31 日，全国首家 3D 打印照相馆落户西安高新区。在那里，只要花 15 分钟将自己的全身外形扫描至计算机，经过 2—3 小时打印便会“凿”出一个立体的“自己”。

You've seen 3D movies and bought 3D televisions, but have you heard of 3D printing? On December 31, 2012, the first 3D printing photo studio in China opened in Xi'an Hi-Tech Industries Development Zone. There, you only need to spend 15 minutes to have yourself scanned by the computer and in two or three hours, you'll get a three-dimensional figure of yourself.

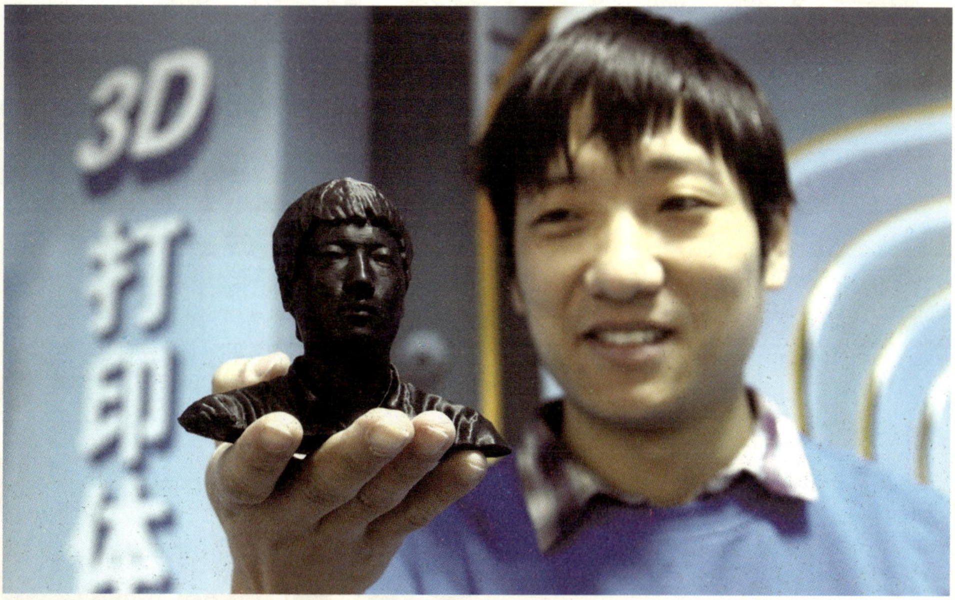


摄影：王燕

**音乐圈**
**Music Circles**

不同于以游客为中心的北京酒吧，西安的酒吧以老板和驻唱歌手为中心，形成音乐圈子。民谣和重金属绝对是不同的场子，最好由当地朋友带着，才能听到最地道的西安音乐圈故事。

Unlike the tourist-centered bars in Beijing, in Xi'an, a number of bars with music circles, singers, and bar owners as the center have formed. Folk rhymes and heavy metal are definitely of different styles and played in different bars. To have a true understanding of the music circles in Xi'an, you'd better find a local guide.

**曲江新区**
**Qujiang New District**

在 2004 年以前，关于西安曲江这个地名，即使许多西安本地人也并不是十分熟悉。如今，这里发生了翻天覆地的变化，成为西安城市的新名片。曲江不再只有大雁塔，亚洲最大的音乐喷泉、大唐芙蓉园、大唐不夜城、寒窑等一个个响当当的新景点，将古朴与现代完美融合，给西安旅游增添了新选择。

Before 2004, even Xi'anese weren't very familiar with Qujiang. Now, the place has undergone tremendous changes to become the new name card of Xi'an. The Giant Wild Goose Pagoda is no longer Qujiang's only scenic spot. New spots like the largest musical fountain in Asia, the Tang Paradise of Lotus, the Great Tang Ever-bright City and the Humble Cave Dwelling, combine antiquity and modernity perfectly and offer tourists more choices in Xi'an.

摄影：王旭东

摄影：王旭东　张宇明

摄影：魏影 王燕

**石榴花**
Pomegranate Flowers

石榴花是西安的市花。逢农历五月初，满城盛开石榴花，灼灼逼人的红，只有火焰与流星可以相比。它的花瓣柔软，外缘下端却有坚实的外壳维护，予人成熟之美、富贵之意。如果你在西安待到农历八月满月之时，吃着硕大如瓜的石榴，更会感知子孙满堂的期待与喜悦了。

Pomegranate flower is the city flower of Xi'an. On the fifth day of the fifth lunar month, pomegranate flowers are in full bloom throughout the city. Only the color of fire or meteors can be compared with their crimson color. With soft petals, and protected by a hard receptacle beneath it, the flower has a beauty of maturity and symbolizes wealth and loftiness. If you stay in the city until the Mid-autumn Festival, you'll feel the bless of having many children as you eat pomegranates as large as melons.

**"孙大圣"带路**
The "Monkey King" as Your Guide

城市发展日新月异，仿佛一眨眼的工夫就多了一条新路，一栋新楼。于是，在城市出入口的高速路边兴起了一种职业——带路人。孙师傅就是其中一员，他打扮成了"孙大圣"的模样，举着 "带路"的牌子，身着金黄色的衣服、手持金箍棒。孙师傅说："这样与众不同，也给往过司机带来欢乐。"

Rapid urbanization brings changes every day. New road and new buildings may pop up in a blink. A new type of job by the highways emerges as the times demand, that is road guide. Mr. Sun is one of them. Dressed in golden yellow like the legendary Monkey King, he holds a magic cudgel in one hand. Beside him stands a sign board that reads, "Here's Your Guide". Sun says, "My unique dress also brings entertainment to passing drivers".

**城中村**
Urban Villages

在西安，一些城中村的配套设施比高档小区还完善。这里是“西漂”的起点，是多数毕业生无奈又自然的选择。南郊沙井村的租客一度多达 10 万人，住进这里的人总梦想着离开，离开了却又忍不住怀念。西安本土原生态电影《沙井村之恋》的片头曲《城中村的那些年》唱出了不少人的青春记忆。

In Xi'an, urban villages may have better accessory facilities than many fancy neighborhoods. This is where "Xi'an drifters" began their life in the city. Most college graduates have no choice but to be drifters in Xi'an. Shajing Village in the southern suburbs once had over 100 thousand tenants. Most of them dream to move out some day as soon as they move in, yet when they do leave, they can't help but miss the place. The theme song "Those Years in the Urban Village" of the film *Love in Shajing Village* reminds so many people of their youthful days.

**粉巷**
Powder Alley

钟楼的西南有条东西向的街道——粉巷。粉是女人的化妆品，粉巷就与女人有关了，传说粉巷是因卖面粉或胭脂而得名，还有说是古时皇帝选妃的地方，此地也曾为青楼之地。今天的粉巷就像北京城的南锣鼓巷一样，是吃喝玩乐一条街，还有条洋气与浪漫兼备的德福巷酒吧街藏匿其中，难怪美女帅哥都喜欢逛粉巷。

To the southwest of the Bell Tower lies Fen Xiang (literally, "powder alley"), a street that runs from east to west. As powder is a kind of cosmetics, so naturally Fen Xiang is related to women. Legend has it that different kinds of powder and blusher were sold here. There is another theory that the alley used to be the venue for the emperor to choose concubines. And it is also said it was once a brothel street. Just like Beijing's South Luogu Lane, Fenxiang is now a street of restaurants, bars, shops and entertainments. Moreover, the modern and romantic Defuxiang Bar Street is also hidden here. No wonder young people like to come to Fenxiang.

**文化商机**
Business Opportunities in Culture

在文化里寻找商机，是西安商业的特色，大雁塔广场西侧的大唐通易坊便是这种特色商业的标志。这里的仿古建筑与大雁塔交相辉映。这里的经营以咖啡酒吧、特色餐饮为主。夜幕降临后，欣赏完大雁塔北广场音乐喷泉的游客，会结伴蜂拥至这里喝一杯。

Looking for cultural opportunities is a unique characteristic of business in Xi'an. Great Tang Tongyifang, located to west of the Giant Wild Goose Pagoda Plaza, is a symbol of this feature. Here architectures modeled after ancient styles and the Giant Wild Goose Pagoda enhance each other's glamour. The businesses here are mainly cafes, bars, and specialty restaurants. In the evening, after enjoying the musical fountain in the plaza located to the north of the pagoda, people would swarm here for a drink with friends.

**独一无二的马拉松**

**A Unique Marathon**

每年在国内举行的马拉松赛有30多个，这其中最与众不同的当属西安的城墙马拉松赛，这是世界上独一无二在历史文物遗迹进行的马拉松赛。在700多岁的明城墙上体验源自古希腊的竞技项目，古今与中外完美结合。一位跑者说："在这里跑步是体验体育的魅力，更是感受历史的温度。"

Of the over 30 marathon games held in China every year, the City Wall Marathon in Xi'an is absolutely unique. This is the only marathon that takes place on ancient relics in the whole world. Running with the athletic spirit of Ancient Greek on the city wall built in the Ming Dynasty is a perfect combination of the old and the new, the Chinese and the foreign. One of the runners remaked, "Running here, I can not only experience the charm of sports, but also feel the temperature of history."

**约会的"老地方"**

**The Place for Dating**

西安人约会的"老地方"是哪儿？开元门前堪称几大约会胜地之首，仅"开元门前的喷泉"就被网友多次提及。选择这里原因是：其一，没人找不到；其二，逛街方便。坏处是"人海茫茫过客匆匆"，不容易一眼找到。现在随着商圈的增多，李家村万达广场、大雁塔广场等地，已成西安人新的约会胜地。

Where is "the place" for dating in Xi'anese opinion? The Tang Kaiyuan Gate is the most favoured choice. "The fountain in front of Kaiyuan Gate" alone was mentioned many times by netizens online for two reasons: first, everyone can easily find it; second, it's a good place for window shopping. Its disadvantage is that it is so crowded that it's hard to spot your date. But with the establishment of new commercial centers, Xi'an residents now have new places for dates such as the Wanda Plaza in Lijia Village and the Giant Wild Goose Pagoda Plaza.

**十大美女聚集地**

**Ten Places to Find Beauties**

西安值得关注的不仅有古迹、小吃，还有美女。有网友就列出了西安十大美女聚集地：东大街（潮流型），高新（职场型），曲江南湖（温婉型），万达广场（御姐型），小寨（活力型），大学城（萝莉型），各大高校（青春型），大雁塔北广场（感性型），各大夜店（火辣型），康复路批发市场（混合型）。

Besides ancient relics and tasty snacks, Xi'an is also famous for beauties. A netizen listed the top 10 places to find beauties: East Street (trendy girls), Xi'an High-Tech Industries Development Zone (office ladies), Qujiangchi Relics Park (sweet and gentle girls), Wanda Plaza (the mature kind), Xiao Zhai (energetic ones), university district (lolitas), other universities (youthful ones), north plaza of the Pagoda of Wild Goose (sentimental girls), clubs (sexy ones), and Kangfu Road Wholesale Market (mixed).

**城墙下的咖啡香**

**The Fragrance of Coffee by the City Wall**

不知从何年月起，顺城巷里开了一家又一家咖啡馆。或以猫咪为主题，或以二手旧书为主打，各种风格的咖啡馆成了城墙根下别致的风景。闲暇时，坐于临窗的沙发，望着城墙青色的边际，你会相信，时间是可以停下来的。

No one could tell since when cafes have emerged in Shuncheng Alley one after another. These cafes all have different theme styles like kittens, second-hand books and so on, constituting a distinct scenic spot by the city wall. When you sit on a sofa by the window and look beyond the greenness of the city wall in leisure, you'll begin to believe that time really could be stopped.

**新旧建筑融合**

**The Harmony of the Old and the New Architectural Styles**

西安的建筑风格显现着新与旧的融合。古城内保留不少明清古建筑，除了城墙，还有很多特色街道如广济街、回坊，既有宗教色彩，又充满生活气息。古城外，新唐风建筑渐成气候，从早期的历史博物馆、唐华宾馆等单个的仿唐建筑，到眼下曲江建筑群，已经更多地与西安人的日常起居、休闲活动结合起来。

The architectural style in Xi'an is a harmonious combination of the old and the new. In this ancient city, many Ming and Qing architectures, not just the city walls, have been well preserved. There are many streets with special features, such as the Guangji Street and Huifang, which are permeated with both religious atmosphere and the flavor of secular life. Outside the ancient city, architectures of the Tang style are gaining popularity. Both buildings modeled after ancient styles like the history museum, Garden Hotel and the architectural complex in Qujiang have taken into consideration of the day-to-day life and relaxation of the Xi'anese.

摄影：尚洪涛

## 城墙根旅社

### Hostels by the City Wall

进了南门，左拐，沿着城墙脚下寂寂的青石板小街西行，很容易找到几家古色古香的青年旅社。这里是天南海北的驴友之家。住在这里，清晨和黄昏，抬眼就能看到城墙，这种仰望历史的姿态非常符合背包客在这个城市的心境，所以这里的青年旅社最受喜爱。这里的人和事在各种旅行论坛不断被提及。

Enter the city through the South Gate, turn to the left, and walk westward along the cobblestone street at the foot of the city wall, you can easily find some old-fashioned youth hostels. These are the homes of travelers. Staying here, you can see the city wall whenever looking up. Since this posture of looking up to history tallies with the mood of backpackers, these youth hostels are most favored by them. The people and what they have encountered here are constantly mentioned at all kinds of travel forums.

 摄影：翟小霄　贾庆华

摄影：贾庆华

**城墙章**
**The City Wall Seal**

只有西安地铁，每一个车站都有属于自己的 logo——方形的“城墙章”。它们在车站立柱、导向牌等显著位置，配合颜楷字体的站名出现，方便乘客查看。最特别的是，这每一站的 logo 上都突出了此站附近的标志性建筑，是不是很有文化、很有特色呢？

Each subway station in Xi’an has a special logo of its own: square seals of the city wall in different patterns. They can be seen in all conspicuous places: on pillars and direction signs, next to the station names of Chinese characters in the Yan Kai style to the convenience of passengers. The most special part is that each logo highlights the landmark building near the station. Isn’t that culturally distinctive?

**交大樱花赛武大**
**Cherry Blossoms in Xi’an Jiaotong University**

每年 4 月中旬，是西安交通大学校园里最拥挤的时节。一年一度的樱花节免费向公众开放，人们相邀赶来赏樱游园。枝头上粉的、绿的、黄的、白的，各色樱花装点了樱花大道烂漫的春日。都说“三月樱花，唯有武大”，其实，您不用跑到长江边，在西安交大就能感受樱花缤纷。

Xi’an Jiaotong University is most crowded in mid-April every year. During the annual Cherry Blossom Festival, the university is open to the public, when people arrange to meet here to appreciate the cherry blossoms and tour the campus together. Pink, green, yellow, and white cherry blossoms on the branches embellish the boulevard with springtime romance. People all say that cherry blossoms in March can be only seen in Wuhan University, but actually you don’t need to run all the way to the bank of Yangtze River. Instead, you can come to Xi’an Jiaotong University to enjoy the beautiful scene of cherry blossoms.

### 都市剧取景圣地
### An Ideal Location for Shooting City TV Dramas

一些外地人对西安的印象还执拗地停留在“黄土高坡”，很多新生代导演却早把镜头对准了这座时尚之都。细数之下，近些年不少热播都市剧的取景地都选择了西安:《请你原谅我》《前妻回家》《宝贝儿回家》《落泪成金》……在导演们眼里，西安的时尚是与文化氛围结合在一起的，大气磅礴又温情脉脉。

A lot of non-locals' impression of Xi'an is still stuck to "the Loess Plateau", but many new directors have already turned their camera to this trendy city. In recent years, many popular urban TV shows were shot in Xi'an, including *Please Forgive Me*, *Ex-wife Going Home*, *Baby Child Back Home*, and *Tears Turn Gold*... In directors' eyes, Xi'an is a modern city permeated with cultural spirit, majestic yet full of tenderness.

### 左手音符，右手丹青
### Music Goes Hand in Hand with Fine Arts

大唐不夜城不仅汇集了流光溢彩的夜景，也汇集了城市的艺术灵魂。路西的西安美术馆，多个大小不同的展厅，尽显唐代建筑艺术风格的沉稳大气。路东是西安音乐厅，交响音乐厅演奏台上方的管风琴是西北地区唯一的管风琴，出自德国管风琴制造世家——约翰尼斯·克莱斯之手，乃“镇厅之宝”。

The Great Tang Ever-bright City converges not only the dazzling night scenes but also the city's soul of art. On its west lies Xi'an Art Museum, whose exhibition halls of different sizes display the grandeur and solemnity of architectures of the Tang Dynasty. On its east side lies Xi'an Concert Hall, which boasts the only pipe organ in Northwest China, majestically standing above the stage of the symphony music hall as its most precious treasure. It was made by Klais Orgenbau, the century-old German family of organ making.

### 穿越历史的地铁
### A Subway Across History

西安修建地铁之初引发的争议不小，人们最担心的莫过于对地上地下文物古建的影响。所以，仅二号线用于文物保护工程的投资就高达 2500 多万，一边在技术上通过避绕、减震降噪保证明城墙和钟楼安全，一边沿线勘探发掘了一批珍贵的文物。所以，西安地铁宣传词称“穿越历史，感受未来”很是贴切。

In the early stage of the subway construction in Xi'an, there were a lot of controversies. People's biggest concern was how its construction would affect ancient architectures and artifacts above and under the ground. As a result, the investment for the preservation of cultural relics for Line Two alone amounted to over 25 million *yuan*. While adopting up-to-date technologies to reduce the noise and vibration in order to protect the city walls and the Bell Tower, excavation was carried out along the route and a batch of precious artifacts were discovered. The propagation slogan of Xi'an's subway "Run through History and Feel the Future" is a most proper statement.

摄影：王旭东

## 骑行游西安
## Cycling Around Xi'an

“开车太快，走路太慢，骑车刚好。”这是西安许多单车骑友常挂在嘴边的一句话。当下，西安越来越多的单车骑行族，选择在周末或节假日时骑车漫游西安。他们多是事先在论坛上约好，或是选择能欣赏秦岭周边风景的环山线路，或是选择绕城墙一周的环城线路来细品古城美景，这已经成了西安的市民旅游新风尚。

“Driving is too fast; walking is too slow; and cycling is just right.” This is what many cyclers in Xi'an always say. More and more Xi'anese choose to roam the city by bike on weekends and holidays. They usually arrange the trip in advance on online forums. Sometimes it'd be a mountain route where they can enjoy the sceneries near the Qinling Mountains. Sometimes it'd be an urban route around the city wall so that they could discreetly savor the elegance of this ancient city. This has become a new trend of tour among the Xi'anese.

## 微博求婚
## Proposing via Weibo

如果要向自己心爱的人求婚，不妨到西安曲江银泰城商场，只要@商场官方微博，来上一段华丽而又真挚的求婚词，商场微博墙大屏幕就会同步显示。据说每天都有人在这里大胆表白，谁说西安人保守呢?

If you want to propose to your beloved, you might as well come to Intime City Mall in Qujiang New District in Xi'an. Just tag the mall's official Weibo account, post your elegantly written and sincere marriage proposal, and the big screen wall in the mall will display it instantly. It is said that people come here to propose every day. Who has alleged that the Xi'anese are shy and old-fashioned?

**西安城里的国际公寓**
**The International Apartment in Xi'an**

西安城市里最具国际化的地方，就在西安外国语大学的东北角。这里是来自十多个国家的50多名外教生活的地方。美国人的快乐、英国人的严谨、意大利人的浪漫在这里共同交汇。Matt来自美国，中文名叫陈新荣，他说：“小时候在旧金山博物馆见到了四个兵马俑，实在太酷了，所以来中国的时候选择了西安。”

The most internationalized place in Xi'an is at the northeast corner of Xi'an International Studies University, where over 50 foreign teachers from more than 10 counties reside. Here, the optimism of the Americans, the prudence of the British, and the romance of the Italians merge together. Matt, from America whose Chinese name is Chen Xinrong, said, "One day in my childhood I happened to see four terracotta warriors at a museum in San Francisco. They were so cool that I chose Xi'an as my destination when I came to China".

**吃尽天下锅**
**Having All the Hotpots in the World**

动漫明星麦兜名句：“今天吃麻辣火锅，明天吃酸菜鱼火锅，后天吃猪骨头火锅，陈老师直夸我，‘麦兜，你终于找到生命的真谛了’。”见了火锅就走不动道的人，或许可以到西门外的西关正街，找一找“生命的真谛”。这里堪称西安的火锅一条街，数十家全国各地风格的火锅云集于此，保证你吃到“扶墙出”。

McDull, a cartoon character, has a famous line, "I have mouth-numbing spicy hot pot today, fish with pickled vegetables hot pot tomorrow, and pig bone hot pot the day after tomorrow. My teacher Miss Chen complimented me, 'McDull, you have finally found the true meaning of life.'" People who find themselves stopping in front of hot pot restaurants could go seek "the true meaning of life" on Xiguanzheng Street outside the West Gate. On this street, a dozen of hot pot restaurants of different styles across China are clustered, and you will eat much more than you can stand.

**樱花街道**
**The Cherry Blossom Avenue**

位于高新区的高新二路不仅有鳞次栉比的写字楼和住宅楼，两侧人行道300多株樱花树是这条路独一无二的名片。春季沿着樱花大道行走，轻风吹过，花瓣翩翩飘散，或洁白或粉嫩。沐浴在花瓣雨中，那一刻，你会感到“西安最美街道”不是浪得虚名。

On the Second Gaoxin Street in Xi'an's Hi-Tech Industries Development Zone, one can see not only row upon row of office buildings and apartments but also over 300 cherry trees lining the street, which compose a unique scene. In spring, walking along the cherry blossom boulevard, when a breeze brushes by and white and pink petals dance in the air, you'll be bathing in a rain of petals. You'll understand then that this street well deserves the fame of "the most beautiful street in Xi'an".

## 音乐喷泉
## Musical Fountain

在古代，西安有许多世界之最。现代西安亦有诸多“之最”，位于大雁塔的喷泉广场就是其中之一。她的坐凳之多、光带之长、音响组合规模之大都是世界之最。她还是世界首家直引水喷泉，八级迭水池中的八级变频方阵也是世界最大的。

Xi'an ranked the world's top city in many aspects in ancient times. In modern days, Xi'an also tops many lists. The fountain plaza in front of the Giant Wild Goose Pagoda holds many world records. For example, it boasts the most benches and the longest light strings and the first fountain using direct water diversion, and is equipped with the most powerful audio system, in the world. The water from the fountain covers an area of 20 thousand square meters. The eight-level-waterscape fountain is also the largest of its kind.

摄影：王幼健

摄影：徐佳伟

# 印象·讲述

Narratives and Impressions

**第一眼和最后一眼**
The First and the Last Look

在古都西安，最有气势和最具王朝标志的，就算是古城墙了。有人甚至认为，每一个到达和离开西安的人，留在眼里的第一眼和最后一眼，都应该是西安的城墙。

In the ancient capital city Xi'an, the age-old city wall is the most majestic and the most symbolic of Imperial China. Some even believe that the first look everyone takes when arriving at Xi'an and the last look everyone takes when leaving Xi'an is its city wall.

**古古的古城**
An Old Old City

西安市曾面向海内外征集"一句话宣传西安"的广告语。贾平凹给出的一句话最质朴：西安是一座古城，古古的古城。

To respond to the soliciting of one-sentence slogan for the propagation of Xi'an at home and abroad, Jia Pingwa, a famous writer, offered the plainest one: Xi'an is an old city, an old, old city.

摄影：王幼健

**说话口气大**
Arrogant Talk

有网友排座中国十大吹牛城市，西安列第八位。点评是这样说的：西安人，不管他是在街头用三轮车拉货的小贩，还是腰缠万贯的富商，说话的口气总是很大，从来不会轻易认输，他们的优越感不同于北京人、上海人，带着西北独有的强悍气息。

Xi'an ranked eighth on a netizen's list of China's "Top 10 Bluffing Cities". The comment reads: Whether a vendor on his tricycle along the road or a millionaire businessman, the Xi'anese always talks big and never admits defeat. The sense of superiority of the Xi'anese is different from that of the Beijingers or the Shanghainese, for there is a unique toughness of northwestern China in the tone.

**父亲一样的城市**
A City Like a Father

歌手郑钧 18 岁离开西安上大学，彼时的心情如逃离一般，以为可以摆脱"兄代父责"的哥哥棍棒式的家教。但多年后他回忆，西安这个城市像是父亲，弥补了自己从小缺失的父亲角色，同哥哥一样严肃、沉重，给人以压力，但爱也在这个过程中体现。"我血液里流淌的就是羊肉泡馍，你说我还能唱别的歌吗？"

When singer Zheng Jun left Xi'an for college at the age of 18 he felt as if he could finally escape from his elder brother, who had always assumed a father's responsibility and got very strict with him, often resorting to physical punishment. Many years later, however, Xi'an was like a father in his memory, who filled in for the role of a father during his childhood. Solemn and oppressive, Xi'an had put pressure on him the way his brother did, but love found expression right here. "Now that *yangrou paomo* has melted into my blood, how could I sing any other kinds of songs?"

**来西安三天没吃"饭"**
No "Meals" for Three Days in Xi'an

曾经有几位外地的媒体记者来西安采访了几日后感慨道："已经三天没有吃到'饭'了。"西安的东道主以为对客人招呼不周，经几位客人解释后才知道，一些省所谓的"饭"就是指米饭，来西安几天光特色小吃都没有吃重样过，还听说西安的面食种类连吃一个月都吃不全，大米饭在这里根本排不上号。

After several days of interviewing in Xi'an, a couple of out-of-town journalists exclaimed that they "hadn't had proper meals for three days". The host first thought that he failed to treat his guests right, but he learned after listening to the guests' explanation, that in some provinces a "proper meal" must include rice. During their stay, the journalists never even had the same local snack twice. It is said that it takes more than a month to taste all kinds of flour food in Xi'an. Rice can hardly squeeze into the menu.

**撞脸**
Identical Face

著名词人方文山在微博上传了一张跪着的秦兵马俑照片，自嘲与古人撞脸。他配文解释称朋友从西安回来，说秦俑馆有个跪姿俑很像他，起初他并不相信，直到亲眼看到这张照片。因兵马俑右膝盖跪在地上，方文山也不忘调侃，“难怪我右膝多年来一直隐隐作痛”。

Vincent Fang, a famous lyricist, once posted a photo on Weibo, and claimed in a bantering tone that he shared the same face as ancient Chinese. He explained that after returning from Xi'an, his friend claimed a kneeling terracotta warrior looked just like him. He did not believe it until seeing the photo. Since the warrior knelt on his right knee, Fang humored: "No wonder there has been pain in my right knee all these years."

**中国的历史**
The History of China

美国前总统克林顿访华，在解释为何选择西安作为其访华第一站时说：“我觉得，了解一个国家要从了解它的历史开始。”网友则说，中国展示给世界人民的应该是一个彬彬有礼、满腹诗书、端庄优雅的形象，西安是最好的代表。

During his visit to China, former American president Clinton explained why he chose Xi'an as his first stop: "I think the best way to know a country is to start with its history." Netizens agree that the image China presents to the world should be one that is polite, cultivated, intelligent, and elegant, the best representative of which is Xi'an.

**作家地位高**
The Superior Status of Writers

莫言在做客东莞莞城“文化周末大讲坛”时，曾经谈到作家的地位。他说：“我想，拉丁美洲地区作家的地位确实是非常高的，拉美作家的地位，有一点像中国西安作家的地位。在我们中国，作家的地位在西安是最高的。”此话从一个侧面说明了陕西是中国文学的重镇之一。

At a "Weekend Forum on Culture" in Dongguan, Mo Yan spoke of the status of writers in Xi'an: "In Latin America, writers enjoy a high social status, similar to that of writers in Xi'an. Writers are accorded a higher status in Xi'an than in other cities." Evidently, Shaanxi holds a significant position in Chinese literature.

**许巍的歌声里**
In Xu Wei's Singing

西安籍歌手许巍曾经唱道：“我只有两天，一天用来出生，一天用来死亡。”有歌迷解读说：陕西人，就像是一张黑白照片，中间色完全省略。

Xu Wei, a Xi'an-born singer, has these words in one of his songs: "I only have two days, one day to be born, and the other to pass away." A fan reads between the lines: The people of Shaanxi are like a black-and-white photograph; there is no intermediate color."

## 一个字的幸福
## Happiness in One Character

在西安入选最幸福城市的新闻发布会上，贾平凹用“biángbiáng 面”里 60 个笔画的“biáng”字，诠释西安人的幸福概念：一个房子，房子里有人、有车，一边能看见月亮，一边还有卫士保卫着我们的幸福。下边有心宽体胖的“政府”，可发表言论，幸福地坐着车子享受幸福生活。

At the press conference at which Xi'an was voted as one of the happiest cities, Jia Pingwa used the 60-stroke character "biáng" in "biangbiang noodles" to demonstrate the Xi'anese understanding of happiness: there is a house, in which there are people and cars; on one side there is the moon, and on the other a guard protecting our happiness; on the bottom of the character sits a benevolent and tolerant "government". This means the Xi'anese sitting in the car enjoy the freedom of speech and a happy life.

摄影：冯炜

**马飞的歌**
Ma Fei's Song

西安乐手马飞用一口纯正的长安口音唱道：“骑着车子来到长安县，来上一个大碗的岐山面……”简单几个场景就勾勒出长安人几千年来都过着这种悠闲的生活。听过歌的人先是被歌里土得掉渣的长安话逗笑，然后又会勾起浓浓的乡愁。当然，唯一需要纠正的是，长安县（区）的姑娘并不像他歌中唱的那样不好看。

In authentic Chang'an accent, Ma Fei, a local singer, sang: "I got to Chang'an County by bicycle, and ordered a huge bowl of Qishan noodles..." With these simple words, he conjured up the laidback lifestyle the locals have enjoyed for thousands of years. Hillbilly and amusing, the Chang'an dialect would evoke a wave of nostalgia. The local girls, however, aren't as ugly as he described in the song.

**“古墓派”弟子**
Followers of the "Ancient Tomb Sect"

“上课如上坟”虽是学生调侃的一句戏言，但在西安却是实情。最近西安科技大学修操场时，就发现了一座古墓，再次印证“在西安随便挖一铲子，便能挖出个古墓来”。而在这之前，西北政法、西安交大等学校也都挖出过规格不同的秦汉唐古墓，难怪西安的大学生在毕业的时候都会说自己是“古墓派”弟子。

"Going to class is like visiting a grave yard" is only a common joke among students, but in a way reflects the true situation in Xi'an. Recently, when Xi'an University of Science and Technology was renovating its sports ground, an ancient tomb was discovered, serving as another piece of evidence of the saying that "Any casual dig may result in a fresh discovery of an ancient tomb". Prior to this, ancient tombs of various scales from the Qin, Han, and Tang dynasties had been unearthed in Northwest University of Political Science and Law and Xi'an Jiaotong University as well. No wonder Xi'an college graduates refer to themselves as followers of the "Ancient Tomb Sect".

**春如四季**
Spring like Weather All Year Round

说到西安的气候，网友一句最经典的总结是“昆明四季如春，咱西安是春如四季”。虽然夸张，但也道出了西安的实情。打开西安人的衣柜，几乎找不到春秋两季的衣服，从穿短袖到穿棉服常常只在一周内就完成过渡。而这样的气候也造就了西安人的性格，要么热要么冷，从不拖泥带水，非常干脆、直爽。

A classic description of the climate of Xi'an, courtesy of netizens, is "the weather in Kunming is like spring all year round, but the weather of spring in our Xi'an embraces all the four seasons of the year". Somewhat exaggerated as it is, it reflects the real situation. In a Xi'anese wardrobe you can hardly find any clothes suitable for spring or autumn. The transition from wearing short-sleeved shirts to cotton-padded coats often takes place within a week. This climate has also shaped the Xi'anese' personality: either hot or cold, but never lukewarm, decisive and straightforward, but never sloppy.

**乡音**
**The Native Accent**

听朋友讲过一个真实故事：上世纪80年代末，一位暮年到了美国的陕西籍台湾老兵，临终前连日合不上眼。后来，一名同乡去探望，病榻前用乡音唱了一句秦腔，老兵便断气正寝了。乡音，实际上是同乡同族间的一丝羁绊，也是濡染着感情汁水的一缕牵挂。

A friend once told me a true story: In the late 1980s, a Taiwanese veteran originally from Shaanxi wouldn't close his eyes on his deathbed in the U.S. It so happened that a friend from his hometown visited him, and sang a line from the Qinqiang opera. It was the hometown tune that helped the veteran depart this life peacefully. Drenched in sentiment and nostalgia, the native accent serves as a special bond between country fellows, kins, etc.

**钟楼**
**The Bell Tower**

"倘若没有钟楼，西安城就像一桌麻将。四座城楼对视对坐，坐看花开花落，坐看风生云起。城池里面无处不在喧响，哗啦哗啦的。"——西安作家鹤坪《围着钟楼转的西安人》

"Without the Bell Tower, Xi'an would look like a table of mahjong. The four city towers sit facing each other, watching flowers blossom and wither, winds blow and clouds float. Inside the city, bustling sounds can be heard in every corner, like the sound of mahjong tiles hitting against each other." ——"Xi'anese Circling Around the Bell Tower" by He Ping, an author from Xi'an.

摄影：翟小雪

### 回到唐朝
### Back to the Tang Dynasty

穿越剧流行的今天，若有人问你愿意生活在历史上的哪个时代，你会怎么说？作家潘向黎的答案是："唐朝！当然是唐朝。"而且在她的想象中，自己不是做雍容华贵的宫廷美人，而是做咸阳塬上的游侠少年，"饮酒纵马，放荡不羁，才能和那个时代的雄浑开阔相称"。

If someone asks you which dynasty you'd like to live in, what's your answer? The answer of Pan Xiangli, a famous female writer, was "The Tang Dynasty! Definitely the Tang Dynasty." In her imagination, instead of an elegant and graceful court lady, she would like to become a ranger roaming the Xianyang Terrace. "To suit to that glorious dynasty, I would live an unrestrained life, drinking uninhibitedly and riding horse wildly."

### 说陕西话的"米五斗"
### A German Who Speaks the Shaanxi Dialect

"不为五斗米折腰"，德国人米五斗的名字就取自陶渊明的这句诗。这位在西安生活了 8 年的陕西女婿，能说一口地道的陕西话，他说："我的一位中文老师，在北京研究甲骨文，他就给我说，你要是想明白中国文化，就学习陕西话。喜欢古诗词的他认为读李白的唐诗，也一定要用陕西话。"

A German named himself "Five Dou of Rice" after a poem by Tao Yuanming (365 - 427), "I won't kowtow for five *dou* of rice". Now son-in-law of a Shaanxier. He has lived in Xi'an for eight years, and speaks fluent Shaanxi dialect. He says: "My Chinese teacher, an oracle bones researcher in Beijing, once told me that if I want to understand Chinese culture, I need to learn Shaanxi dialect. A fan of ancient Chinese poetry and culture, the teacher also believes that Li Bai's poems should be recited in Shaanxi dialect."

摄影：翟小雪

**"治愈系"城市**
A "Healing" City

20 世纪末，一种名为"治愈系"的音乐开始在日本流行。从此"治愈系"成为舒缓压力抚慰身心的泛称。有位资深导游说，当你对风光景色熟视无睹、对民俗小吃如数家珍，失去了所有新鲜感，城市对你的唯一吸引，就是无异于当地人的那份舒缓和宽和。西安，就是这样的"治愈系"城市。

A type of music called "healing music" started gaining popularity in Japan at the end of the 20th century. Since then, the word "healing" has extended to refer to anything that relieves pressure and conciliates the soul. An experienced tourist guide once explained that when you have seen all the beautiful sceneries and landscapes, and tasted all kinds of ethnic cuisine, the only thing in a city that attracts you is the gentleness and the inclusiveness of the locals. Xi'an is such a "healing" city.

**读书人的情结**
The Literati's Obsession

诗人余光中曾在诗作《寻李白》中写道："酒入豪肠，七分酿成了月光，余下的三分啸成了剑气，秀口一吐就是半个盛唐。"2012 年，来到西安的余光中感慨："长安是天下读书人的一个情结，只要想到长安，就会想到朝廷、庙堂、君王、国运。我对这里的历史充满敬畏，这里满足了我对中国文化内心的憧憬。"

Poet Yu Guangzhong wrote in his poem "In Search of Li Bai": "As wine flows into the bold and exuberant soul, 70 percent is distilled into the moonlight, the remaining 30 percent is forged into a sword's spirit. A single utterance reveals half the prosperity of the Tang Dynasty." When he arrived in Xi'an in 2012, Yu was moved: "Chang'an is an obsession to all literati in China. The mere thought of it brings up images of the imperial courts, temples, emperors, and the fate of the nation. I am filled with awe in regard to its history, which quenches my thirst for traditional Chinese culture."

**古物中心**
A Center of Ancient Artifacts

清末民初是西方人前往西安较集中的时期，外国传教士、医生、商人、探险家等在此活动，留下不少文字史料。美国旅行家、地理学家威廉·埃德加·盖洛 1911 年游历西安后，在其《中国十八省会》中赞誉说："西安及其附近地区浓缩了中国的历史，一位古文物收藏家很难找到比它更好的古物中心了。"

From the end of the Qing Dynasty to the early days of the Republic of China, foreigners, including missionaries, doctors, businessmen, and explorers, flooded to Xi'an and left many historic documents. William Edgar Geil, a famous American explorer and geographer, praised Xi'an in his *Eighteen Capitals of China* after he visited the city in 1911: "The history of China is condensed in Xi'an and its surrounding area. There is no better ancient artifacts center for a collector than Xi'an."

摄影：王旭东　李念

**张朝阳的习惯**

An Internet Baron's Habits

搜狐老总张朝阳是地道西安人，他在一次接受采访时说，小时候成长的环境，是黄土地与蓝天，不是喧嚣的尘世。色调、景物、声音都比较单调，因此潜意识里的许多东西就是不动的、不变的。面对不善变的一切，自己养成了对本质、本源深刻追求的习惯。

Charles Zhang, CEO of Sohu Inc., a Xi'anese, once recalled in an interview that the environment in which he grew up was a paradise of yellow earth and blue sky, free of worldly chaos. Since the colors, sceneries and sounds were pure, he naturally believed that all things were timeless and perpetual. The seemingly unchanging environment has helped him to develop a habit of seeking the nature of things.

**罗大佑眼中的西安**

Xi'an in Lo Ta-yu's Eyes

罗大佑：假如说龙是中国的象征，西安应该就是龙的心吧！这百闻不如一见的古都给我最强烈的印象是——它重击到你心灵深处的神秘力量，都是看不到的；你必须亲临现场踏上斯土，才会感受到。历史，不在西安的土地上，而是在地下，或空气中。你看不到它，却被它强烈地摇晃着。

Musician Lo Ta-yu said, "If the dragon is the symbol of China, Xi'an should be the dragon's heart! My strongest impression of this legendary ancient city was the invisible and mysterious power that rocks the soul. You could never perceive it without stepping on the soil. History is not on the surface, but in the earth and in the air. You cannot see it, but it moves you strongly".

**茅坡国际**

Maopo International

城南大学城的崛起，离不开周边的乡村。高校学府与乡土农村两种文化形态从碰撞走向交融，彼此难舍难分。就像陕师大旁的茅坡村，被称作 MPI（Maopo International）。这里有小摊的烤面筋、臭豆腐，有乱糟糟的二手书店，有成堆的小旅社，飘散出涩涩的青春。

The rise of the university district in the southern part of Xi'an couldn't have happened without the neighboring villages. The two different cultures of universities and of rural areas first clashed, and then harmoniously merged, and have become inseparable. For example, Maopo Village beside the Shaanxi Normal University is jokingly referred to as "Maopo International". There are street stands of barbequed gluten, stinky tofu, messy second-hand bookstores and a number of hotels. Everything has a tinge of budding youth.

摄影：翟小雪

### “泡”在泡馍馆
### Hanging Around in *Paomo* Restaurants

在外人眼里，西安人性子急，做事风风火火。但在吃泡馍时，讲究的西安人会仔仔细细地慢慢掰馍。在他们看来，掰馍是对待美食的一种态度。小小两个馍，他们要耗费个把小时掰碎，“杰作”完工时，似乎还会有几分成就感。即使再急，进了泡馍馆，怎么也要泡上一两个小时。

Nonlocals think that the Xi'anese are so impetuous that they always act hastily. Yet when they eat *paomo*, they shred the cake in a particularly slow fashion. For them, cake shredding shows their serious attitude toward the delicacy. They spend nearly an hour tearing two cakes into small pieces. When the “masterpiece” is finished, they even feel a sense of achievement. No matter how much of a hurry they are in, they will spend one or two hours in a *paomo* restaurant.

### 西安作家的特色
### Local Color Writers

“巴蜀鬼才”魏明伦曾多次来西安。谈及陕西作家，魏明伦总结了两点：一是都不讲普通话，比如陈忠实、贾平凹等，个个都是一口“秦腔”；二是个个能写一手漂亮的毛笔字，用魏明伦的话说，“这在全国其他省份是没有的”。

Wei Minglun, a Sichuan-based genius playwright who has visited Xi'an several times, drew two conclusions regarding Shaanxi writers. Firstly, none of them speaks mandarin Chinese. Writers like Chen Zhongshi and Jia Pingwa all have a heavy accent. Secondly, every writer knows calligraphy. According to Wei: “Such talent is not so readily found in writers in any other provinces.”

**愈夜愈美丽**

The Charm of the Night

有人说，到西安不可错过的一件事就是要“沉浸在迷惑而内敛的西安夜色中”。“斑驳的古城墙上挂满了红灯笼，有着久远历史的建筑在现代灯光映射下焕发了青春。在夜色中走入西安，你会看到一个不一样的西安。”西安的许多景点都会在晚上绽放更迷人的色彩，像钟鼓楼、大雁塔及音乐喷泉、大唐芙蓉园……

It is said that one must-do in Xi'an is to "immerse yourself in the enchanting yet unassuming night". "With red lanterns hung around, the city wall, ancient and mottled, radiates the vigor of youth in the modern lights. Walking into the city in the evening, you will see a different Xi'an." Many of the sights are much more enthralling at night, like the Bell and Drum Towers, the Giant Wild Goose Pagoda and its musical fountain, the Tang Paradise of Lotus and so on.

**打“飞的”吃小吃**

Take a Plane for Snacks

郭达说，在北京和老乡聚在一起，谈论最多的话题就是哪里的面好吃，如果谁发现了好的面馆，一群人就开着车去吃，每次都是这样，乐此不疲。歌手郑钧更为夸张，他说自己经常会出现这样的情况：每当想起西安的小吃，想得厉害，就会不顾一切地飞回西安，吃够了小吃，再飞回北京。

Guo Da, a successful actor, says that whenever he and other fellow Xi'anese get together in Beijing, the topic they discuss the most is which restaurant serves good noodles. Every time someone discovers a good place, they drive there together, never seems to be tired of the activity. Zheng Jun, a talented singer, is crazier. Zheng says whenever he misses Xi'an snacks, he flies back to Xi'an. Only when he has had enough would he fly back to Beijing.

**城墙赏月夜**

The Moon over the City Wall

海边之明月，使人欲仙；山上之明月，使人高洁；草原之明月，使人眷恋。这些地方赏明月，固然各有其妙，但作家朱鸿却独爱城墙赏月夜：月光之下，“仰观白星远芒，俯察青砖古色”；“脚下有历史，四边有人类”。在他看来，“城墙上的明月，是兼容了宇宙泱茫与尘世温暖的”。

The bright moon by the sea makes one feel like a god. The moon on the mountain makes one feel noble, and the moon on the prairie makes one feel nostalgic for it. When gazing the moon, your feelings vary with contexts. Yet writer Zhu Hong prefers the city wall because in the moonlight "silver stars shine overhead and grey bricks emanate ancient colors down below". "Under the feet lies history while humanity abound". Zhu believes that "the bright moon over the city wall blends both the infinity of the universe and the warmth of this world".

## 走城墙

### Walking along the City Wall

有资深“驴友”在洋洋洒洒上万字的西安游记中写道：如果有一天你能去西安，那么千万请你去走一走这座古城的城墙。已经没几座有完整城墙的都市了，幸好还有西安城墙，值得我们在清晨黄昏的时候，去行走，去驻足，去用心聆听，去收获一些在都市中永远无法收获的东西。

In a 10,000-word Xi'an travel notes, an experienced backpacker wrote, "If you get to visit Xi'an one day, please remember to take a walk on the ancient city wall. It is hard for you to find such well-preserved city walls elsewhere. Lucky for you, Xi'an city walls are still there. At dawn or dusk, you can take walks, stop and ponder, listen intently and attain what you could never get in a metropolitan area.

摄影：尚洪涛

**一个外国人眼中的陕西人**

Shaanxi People Through a Foreigner's Eyes

尼克尔斯在《穿越神秘的陕西》中这样描述陕西人：陕西人更为达观冷静、富有思想，并且热爱学问，有着温文尔雅的正义感。陕西人对自己的传统了然于胸、引以为豪，喜欢谈论伏羲时代的事件，仿佛就发生在昨天。说起本国的历史，他们很少提到最近1500年来发生的事情。

In *Through Hidden Shensi*, Francis Nichols described Shaanxi people thus: Shaanxi inhabitants are more open-minded, calmer, and more intelligent. They share a love for knowledge, as well as a gentle understanding of justice. They are familiar with and proud of their tradition. They like to talk about events from the Era of Fuxi (a legendary Chinese ruler who taught people how to fish, hunt, and raise livestock) as if they happened only yesterday. When they discuss China's history, they rarely bring up things that happened over the recent 1,500 years.

**本真的秦腔**

Soulful Qinqiang Opera

学者蒋勋生于西安，长于台湾。80年代末，回到西安的蒋勋无意中在城墙下听到一对盲人夫妇唱秦腔，汉唐盛世的故事瞬间在裂帛一样的唱腔中直上九霄，一旁的蒋勋泪流满面。蒋勋说，那种悲怆的感觉太强烈，有太多的撞击在里面。心慌意乱是没有办法把最美的部分呈现出来的，内容可以伪善，但声音骗不了人。

Chiang Hsun, a scholar in aesthetics, was born in Xi'an and grew up in Taiwan. In the late 1980s, back to Xi'an, Chiang accidentally heard a blind couple singing Qinqiang opera by the city wall. The sonata about the heyday of the Han and Tang dynasties reached up to the sky, and Chiang was moved to tears. The tragic sensation was so overwhelming that as to hit him close to heart. A troubled state of mind would deter a singer from presenting the most beautiful aspect of a piece. Lyrics can be pretentious, but the voice tricks no one.

**伙计们喊你回西安**

A Call Back to Xi'an

“拍张照片发个微博，中午又吃炸酱面，面里没有油泼辣子……”《回西安》，这首北漂创作的歌勾起了集体回忆，最后那句“回西安吧，北京有啥好”更是戳中泪点。网络上立现神回应：“额也想回去，早晨吃俩肉夹馍，中午咥碗泡馍，黑了咥碗燃面。神仙日子也奏是这样子过！”

“Take a picture and post it on Weibo. Eat Beijing-style noodles at noon again, and there's no spices...” The song about the life of drifters in Beijing, *Return to Xi'an*, aroused some collective nostalgia. The last line “Let's return to Xi'an; what's so great about Beijing?” moved many to tears. A great response online read, “I want to go back, too. Eat two *roujiamo* in the morning; devour a bowl of *paomo* at noon, and then a bowl of Shaanxi noodles in the evening. This is the most wonderful life!”

**搬到西安去浪漫**
Move to Xi'an for Romance

2010年，一则名为《假如在西安拥有爱情》的网帖走红网络。大雁塔音乐喷泉、回民街泡馍、德福巷酒吧、青龙寺樱花……这些西安人再熟悉不过的地方，都出现在网帖所描绘的爱情故事里，是那么的浪漫。以至于有网友大呼在西安生活很惬意，更有网友直言"要搬到西安去感受浪漫"。

In 2010, an online post titled "If You Had Love in Xi'an" went viral. The musical fountain at the Giant Wild Goose Pagoda, the *paomo* on Muslin Street, the bars on Defu Alley, and the cherry blossoms in Qinglong Temple... These places that the Xi'anese couldn't be more familiar with all made their way into the post. The story was so romantic that some netizens cried out how comfortable it is living in Xi'an, and some even declared that they would "move to Xi'an for romance".

**骑行赏景**
Sightseeing by Bike

放慢旅行的节奏，骑自行车漫游城市街巷，或许你会看到更细致的风景。骑行西安有不同主题的线路：赏花踏青线（交大—兴庆宫公园—植物园—杜陵）、穿越历史线（陕西历史博物馆—大雁塔—大唐芙蓉园—曲江池）、红色主题骑行线路（张学良公馆—碑林—书院门—八路军办事处—止园）等。

Slow down the pace of your travels and roam the city streets by bike, and then perhaps you'll see sceneries in detail. Bike tours in Xi'an boast different themes: the flower appreciation route covers Jiaotong University, Xingqing Palace Park, Botany Garden and Du Mausoleum. The history route includes the Shaanxi History Museum, the Giant Wild Goose Pagoda, the Tang Paradise of Lotus and Qujiang Lake. The recent history route: the Former Residence of General Zhang Xueliang, the Stele Forest Museum, the Academy Gate, the Eighth Route Army Xi'an Office and General Yang Hucheng's former residence, Zhiyuan Garden.

**最柔软的时光**
Romantic Moments

网友说，即使如西安这样沧桑的城市也有柔情的一面：一、在大雁塔徜徉；二、在大唐西市感受风情；三、和恋人漫步南湖；四、城墙上放风筝；五、环城公园观四季；六、大唐通易坊享下午茶；七、傍晚登钟鼓楼；八、在未央湖烧烤；九、在白鹿原登高望远；十、欣赏兴庆湖畔倒影。你心中最柔软的时光是什么？

Netizens say, though Xi'an is so weathered, you will enjoy some romantic moments: 1. Strolling at the Giant Wild Goose Pagoda; 2. Sightseeing at the Tang Dynasty West Market; 3. Roaming around South Lake with your beloved one; 4. Flying kites on the city wall; 5. Watch the four seasons pass in City Wall Park; 6. Sipping afternoon tea at Datang Tongyifang; 7. Climbing the Bell and Drum Towers at dusk; 8. Barbequing by Weiyang Lake; 9. Ascending the White Deer Plain for a distant view; 10. Appreciating the reflections in Xingqing Lake. What do you think your romantic moment should be like?

**怀古幽思**
Nostalgia for the Past

西安是美食之都，但作家马伯庸却说，去其他城市，第一反应就是找美食，唯独到西安后，思绪根本无法旁骛，完全被密密麻麻的怀古幽思所填满。一想到自己和那么多历史和传说在空间上重叠，就有种深切的沉静弥漫四周。

Xi'an is a paradise of cuisines. Yet Ma Boyong, a famous writer, says that although the first thing he does when he arrives in other cities is to look for delicious food, when he arrives in Xi'an, his mind is so occupied by an overwhelming amount of nostalgia for the past that he could think of nothing else. The thought of him being in a place where so many historic events and legends took place evokes a sense of profound tranquility.

**千人千面兵马俑**
Each Terracotta Warrior is Unique

演员张嘉译小时候听老师说兵马俑一人一个样，没有重样的。上北影之后听老师讲个性化形象塑造，脑子里就浮现出千人千面的兵马俑。放假回家又去看兵马俑，趴在栏杆上，一看大半天。"先人们两千多年前就懂得塑造人物要有区别、不能雷同。演戏时，我对近似的角色也努力演出不同的地方。"

When Zhang Jiayi, a noted actor, was little, his teacher said that each terracotta warrior looked unique. Later on when he took a class on personalizing characters at the Beijing Film Academy, he thought of the terracotta warriors immediately. On the holiday, he went to see the Terracotta Army back home. Leaning against the bar and staring long at the clay figures, he pondered: "Over 2,000 years ago, our ancestors already knew that when portraying an image, there should be differentiation, and none should be identical. When acting, I also try to give different interpretations to similar characters."

摄影：王旭东

## 靠着城墙发会儿呆

## Daydreaming Against the City Wall

贾平凹说，在全世界的范围内最具古城魅力的，也只有西安了。它的城墙赫然完整，独身站定在护城河上的吊板桥上，仰观那城楼、角楼、女墙垛口，再怯弱的人也要豪情长啸了。而在众多网友心中，靠着城墙发会儿呆，十足的文艺范儿。

According to Jia Pingwa, a famous writer, Xi'an is a city of the greatest ancient charm in the world. The city wall is complete and well preserved. Standing alone on the drawbridge over the moat, looking up at the gate tower, turret and crenels, the most timid man will be compelled to give a shout. To many netizens, daydreaming against the city wall is artsy enough.

摄影：王幼健

摄影：翟小雪

**这城市那么重**
A City So Rich

对于台湾当代作家白先勇来说，西安是他多年的梦。因为年轻时念诗词，读史书，里面都会提到渭水、终南山这些地理名词，他一直很向往。来之前，白先勇称，“西安，一直是文学的想象。”亲临这座古城后，他觉得圆了自己的一个梦，但称这座城市太重，不能轻易去写。

To Pai Hsien-yung, a contemporary Taiwanese writer, Xi’an has been in his dream for many years. When he was young, he often came across such geographic terms as the Wei River and the Zhongnan Mountains in his history and poetry books. He had always longed for them. Before he visited the city, Pai said, “Xi’an has always been a literary image.” After he finally came to this ancient city, he felt that his dream was fulfilled. Yet this city is so rich that it shouldn’t be rashly written about.

**下一站，西安**
Next Stop, Xi’an

“我要离开北京啦！工作已辞啦，房子已卖啦！下一站，西安。”网友@花无影 微博上的一通告白被转发两万多次。他称要换个城市，不那么拥挤，不那么现实，有文化背景，有 IT 环境，空气不潮湿，冬天有暖气。最后西安胜出！他说：卖了北京的房，可在西安搞定一住宅三公寓，出租月入五千，还工作个辣子！

“I'm leaving Beijing! I’ve already quit my job and sold my apartment! Next stop: Xi’an.” An announcement on Weibo was reposted over 20,000 times. The netizen was determined to move to another city, not so crowded, not so materialistic, not so humid, with rich cultural heritage, an ideal environment for IT, and heating in the winter. Well, Xi’an turned out to be the winner! He exclaimed, “Having sold my apartment in Beijing, I could get a house and three apartments in Xi’an. In other words I’ll get 5,000 *yuan* in rent per month. Why still work!”

**嗅到台北特质**
A Reminder of Taipei

台湾一家报纸曾刊载一篇题为《嗅到台北特质》的文章称赞西安公交。来自台北的作者描述说：很难想象能在西安市坐到童年时期的“普通公交车”，可以打开车窗，让徐徐的微风吹在脸上……友善的西安公交车有台北特质，乘客有礼貌地让座……车掌的亲切报站与司机的敬业精神，抚慰了一个彷徨的旅人内心的一角。

An article titled “A Reminder of Taipei” in a Taiwanese newspaper once praised the buses in Xi’an by saying, “I could hardly imagine taking the ‘bus’ from my childhood in Xi’an. With the windows open, a faint breeze fondled my face... I noticed the friendly Taipei characteristic on buses in Xi’an: passengers give up their seat for seniors... The conductor’s amiable stop announcements and the driver’s professionalism consoled a traveler’s heart.”

摄影：阮班慧

# 逸闻·趣谈

Tales and Anecdotes

### 微西安
### Microblogs About Xi'an

微时代，了解一个城市不妨从 @ 开始。除了政务微博、媒体微博、名人微博外，草根微博不可或缺。看城市动态，@ 在西安 ；看历史掌故，@ 寻找老西安 ；身为吃货，一定别忘了 @ 老妖带你吃西安 。就算你什么都不想看，只想感受来自远古的声息，也可以 @ 古城钟楼 ，听他每个整点为你“铛、铛、铛……”报时。

In the era of microblogging, Weibo, a Chinese version of Twitter, might be the best way to know a city. Aside from government accounts, media accounts and celebrity accounts, grass-roots accounts cannot be missed. To keep up to date with the city, you'd better follow "In Xi'an". For historical anecdotes, you should follow "In Search of Old Xi'an". As a foodie, you should not miss "Visit the Eateries in Xi'an with Laoyao". If you are interested in nothing but the echo from ancient times, you could just follow the "The Ancient Bell Tower". You can hear it ringing the bells for you on the hour.

### 您对西安有几分熟？
### How Familiar Are You with Xi'an?

要想判断一个人对西安有几分熟？有网友调侃说，只听一句话就能听出来。“哎，钟楼在哪儿呢？”这是刚到西安的外地人，一分熟。“走，逛小寨去。”这是到西安一年的外地大学生，五分熟。“来碗凉皮，再来瓶冰峰，嫽咋咧！对了，再加个肉夹馍。”这是深得西安美食精髓的西安娃，全熟。

To tell how familiar someone is with Xi'an, a netizen said jokingly that it only takes one sentence. "Hey, where is the Bell Tower?" This must be a question asked by someone totally new. "Let's go hang out in Xiaozhai." That must be an out-of-town college student who has just been in Xi'an for a year. "A bowl of *liangpi* (cold noodles), and a bottle of Ice Peak soda, wonderful! Wait, and a *roujiamo* please." That must be a Xi'anese who gets the essence of Xi'an cuisine.

### 吃不胖的肉夹馍
### Never Get Fat on *Roujiamo*

贾平凹讲过一则肉夹馍趣闻：有上海女子来西安，束腰节食要苗条不要命，在一家店铺前踌躇半晌却不敢吃。店主明白，大口咬嚼，满嘴流油，说：“我家经营腊汁肉三代，我每日六个肉夹馍吃过五十年，你瞧我胖不堆肉，瘦不露骨。”女子连走了八十家店铺，见卖主个个干练，遂大开牙戒。

Jia Pingwa once told an anecdote about *roujiamo*: A Shanghai girl came to Xi'an. She was such a dieter that she would give anything for a slim waist. She had been hesitating in front of a restaurant for a long time without the guts to have one. The owner understood at once, took a big greasy bite, and assured her: "My family has been in this business for three generations. I've lived on six *roujiamos* a day for 50 years. Yet look at me, there is no excess fat on my body, nor am I bone skinny." After checking 80 restaurants, whose owners are all in good shape, she finally decided to break her diet.

**"没文化"**
**Lacking Culture**

陕西人鄙视别人的欠缺时常说"没文化"，而不论别人欠缺什么，哪怕他只是不知道羊肉泡馍的吃法。

Ignorance of any kind is often described as "lacking culture" in Shaanxi, even if it is about an improper way to eat *yangrou paomo*.

**三震三合**
**Three Quakes and Three Recoveries**

1300 多年间，小雁塔历经十多次地震，其中"三震三合"完好无毁是最广为人知的传奇。1965 年，在修复小雁塔时，专家揭开了谜团，原来古代工匠根据西安地质，特意将塔基用夯土筑成一个半圆球体，如同一口"大锅"，使得屹立于"锅"上的塔身受震后压力能均匀分散，就像一个"不倒翁"。

Throughout its 1300-year history, the Small Wild Goose Pagoda has survived over 10 earthquakes, three of which found the pagoda cracked and soon closed again. During a 1965 renovation, experts unraveled the mystery: Ancient architects built the pagoda's base into a hemisphere in the shape of a gigantic wok, thus distributing the weight of the pagoda evenly and rendering the structure like a roly-poly toy.

摄影：翟小雪

摄影：张宇明

**碑字少一撇**

The Missing Stroke

林则徐生前曾三次踏上西安的土地，一次是在被流放途中路过留居，另有两度在西安任职。如今在西安碑林，还留有他的两处墨宝。传说“碑林”两字是林则徐所写，因当时被皇帝罢了官，故“碑”字少写了一撇，就像那丢了的乌纱帽。

Lin Zexu (1785 - 1850), an official of the Qing Dynasty, went to Xi'an three times. Once, he sojourned there when sent exiled; the other two times, he held office. Two of his calligraphic works are still found in the Beilin Museum. Legend has it that it was Lin who wrote the two characters “碑林” (*beilin*, Stele Forest). The missing stroke in the first character has been held to imply that he was removed from his position.

**“邪”得很**

Somewhat “Supernatural”

不少人都发现，西安这地方“邪”得很。往往前一秒你还在想着一个朋友，后一秒他的电话就打过来了。刚和别人聊到哪位朋友，转眼就能和他打个照面。西安人习惯开玩笑这么解释：那是脚底下的先人们在听着呢！在西安，可别随便在背地说人坏话。

Many people find Xi'an somewhat “supernatural”. One second you are thinking of a friend, and the next second he calls. A friend who has just come up in a conversation may suddenly show up around the next corner. It is a standing joke that the ancestors buried beneath our feet are listening! So in Xi'an, don't speak ill of anyone behind their back.

**“北京时间”来自西安**
**"Beijing Time" from Xi'an**

全国人民都遵守的“北京时间”原来并不诞生在北京，而是来自西安临潼的中科院国家授时中心。这里承担着北京时间的“守时”工作，即通过原子钟系统，来保持和比对标准时间的产生。接下来，这个时间还必须由位于蒲城的国家授时中心二部（原陕西省天文台）通过无线电波发播到全国各地，这就是“授时”。

The “Beijing time” that the whole nation abides by is not generated in Beijing, but in the National Time Service Center (NTSC) of Chinese Academy of Sciences in Lintong, Xi’an. This institute is responsible for keeping the Beijing Time via the atomic clock, which tracks and compares standard times. Then, the national standard time is transmitted across the nation from the NTSC base in Pucheng (formerly Shaanxi Astronomical Observatory). This is time service.

**里根到兵马俑“拍马屁”**
**Reagan Buttering China's Butt**

1984 年，作为中美两国建交以来第一位访华的美国在职总统，里根被特许下到兵马俑坑底参观。在得到允许后，里根伸手轻拍了一下马俑的屁股，并在离开时幽默地冲着兵马俑喊了声“解散”。事后一位记者在报道这条新闻时附上的标题是“里根总统拍中国的马屁”。

In 1984, as the first sitting president to visit China since the re-establishment of Sino-American relationship, Mr. Reagan was given special permission to get into a pit for an intimate contact with the terracotta warriors. He gently tapped a terracotta horse’s butt. Before departure he humorously shouted to the terracotta army: “Dismiss!” Later, a news report emerged with the title “President Reagan buttered China’s butt”.

**爱情其实很简单**
**Love Is Simple**

作为陕师大物理系的师兄妹，李祥生和姚世瑗已经牵手相爱近半个世纪。几年前李老生病，只能坐轮椅，而姚奶奶除了照顾他的起居外还会在天气好的时候陪老伴儿打乒乓球。他们在夕阳下打球的照片在网络上感动了无数人，但姚奶奶却说：“牵了手，就要走完一生。你照顾我，我照顾你，这不是应该的吗？”

Schoolmates at Shaanxi Normal University’s Physics Department, Li Xiangsheng and Yao Shiyuan have been in love for nearly half a century. When Li fell sick and was confined to a wheelchair several years ago, not only did Yao take up his daily caring, she also played ping pong with him on fine days. Photos of them playing ping pong in the setting sun moved many netizens, but granny Yao merely replied: “Once you get hitched, you should walk through a lifetime together. Isn’t it appropriate to take care of each other?”

**“东西”的来历**

The Origin of "Dongxi"

相传东汉时，洛阳和长安是当时商业繁华的城市，洛阳被称为“东京”，长安被称为“西京”。有人到东京、西京购物，就说“买东”或“买西”。还有一种说法，公元7世纪初，长安城内的东市和西市，是两大商业中心，也是当时朝廷指定的商品交易场所，人们购物都要到这两个地方，因此有了“买东西”。

During the Eastern Han Dynasty, Luoyang and Chang'an were the most prosperous cities: Luoyang was called "Dongjing" (the eastern capital), and Chang'an "Xijing" (the western capital). Shopping at either would be described as "buying East" or "buying West". Another story about the origin of the phrase "*maidongxi*" (to buy things) is that in the early 7th century, the East Market and West Market were two major commercial centers in Chang'an, and also major fairs designated by the state. Whenever people shopped, they came to the two venues, thus the term "*maidongxi*".

**过去和现在的爱情**

Love: Past VS. Present

传说王宝钏与薛平贵的爱情见证地寒窑就在西安曲江池。相传王宝钏是唐朝宰相的女儿，却执意嫁给一贫如洗的流浪汉薛平贵。后薛平贵从戎，王宝钏独守寒窑等夫十八年，直到薛平贵回乡。现如今，网友说：“别说十八年，现在能有个人愿意等你十八个月，已经证明他（她）是相当地把你放心上了。”

Legend has it that the romance of Wang Baochuan and Xue Pinggui happened at the Humble Cave by Qujiang Lake. Wang Baochuan, a daughter of a Tang Dynasty premier, insisted on marrying Xue Pinggui, a destitute scholar. More strikingly, Wang waited for Xue faithfully during his 18-year-long military service. A netizen commented: "Today if someone waits for you for 18 months, let alone 18 years, you matter to him or her tremendously."

**天秤座的城市**

A Libra City

有网友说：“高原圣域的拉萨是神秘的天蝎座；四季如春的昆明是不喜变化的金牛座……中国地理版图中心点的西安，正好属于不偏不倚的天秤座。”什么？西安是中国的中心？北纬34° 32′ 27″，东经108° 55′ 25″，中国大地原点位于西安以北30多公里的泾阳县永乐镇。中国的中心就在这里。

A netizen once said, "Lhasa on the Tibetan Plateau is a mysterious Scorpius. Kunming, the city of spring, is a Taurus that is unwilling to change... Xi'an, the center of China, is a Libra straight and square." Wait, Xi'an is the center of China? Coordinates for the geographic center of China indeed falls 30 kilometers north of Xi'an at Yongle Town, Jingyang County: N34°32'27", E108°55'25"". That is where China's center is.

**成龙“偷”了一瓶土**

**Jackie Chan “Stole” a Bottle of Earth**

成龙在拍摄电影《神话》时，曾在西安获准进入临潼秦始皇陵兵马俑的一号坑实地拍摄。完成拍摄后，成龙却不舍得离开，忍不住“偷”回了坑里的一小瓶土。他这样解释自己的举动：“这样我带回家里，还是感到能真切地接触到每一个兵马俑。”

When Jackie Chan was filming *The Myth*, the crew were permitted to shoot part of the Terracotta Army in Qinshihuang mausoleum. After the location shoot, Jackie could hardly tear himself away from the scene and he couldn't help "stealing" a small bottle of earth in the pit. He explained, "The earth I took home would give me a feeling that I'm still with all the terracotta warriors."

**中国式“比萨斜塔”**

**The Chinese Leaning Tower of Pisa**

大雁塔坐落于西安南郊，始建于公元652年，是古城的标志性建筑。由于多种因素影响，大雁塔已经倾斜，偏离中轴一米多，被戏称为中国式“比萨斜塔”。从1997年起，通过回灌地下水等多种保护方式，大雁塔塔身开始停止倾斜，并以平均每年1毫米的速度缓慢回弹复位，如此计算，要想复原得一千年。

The Giant Wild Goose Pagoda in the southern suburbs of Xi'an was built in 652. It is an iconic architecture of the ancient city. For a number of reasons, the old structure has tilted to one side, with its top displaced horizontally one meter from where it would be if the structure were perfectly vertical, hence the nickname the Chinese "Leaning Tower of Pisa". Since 1997, various measures such as injecting underground water have been implemented to stop the pagoda from tilting further. The tilt decreases at a rate of one millimeter a year, hopefully getting completely corrected in 1,000 years.

摄影：王幼健

**蓝桥之恋**

**Love at the Blue Bridge**

《庄子·盗跖》中记载过一个哀怨凄婉的爱情故事：一名叫尾生的男子和心爱的姑娘约在蓝桥相见，姑娘迟迟不来，桥下水势却一直上涨，尾生抱柱而死。蓝桥就在今天蓝田西南的兰屿水上。电影 Waterloo Bridge 引进国内时，为了让影片更有文化品位和凸显感情色彩，发行商用《魂断蓝桥》替代了原名《滑铁卢桥》。

Chuang Tzu documented a beautiful yet tragic love story. Wei Sheng made a date with his beloved girl under the Blue Bridge. The girl failed to show up as the water kept on rising. To keep his date, Wei Sheng drowned with his arms wrapped around a pier. The Blue Bridge is located in Lanyu, southwest of Lantian. When the film *Waterloo Bridge* was introduced into China, the release company used "魂断蓝桥" (Soul Broken on the Blue Bridge) instead of a direct translation of the title to give the film more context and emotional affect.

**唐朝的神马和浮云**

**The Divine Horses on Floating Clouds from the Tang Dynasty**

唐朝 20 位帝王除了末代 2 位外，都安葬在长安以北的塬上，称为"唐十八陵"。这些陵墓中最让人赞叹的是堪称中国石刻艺术巅峰的石雕，尤其是唐独有的翼马，更是象征了大唐的盛世气魄。而高大的"神马"配上脚下的"浮云"，让"神马都是浮云"这句现代流行语，非常巧合地出现在一千多年前的唐代雕刻上。

Of all the 20 emperors of the Tang Dynasty, 18 were buried on the Loess Plateau to the north of Chang'an. The royal tombs are generally referred to as the "Eighteen Tang Mausoleums". Most amazing about them are the stone carvings which are reputed to be the epitome of the Chinese stone sculptures. Among them, the winged horses, in particular, claim to be the symbol of this golden era. These giant divine horses with floating clouds under their hoofs, created over 1,000 years ago, seem to be an unintentional annotation to a saying popular today, "神马都是浮云", implying that nothing, divine or earthly, gives cause for concern.

**买电影票就像春运买火车票**

**Movie Tickets Are Really Hard to Get**

2012 年岁末，一位女士和爱人去看贺岁电影，结果买票排了 40 分钟队。网友在微博上感叹："在西安买电影票就像春运买火车票，真是难上加难啊。"有数据显示，2011 年西安票房收入突破 2 亿，有超过 500 万人次走进电影院，增长速度连续三年全国第一。

When a lady went to see a New Year's film with her husband at the end of 2012, she spent 40 minutes queuing for the tickets. A netizen exclaimed, "Buying movie tickets in Xi'an is like buying train tickets during the Spring Festival, extremely difficult". Statistics show that in 2011 the box office takings in Xi'an exceeded 200 million yuan; the number of movie-goers was over 5 million. The growth speed has been number one in China for three consecutive years.

**城墙上下看市井百态**

**Everyday Life on the City Wall**

如果想了解西安人最鲜活生动的市井百态，一定要到城墙上下走走瞧瞧。这不，几位吉林游客就在城墙上有了别样发现：86 岁的老大爷杨志龙在城墙上一边晒太阳，一边用钩针织红披肩。杨大爷说，50 年前因病住院时闲着没事和病友学钩织，退休后又拿起来，现在能织 30 多种衣物，还给很多女士都传授过技艺。

If you want to see the liveliest parts of Xi'an, you have to check out the city wall. A couple of tourists from Jilin, for example, found something interesting: an 86-year-old man, called Yang Zhilong, was knitting a red cape while enjoying the sun on the wall. Yang said that he took up knitting 50 years ago when he was hospitalized for an illness. He picked it up again after he retired. Now, he could knit over 30 kinds of clothing, and had even taught his skills to a lot of ladies.

摄影：尚洪涛

## 国人的 DNA
### The DNA of the Chinese

来西安，一定要去参观秦兵马俑，在那里，你或许能在兵俑中找到另一个“自己”。据研究，兵马俑的脸型总共有八种，分别是“国”“用”“田”“目”“甲”“申”“由”“蛋”八种，这八种脸型基本涵盖了所有中国人的脸部特征。中国任何地方的人，都能从秦俑中找到自己的影子。

While exploring Xi'an, you must visit the terracotta warriors, among whom you may find another self. Research concludes that there are eight types of warriors in terms of face shapes, each corresponding to a Chinese character: 国, 用, 田, 目, 甲, 申, 由, and 蛋. These eight shapes cover almost all Chinese's facial characteristics. Wherever a Chinese comes from, he can always find a terracotta warrior who resembles himself.

摄影：王旭东

**北方最炎热城市**
**The Hottest City in Northern China**

国家气候中心公布的近 31 年全国夏季炎热程度靠前的 10 个省会城市或直辖市排行榜，西安名列第七。从地理位置来看的话，西安是北方最炎热的城市，也是长江流域以北唯一入选此排行榜的城市。有网友调侃说："西安天气实在太热了！买了筐鸡蛋到家变小鸡了；买了个凉席，一睡变成电热毯了。"

On the list of the top 10 hottest provincial capitals in the summer in the past 31 years, issued by the National Climate Center, Xi'an ranks number seven. Geographically speaking, Xi'an is the hottest city in Northern China and the only city to the north of the Yangtze River to make the list. A netizen joked, "Xi'an is way too hot! I bought a basket of eggs, and they turned into chickens when I got home. I bought a bamboo mat, and after a nap it turned into a hot blanket..."

**厕所标志也用手书**
**Handwritten Signs of a Restroom**

西安城里爱舞文弄墨的人多，很多裤兜里就装着笔和印章，只要有人敢求，就有人敢写。作家穆涛曾在一篇文章中这样写道："我家楼下的公厕，入口处的标志原来是男女简笔画像，有一天突然换了手书，笔力倒也清俊，只是没有落款，不知出自哪一只闲手。我早上去蹲急，常听到议论，某某某字写得不好怕没前程了。"

There are a lot of calligraphy lovers in Xi'an who carry brushes and seals in their pockets. As long as there is a request, someone will oblige. Mu Tao, a writer, once wrote in an article, "The signs at the entrance of the restroom by our building used to be cartoons of a man and a woman. One day, they changed into written scripts. The writing was rather elegant, but it wasn't signed, so no one knows who did it. When I rush there in the mornings, I often heard people discussing that someone's writing is not good so that he or she won't have much of a future."

**说不清的西安**
**A City Beyond Description**

陕西电视台《开坛》节目有一期请来嘉宾余秋雨，现场一学生问他："《文化苦旅》里为什么单单不评价陕西，不评价西安？"一向侃侃而谈的余秋雨顿了一下，说："西安太厚重，我需要用很大篇幅、很长时间才能说清。"当然直到今天他也没能说清。倒是陈忠实，用一系列的散文结集《吟诵关中》，解读了陕西人的形象。

On *Open Forum*, a talk show on Shaanxi TV, a student asked the guest star, Yu Qiuyu, a noted writer, that why he did not write about Shaanxi in his masterpiece, *A Bitter Journey Through Culture*. Yu, being famous for his witty tongue, thought for a while and answered, "Xi'an is so profound as to defy description." He has not been able to write about it to this day. Instead, Chen Zhongshi, a local writer, managed to portray Shaanxi people via a collection of essays titled *Ode to Guanzhong*.

### 冰窖巷不冰
### The Ice Vault Alley Is Not Cool

有网友曾盘点西安街道之最，例如：最“炫富”的街道洒金桥，其实压根儿没人在此散财；最“黑”的街道炭市街，你也找不到一块炭；炎炎夏日，你走在冰窖巷，自然也不会有多凉爽惬意。

Some Netizens bantered about the street names in Xi'an. The "most luxury" street is "Sajin Bridge" because it literally means to throw gold, although no one ever distribute money here. "Tanshi Street" is nicknamed the darkest street because the name suggests selling coal. In reality, no single block of coal is to be found here. Likewise, you won't feel cool in the summertime when walking along "Bingjiao Alley", which purports to ice vault.

### 陶醉在古城
### Fascinated by the Ancient City

挪威科技大学建筑教授哈罗德在西安讲学多年，这个城市散落在大街小巷的历史遗迹都令他着迷。漫步城墙或街巷，他总会闭起眼睛深深呼吸，一副陶醉的表情。他和西安的同行一起参与民居保护，还为此争取了挪威政府的资金援助。

Harold is a professor in Architecture from Norwegian University of Science and Technology. He has been a lecturer in Xi'an for many years. The historic relics around the city's streets and alleys fascinate him. When he roams along the city wall or streets, he always closes his eyes and takes a deep breath, with a look of intoxication on his face. He and his fellow architects in Xi'an are trying preserving local architecture, for which he obtained fund from the Norway government.

摄影：翟小雪

**人名车站**
**A Bus Stop Named After a Person**

公交站命名，多是以地名、路名、地标性建筑为依据，但西安907路公交线路上，有一站的站名却是以人名命名的，叫“骆小朋站”。原来，因该站附近骆宋村多次申请，才在村口设立了临时停靠的便民招呼站。村民认为，是村主任骆小朋的努力才使大家出行更加方便了，所以把他的名字印上。

Bus stops are usually named after a place, a street, or a landmark, but one stop along the route of bus No. 907 in Xi'an is named after a person. It is called "Luo Xiaopeng Stop". The stop was not set up until Luosong Village, a village nearby, applied to the local government many times. Villagers believe that it is thanks to the incessant efforts of their village director Luo Xiaopeng that they can now travel more conveniently. That is why the stop carries his name.

**最美的公厕**
**The Most Beautiful Restroom**

有花有鱼有彩灯，圣诞节会装上圣诞树，春节又会挂起红灯笼……位于凤城四路的长庆免费公厕被附近的居民称为“西安最美公厕”。而这些漂亮的装饰品，全是年近六旬的公厕管理员孟庆义花数千元自费购买的。孟庆义说：“人无论干什么都要干好，能把公厕打扫得让人不嫌弃，也算是我老有所为了。”

It is hard to imagine colored lights, flowers and fish, even a little decorated tree in the Charismas season and red lanterns during the Spring Festival, all in a restroom. The Changqing Restroom on Fengcheng No.4 Road is called "the most beautiful restroom in Xi'an" by residents nearby. These beautiful decorations that cost several thousand yuan were all purchased by the 60-year-old janitor Meng Qingyi. Meng said, "Whatever you do, you have to do it well. I'm proud that I keep the restroom so clean that people all like to use. Isn't this a big accomplishment for an old man like me?"

**一句话概括常住客**
**Salient Features of Different Communities**

最近，一条概括了西安常住客特点的微博在网上热传：待在曲江的人普遍清高，待在南郊二府庄的人普遍文艺，待在粉巷的人普遍疯癫，待在书院门的人普遍都宅，待在友谊路的人普遍豁达，待在二马路的人普遍执着，待在幸福路的人普遍乐观，待在莲花池的人普遍能吃苦，待在崇业路的人普遍富裕……

Recently, a Weibo post about the characteristics of Xi'an residents went viral. According the post, people in Qujiang are lofty. People in Erfu Village in the southern suburbs are artistic. People in Fen Xiang are unrestrained. People in Academy Gate enjoy the pleasures of home. People on Youyi Road are broad-minded; whereas people on Erma Road are perseverant. People on Xingfu Road tend to be optimistic. People at Lianhuachi are mostly hard-working. And people on Chongye Road are generally rich.

摄影：尚洪涛

### 胖子的美丽
### Plump Beauty

红润的脸蛋，丰腴的腰身，XXXXXXL 号的飘逸纱裙……西安博物院馆藏 107 件（组）与唐朝女性生活息息相关的文物壁画、雕像集中展出，还原出一个个千年之前的“重量级美女”，展示出唐代崇尚的丰腴美感。欢迎那些正发愁“五月不减肥，六月徒悲伤”的姑娘们随时前来找自信。

Rosy cheeks, voluptuous waist, and size XXXXXXL flowy chiffon dress… The Xi'an Museum houses and exhibits 107 mural paintings and statues about the lives of women in the Tang Dynasty, restoring one after another "heavy beauty" from thousands of years ago, displaying the sensual beauty of plum figure promoted in the Tang era. Girls obsessed with losing weight are welcome here to reclaim their confidence.

### 关中人最尊重女性
### Guanzhong People Respect Women the Most

若问全国各地哪里最尊重女性，西安市作协主席吴克敬定会回答“关中人”。其他地方，把年轻女性或叫姑娘，或叫闺女等，关中人也有这么叫的，但最普遍的叫法还是“女子”。吴克敬说，被冠以“子”的，若非先贤亦为大哲，譬如孔子、老子等，“女子”之称不正是对女性的大尊重大爱戴吗?

If you asked Wu Kejing, president of the Xi'an Writers Association, which place in China respects women the most, he would answer Guanzhong. In other places, young women are called " 姑娘 " (damsel) or " 闺女 " (lassie, literally, "daughter"). People in Guanzhong use these terms as well, but the most common one is still " 女子 " or "nüzi". Wu Kejing explains that the "zi" is usually used on great scholars and philosophers such as Kongzi (Confucius) and Laozi, the fact that "nüzi" is placed on the same level as them suggests the great respect and admiration for women.

### 面皮火车站
### Cold Noodle Railway Station

坐火车甫抵西安，出站后便能看见城墙。如果你从对面的城墙上看西安火车站，或许除了那川流不息的旅客外，还能发现点什么。比如就有网友说，火车站上边的“西安”两个题字，像极了“面皮”二字。因此有网友调侃，西安是美食之都，到了面皮火车站就该下车当吃货了。

If you travel to Xi'an by train, you'll see the city wall the moment you step out of the station. If you look at the Xi'an Railway Station from the city wall across, you could probably discover something other than the endless flow of travelers. For example, one netizen claims that " 西安 ", the characters for Xi'an, at the top of the station, closely resembles the two characters " 面皮 " (cold noodles). As a result, other netizens joke that Xi'an is indeed the capital of food, and that once you reach the Cold Noodle Railway Station, it is time for you to be a foodie.

**“坚刚”不是“肩章”**

“Resistant”, Not “Epaulet”

有个人发帖说：西安人打招呼叫人“伙计”，这是旧时老板对店员或长工的称呼，说明西安人自大狂妄，把别人低看一等；又说西安人把铁哥们儿称作“肩章”，“肩章”代表级别，说明西安人爱用朋友炫耀身份。这杜撰把西安人逗乐了，跟帖说：叫“伙计”透着亲热；称朋友“坚刚”，不是“肩章”，意思是交情深。

A nonlocal posted an article online and pointed out that when the Xi'anese greet others, they use the word “伙计” (fellow), a term bosses used to call his clerks or workers in the past. This shows that the arrogant Xi'anese hold others in contempt. Meanwhile, the Xi'anese call their best buddy “肩章” (epaulet), with a connotation of ranking. The interpretation: the Xi'anese enjoy flaunting their social status via their friends. Finding this fabrication amusing, the Xi'anese explained that “伙计” implies familiarity, and friends are called “坚刚” –instead of “肩章”–which implies that their friendship goes deep.

**老外评西安**

How Foreigners See Xi'an

《西安晚报》曾组织过一次针对外国游客的百份英文问卷调查，看老外如何品评西安。结果显示，94% 的外国游客就是冲着兵马俑来的，城墙、大清真寺、小吃街、大雁塔也是他们喜爱的景点。至于食物嘛，饺子、面条、烤肉、炒饭……西安丰富的特色小吃，品类繁多，让他们果断抛弃了汉堡、三明治。

*Xi'an Evening* Post once surveyed over 100 foreign tourists in English and found that 94 percent of them came to Xi'an for the Terracotta Army, and among other favorite attractions: the city walls, the Great Mosque, the snack street, and the Giant Wild Goose Pagoda. As for food, such a variety of delicacies like dumplings, noodles, barbequed meat, and fried rice, etc. draw their attention immediately away from hamburgers and sandwiches.

**上辈子的家**

Home in a Previous Incarnation

到了长安，青春才刚刚开始。哈尔滨姑娘心蓝 2008 年首次来西安旅行，第二年就不顾阻力来到西安定居。她遍访唐十八陵，会为在某个唐陵捡到残破墙砖而彻夜激动，会与田野里的石兽唠嗑，乐在其中。“长安是我上辈子的家啊！前世故土，所以我来长安，是回家的感觉。”

Youth does not start until one steps on the soil of Chang'an. Xinlan, a young lady from Harbin, took her first trip to Xi'an in 2008. The following year she decided to settle down in this city at all costs. She visited all the eighteen imperial Tang tombs. She would be up all night out of the excitement from picking up a piece of brick at a Tang mausoleum. And she enjoyed talking to the animal-shaped stone statues in the fields. “Chang'an was my home in my previous incarnation! For me, Coming to Chang'an is coming back home.”

**比姚明脚还大的巨人俑**

**A Giant Terracotta Figure**

2012 年 6 月，秦兵马俑一号坑第三次发掘成果公布。考古专家在百戏俑坑中发现了一个“巨人”。这件平躺的无头陶俑表面已经呈现烧过的黑色痕迹，测量后发现它在无头状况下就有 2.2 米高，散落在旁的脚掌也不小，长 32 厘米，大概要穿 54 码的鞋，比小巨人姚明 52 码的脚还要大。

In June 2012, findings of the third excavation of the Terracotta Army Pit One were announced. Archeologists discovered a “giant” in the *baixi* (acrobatics) site. Lying on the back, the headless clay figurine showed some traces of burning. It is measured to be 2.2 meter tall, the head excluded. Its feet, placed near the body, are also quite large, measured 32 centimeter long, about 54 in shoe size, which are larger than Yao Ming’s 52-size feet.

摄影：张宇明

**原始车载音响**

Primitive Car Radio

头戴草帽，身穿蓝布褂，骑上自行车去赶集，赶路的关中老汉不忘给车头挂上一个小广播，任凭浑厚的秦腔陶醉前行的自己。这或许是最原始、最省钱的车载音响吧。

Wearing a straw hat and throwing on a blue coat, the Guanzhong man would not forget to hang a radio on the head of the bike despite his rush to the fair. On his way, he would abandon himself to the intoxicating and vigorous Qingqiang opera on the radio. Perhaps this is the simplest "car radio" with the lowest price.

**钟楼燕影**

Swallows Around the Bell Tower

每年春，成群的燕子来到钟楼定居，8 月立秋后，就飞走了。楼体的一、二檐是小燕子们的居住地。清晨与傍晚，燕子群绕着钟楼轻舞，在新旧建筑之间飞快穿梭。清洁工康师傅望着天空说："小燕子在上面飞，好像干活时有个伴儿，每年天冷它们飞走时，还怪想它们的。"

While every spring finds flocks of swallows settling down in the Bell Tower, early autumn sees them fly away. The roofs of the first and second floors are their habitats. At dawn and dusk, swallows swirled gracefully around the Bell Tower, fluttering between the old and new structures. Janitor Kang, looking up at the sky, said, "The swallows flying up there are like my companions while I'm working. When they fly away in winter, I miss them quite a lot."

摄影：刘珂

### 西安“闲人”
### Loafers in Xi’an

闲人，西安话读“hán 人”，不是指简单意义上的混混儿，而类似于北京的顽主，且更彪悍。贾平凹写过一篇散文为西安闲人画像，一条条读下来，你会以为是写张嘉译。在西影厂的那些年，张嘉译常夹个包、走路一晃一晃，直不起背，活脱脱一个街头闲人。现在形象变了，但讲义气、爱出头仍是闲人本色。

闲人 (loafer), pronounced “han 人” in the Xi’an dialect, does not refer to a loafer in the normal sense, but someone more valorous than a “顽主” (playful guy), a term with a derogatory sense in the Beijing dialect. Jia Pingwa wrote a piece of prose to portray loafers in Xi’an. Yet when you read it over, you’d think that Jia was writing about Zhang Jiayi, a famous actor. During his years at Xi’an Studio, Zhang always clutched a briefcase under his arm, walking in a staggering and slouchy way. What a true loafer on the street. Now his image has changed, but his devotion to friendship and willingness to act out remained true characteristics of the Xi’an loafer.

### “达克宁”治兵马俑
### “Miconazole Nitrate Cream” to Treat Terracotta

西安土壤潮湿、空气湿度较大，处于地下展厅的兵马俑深受各种霉菌的困扰。比利时的杨森公司提供了上千万的捐款，签下协议为兵马俑除菌祛病。一时间，“达克宁”治兵马俑的消息引起轰动，有人称杨森借兵马俑营销，而杨森老总说，之所以把分公司建在西安，是出于对这里文物的热爱。

The earth of Xi’an is slightly moist and the air humid, so the terracotta warriors in the underground exhibition hall are prone to various moulds. The Belgium-owned company Johnson & Johnson donated over 10 million *yuan* and signed a contract to help protect the warriors from moulds. The news of using the “Miconazole Nitrate Cream” on terracotta warriors instantly caused a sensation. When Johnson & Johnson was criticized for turning the terracotta warriors project into a marketing campaign, its CEO explained that he set the location of the company branch in Xi’an out of his love for the artifacts here.

### 特色指示牌
### Distinctive Street Signs

西安的街道指示牌也是一道人文风景线。在箱式路牌上，标注有地名来源、逸闻趣事、历史文化事件、特色文化习俗及老照片和新景观。旧路牌更有特色：南北方向的路牌是绿色，东西方向的路牌是蓝色。您发现了吗？

The street signs in Xi’an make another distinct cultural sight. On the box-shaped street signs, you can find the origin of the location’s name, anecdotes, historic and cultural events, special customs, old photographs and recommended new sights. The old ones are even more distinctive with those for north-south streets painted green, and those for east-west streets painted blue. Visitors in Xi’an, have you noticed that?

**文物大省地位不可撼动**

**The Incontestable Position in Cultural Heritage**

第 7 批全国重点文物保护单位公布，山西以 452 处高居榜首，陕西则以 235 处屈居第四。不少老陕疾呼："咱还是文物大省吗？"文物官员解释说，陕西 11 座西汉帝陵算一处国保，18 座唐陵也算一处国保，所以数量统计"吃了亏"，好在文物大省不靠数量说话，咱虽量少，但质量高、范围大，地位无可撼动。

The seventh list of Important Historical Sites under State Protection showed that Shanxi topped it with 452 sites and Shaanxi was only in fourth place with 235 sites. Many Shaanxi natives protested, "Are we still the biggest province of ancient artifacts?" Officials explained that the 11 imperial mausoleums of the Western Han Dynasty in Shaanxi only count as one site, so do the 18 mausoleums of the Tang Dynasty, hence Shaanxi is statistically inferior. Fortunately, a province rich in ancient artifacts does not rely on the number. Shaanxi may have less historical sites, but the quality of the sites is higher, and the areas of the sites are larger, so the prestige of Shaanxi remains uncontested.

**不解之缘**

**A Predestined Relationship**

将秦始皇兵马俑比作"世界第八大奇迹"的是法国前总统希拉克。似乎法国总统与兵马俑有一种不解之缘，2007 年，萨科奇首次访华首站就定在西安，并且参观了兵马俑。2010 年，当他再次访华时，仍然将西安作为第一站。不难看出他对这座历史古都的向往。

It was Jacques Chirac, the former French president, who took Qinshihuang's Terracotta Army as the eighth wonder of the world. It seems that French presidents and terracotta warriors have something predestined. In 2007, Nicolas Sarkozy set Xi'an as the first stop of his first trip to China, and he visited the terracotta warriors. In 2010 when he visited China again, Xi'an was still chosen as the first stop. One could easily tell his passion for this historic city.

**城墙下的二小子**

**The Naughty Kids by the City Wall**

爬城墙，城墙根下男孩子们幼年必玩的一个娱乐项目。如同蜘蛛侠一般，身子紧贴城墙，踩着青砖边沿，手脚并用向上爬，还要防着青苔湿滑。若是哪个二小子爬得最高，就被视作一群孩子的"老大"。当然，若是被家长盯见了，呵斥一声，他们也只好仓皇跳下来赶紧跑。

Climbing the wall is a sport that every boy living near the city wall has enjoyed. Like the Spiderman, they keep their bodies really close to the wall, place their feet on the edges of bricks, and climb up on all fours while looking out for the slippery moss. Whoever climbs the highest would become the leader of the gang. Of course, when caught and scolded by their parents, they will jump down hastily and scurry away.

**东稍门**

**The East Checkpoint**

西安为什么没有东稍门呢？原来，东关是块高地，行车无法直接上坡，于是道路就迂回了一下，向北拐到八仙庵那个地方。所谓的稍门其实是哨门，主要是指城墙外的军事放哨城，但东门外军事上难攻，就没必要在正东建造东哨了。

Why isn't there an east checkpoint in Xi'an? Well, the east pass is on a highland, inaccessible by carts in ancient times, so the people had to detour to the north, passing the Temple of Eight Immortals. The so-called "checkpoint" is in fact a post where sentinels kept watch outside the city walls. The east pass itself is difficult to attack from the outside, so there was no need to build a checkpoint.

**是谁制作了兵马俑**

**Who Made the Terracotta Warriors?**

考古专家在陶俑身上发现过 80 多个工匠的名字，藏在腋下、臀部等隐蔽处。被誉为"秦俑之父"的专家袁仲一称，来自宫廷的工匠姓名前带个"宫"字，如宫得、宫进、宫海；另一部分工匠是从各地选拔来的，他们创作风格各异，陶俑也是千人千面。"看得久了，会看出哪些俑是哪些大师的风格。"

Archeologists have found over 80 names of craftsmen on the clay figurines, hidden in covert spots like the armpit, butt, etc. According to expert Yuan Zhongyi, the so-called "Father of Terracotta Army", imperial craftsmen have the prefix "宫" (*gong*, meaning "palace") to their names, such as Gong De, Gong Jin, and Gong Hai; other craftsmen, selected from various places, with their unique style, gave the clay figurines numerous differing appearances. Yuan noted, "After looking at them long enough, one could tell which figurines are in the style of which master."

摄影：张宇明 谢伟

# 参考文献 | References


Lonely Planet《中国旅行指南系列：陕西》，生活·读书·新知三联书店，2011 年。

艾绍强《当戏楼已成往事》，商务印书馆，2011 年。

长安正美《西安，我的神呀！》，陕西师范大学出版总社有限公司，2011 年。

陈凯歌《秦国人》，《当代电影》1985 年第 4 期。

陈忠实《陈忠实解读陕西人》，陕西师范大学出版社，2012 年。

陈忠实《我的关中我的原》，学林出版社，2007 年。

和谷《回到秦朝：寻找中国男人最早的脸》，《中国国家地理》2012 年 1 月。

贺少坤《家住西安》，三秦出版社，2005 年。

鹤坪《老城坊》，太白文艺出版社，2003 年。

胡婕《本色西安》，中国青年出版社，2009 年。

惠焕章《关中百怪》，陕西旅游出版社，1999 年。

季羡林《季羡林散文》，浙江文艺出版社，2008 年。

贾平凹《西安这座城》，《读城》，清华大学出版社，2010 年。

贾平凹《贾平凹长篇散文：静水深流》，河南文艺出版社，2008 年。

贾平凹《贾平凹文集·散文（壹）》，陕西人民出版社，2008 年。

贾平凹《老西安》，中国社会出版社，2011 年。

刘小荣《最后的潼关》，西安出版社， 2010 年。

逯耀东《寒夜客来》，生活·读书·新知三联书店，2005 年。

潘向黎《东边我的美人西边黄河流》，央视国际电视散文，2003 年 12 月 10 日。

人在旅途编辑部《西安玩全指南》，旅游教育出版社，2012 年。

商子秦《城韵秦风》，太白文艺出版社，2006 年。

史红帅《明清时期西安城市地理研究》，中国社会科学出版社，2008 年。

王珑锟《托尼和黄河慈善厨房》，《三联生活周刊》2012 年 41 期。

《西安攻略》编写组《西安攻略》，中国旅游出版社，2011 年。

西安市碑林区地方志编纂委员会《碑林区志》，三秦出版社，2003 年。

西安市地方市志编纂委员会《西安市志》第七卷，西安出版社，2006 年。

姚宝荣、陈锋仪《陕西导游词》，中国旅游出版社，2006 年。

游多多旅行网《西安自助游》，人民邮电出版社，2011 年。

袁林《春发生传奇》，陕西人民出版社，2012 年。

岳路平《一群独立的幽灵在西安徘徊》，《艺术世界》2004 年第 4 期。

张建忠《陕西民俗采风（关中）》，西安地图出版社，2000 年。

张振楣《张振楣谈吃》，北方文艺出版社，2006 年。

《中国自助游》编辑部《西安自助游》，广西师范大学出版社，2010 年。

朱鸿《关中——长安文化的沉积》，商务印书馆，2011 年。

朱鸿《文学演讲录》，太白文艺出版社，2011 年。

朱鸿《西部心情》，陕西人民出版社，2006 年。

朱鸿《关中是中国的院子》，三秦出版社，2009 年。

朱鸿《三石纪唐》，《西安晚报文化丛书》，陕西出版集团三秦出版社，2012 年。

《西安日报》《西安晚报》《华商报》2000—2014 年。

# 索 引 Index

## A



## B

# G



# H

## J



## K

## *N*



## *P*



## *Q*

## *T*

## W



## X

## y

## Z

# 后记

2012年底的一天，我的好友、新华社昔日的同事聂晓阳，给我寄来他主编的《微观西藏》。一向关注西藏的我，立刻被这本采用微博体、通过大量有血有肉的文图细节展示藏地的著作所吸引。晓阳告诉我这是商务印书馆计划出版系列丛书“微观中国”的第一部。第二部“微观”哪儿尚未确定。他认为“微观”西安最合适，如果我愿意领衔主编，他就跟商务印书馆的总编辑周洪波先生说，必要时他会和周总编一起到西安，同编写人员座谈，启发大家思路，释疑解难。

虽然心里有点痒痒，但我没有当即答应。一是西安和西藏不同。西藏对更多的人来说，还比较神秘而陌生。那里众生的习俗服饰甚至蓝天白云风景，都引人眼球。而西安从三皇五帝始，世界就关注她，人们就书写她。现在每年一个多亿的游客从世界各地来亲近她，审视她。微博这种每条不超过140字的鳞片化的东西，如何能反映她的风骨面貌？二是商务印书馆这个老牌出版社，在我印象中，出版的都是典籍精品。我在报社的工作较忙，张罗主编《微观西安》，怕沉不下心来，辜负了晓阳的好意，耽搁了商务印书馆的出版计划。我回复晓阳说，我可以推荐更合适的人来做这件事。晓阳却坚持要我来领头。

由此，我只好应承下来。我找喜欢在微博里躬耕的我们的编辑记者，征询他们是否愿意在工作之余参与写作《微观西安》。很快，陈静、陈颖、高雅、闫斌、王晓英、刘瑾、常宇江、孙欢、翟小雪、贾庆华、李平选等十几位同事报名。这些同事都是写微博的好手，看问题敏锐。长期的采编生涯造就了他们积累、筛选、提炼材料以及拍摄和选图的过人功力。更重要的是，他们生活在这座城市，热爱这座城市，天天关注着这座城市并竭力向人们介绍推介她。因此，晓阳和商务印书馆编辑储丹丹来西安座谈交流时，大家不仅很快明白了出版社的意图，而且还从这座13朝古都和正在建设国际化大都市的现代文明之城的人文、地理、建筑甚至饮食等方面，讲了许多令二位欣喜的事例。后来的事实证明，我们这个团队确实没让人失望。大家思维活跃，眼光既能观照西安的历史，又能审视今天。用大量的图文凝聚西安的厚重和鲜活，沉稳及浪漫，刻画她独特的城市性格，精心描摩展示她富有特色的生活。最终在近千条浓缩

的博文中选出了约500条、在700余幅图片中挑出了210幅，浓缩成这本《微观西安》。

在《微观西安》的编著过程中，我和我的团队也深深感受到了商务印书馆这个老牌出版社的严谨和对图书质量的一丝不苟。每个条目的来源、引文的出处、图片的作者等，储丹丹编辑反复订正。一次一次地返工，一次一次地推倒重来，不厌其烦。最初计划只出汉语简本，但后来确定出汉英双语本时，丹丹又做了大量事务性工作，并诚邀《英语世界》杂志的主编魏令查老师做英译审订。魏先生是咸阳人，曾任教于西安外国语大学，审订这本书再合适不过了。除此之外，北京外国语大学教授，73岁的陈德彰先生也拨冗加入，帮助审订。他们逐字逐句审读英文，使西安又多了通过本书了解她的英语读者。在丹丹的建议下，我们请通晓西安历史文化并编著过《中国古典戏曲词典》的专家——西安文理学院教授王广新作为第一读者，通读校勘中文稿，排除硬伤。在此，我们一并表示诚挚而深深的谢意！

我们还要衷心感谢陕西省委常委、西安市委书记魏民洲同志，百忙之中欣然为本书撰写序言。魏书记在西安生活几十年，虽为官员却学养深厚，对这座城市知之深、爱之切、望之远，在他高屋建瓴的序言中，对西安的文化解读，提升了这本书的价值。

从确定选题到成书，我们中的大部分人，把将近两年里的业余时间都贡献给了这部书，也可以说贡献给了我们生活的这座城市。两年里，西安在一刻不停地向前发展，政治、经济、社会、科学、文化等，日新月异。我们虽然每天都在感受着她的变化，通过我们的新闻工作传播着这种变化，但能利用商务印书馆这个平台，再为她的美丽和发展贡献出一份微薄力量，仍感荣幸和自豪。

屈胜文

2014年8月

# Afterword

One day at the end of 2012, I received a book, *Tibet: Fast and Furious,* from Nie Xiaoyang, a friend and former colleague of mine at the Xinhua News Agency. With a close interest in Tibet, I was immediately absorbed in the book that presented Tibet in a microblog style, abundant with vivid details and nice illustrations. I was told by Xiaoyang that this was the first of a series of books under the title of *One-Minute China* that the Commercial Press planned to publish. Which city to feature in the next book remained unknown, but he believed that Xi'an might be the best choice. He suggested to me that if I was willing to be its chief editor, he would gladly tell Zhou Hongbo, editor-in-chief of the Commercial Press, and go to Xi'an with Zhou if necessary. There they would have a brainstorm, addressing problems concerned.

I positively itched, but did not accept the offer immediately for two reasons. Firstly, Xi'an and Tibet are very different. To most people, Tibet is mysterious and unfamiliar. Tibet's customs, clothing, sceneries, even its blue sky and white clouds, are more than enough to grab attention. Xi'an, however, has long been a focus of attention, and writings about it abound. Every year over 100 million tourists pour in from all over the world to have a close observation of Xi'an. How can microblogs of no more than 140 characters for each piece portray the soul of Xi'an? Secondly, in my impression a prestigious publishing house like the Commercial Press only publishes classic works. I was fairly busy with the work at the newspaper, thus afraid that I might not have enough time to settle down for *Xi'an: Back to the Future* and might let Xiaoyang down and delay the Commercial Press's publishing plan. So I replied to Xiaoyang, promising to recommend a better candidate for the proposed project. Yet Xiaoyang insisted that I take charge.

So I had to take on the project. I looked for editors and reporters of our newspaper who love to microblog and asked if they were willing to devote their spare time to the project. Soon, over a dozen of my colleagues expressed their intention to take part. They were: Chen Jing, Chen Ying, Gao Ya, Yan Bin, Wang Xiaoying, Liu Jin, Chang Yujiang, Sun Huan, Zhai Xiaoxue, Jia Qinghua, and Li Pingxue, all of whom are exceptionally good at microblogging. Besides, they all have a discerning eye and rich journalistic experience, gifted at accumulating, screening and rendering source materials and photography. More importantly, they all live in Xi'an, love this city, care about this city and are willing to do their best to introduce her to the world. Hence, when Xiaoyang and the Commercial Press editor Chu Dandan came to solicit ideas in Xi'an, we soon got the gist of the publisher's intention and cited many anecdotes about the culture, geography, architecture and cuisine of Xi'an, a modern metropolis which served as the capital of 13 dynasties. Our team didn't leave anyone disappointed. All our members have flights of ideas that view Xi'an both through her historical background and current aspect. We employed a great number of pictures and essays that condensed dignity and freshness, steadiness and romance, to provide a vivid description of the city's unique traits and dinstinctive lifestyle. About 500 microblogs and 210 photos were finally compiled into *Xi'an: Back to the Future.*

In the course of compilation, my team and I were deeply impressed with the meticulousness of the Commercial Press. Editor Chu Dandan took great pains to check and correct again and again the origin of each entry, the source of each quote, and the photographer of each picture. Initially, the plan

was to publish the book in simplified Chinese characters only. Later when it was decided to publish the book in both Chinese and English. Dandan invited Wei Lingcha, chief editor of *The World of English* magazine, to review and polish the English translation. A native of Xianyang—a city in Shaaxi—and former professor at Xi'an International Studies University, Wei was an ideal reviewer. In addition, Chen Dezhang, professor of Beijing Foreign Studies University was also enlisted to help with proofreading. They checked the translation line by line to assure smooth understanding for readers abroad. At the suggestion of Dandan, we invited Professor Wang Guangxin from Xi'an University, an expert in local history and culture and author of *Chinese Classic Opera Dictionary*, to be our first reader to proofread the Chinese draft. Wang corrected a fair few errors and ensured the book's quality. We owe our sincerest gratitude to all of them!

We would also like to thank Wei Minzhou, member of the Standing Committee of the Shaanxi Provincial Committee and Secretary of the Xi'an Municipal Committee of the CPC, who gladly wrote the foreword to this book. Having lived in Xi'an for decades, Wei, an erudite official, knows this city very well, loves it with passion, and expects much for it. The broad perspective he adopted in the preface elevates the value of the book.

From the proposal to the completion of this book, most members of our team have devoted almost all our spare time to the book or the city concerned in the past two years. The last two years has witnessed Xi'an's rapid development in politics, economy, society, technology and culture. We have been experiencing the dramatic change, and as journalists we have also been reporting it to the world. However, we feel honored and proud to add to Xi'an's charm and development through this book published by the Commercial Press.

*Qu Shengwen*

August, 2014

摄影：王幼健

**图书在版编目(CIP)数据**

微观西安:汉英对照/屈胜文主编;陈静等编写.—北京:商务印书馆,2014
ISBN 978-7-100-10777-8

Ⅰ.①微… Ⅱ.①屈…②陈… Ⅲ.①西安市—概况—汉、英 Ⅳ.①K924.11

中国版本图书馆CIP数据核字(2014)第229699号



**微观西安**
(汉英版)
**XI'AN: BACK TO THE FUTURE**
屈胜文 主编

---

商务印书馆出版
(北京王府井大街36号 邮政编码100710)
商务印书馆发行
北京中科印刷有限公司印刷
ISBN 978-7-100-10777-8

---

2014年11月第1版 开本787×1092 1/16
2014年11月北京第1次印刷 印张17¾
定价:68.00元